There and Back Again

Joanne Sandstrom

EARENDIL PRESS   *Oakland, California*

EARENDIL PRESS
1958 Manzanita Dr.
Oakland, CA 94611

Library of Congress Cataloging in Publication Data

Sandstrom, Joanne, 1938–
    There and back again

1. Anduril (Yacht) 2. Sandstrom, Joanne, 1938–
3. Voyages around the world—1951–   . II. Title.
G440.A545S36 1983   910.4'1   83-48925
ISBN 0-914577-07-7

Photographs by Donald and Joanne Sandstrom (with discussion still going on about who is
responsible for which ones).
Selections from "The Birth of the Dream," "Down to the Sea," "The Sea Not Traveled"
(Robinson Crusoe Island adventures), and "Pacific Paradises" (grounding at Wallis Island)
first appeared in *Multihulls*. The Pitcairn Island story from "The Sea Not Traveled" first
appeared in *latitude 38*.

Contents

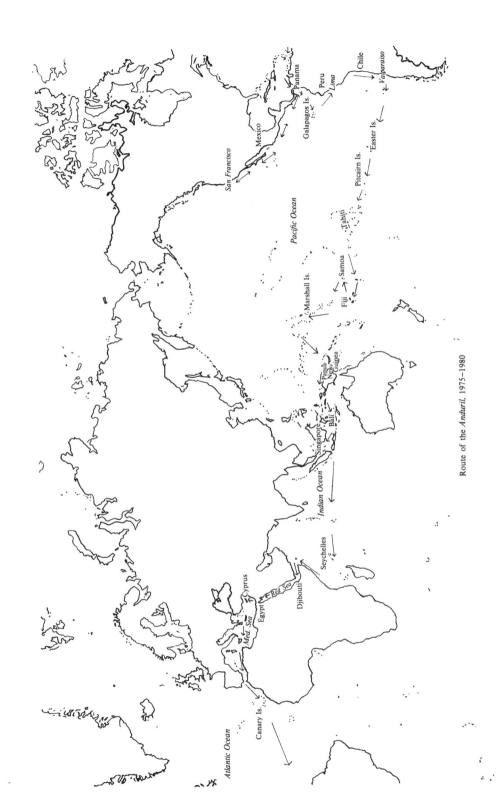

Route of the *Anduril*, 1975–1980

The Birth of the Dream

I sent birth announcements when we launched *Anduril* because Don had often compared his building the boat to a woman's having a baby. And he did suffer many of the symptoms of pregnancy—some nausea, some euphoria, some uncertainty, and great emotional involvement. Even after two and half years of labor, however, the birth was premature. The boat really wasn't completed. But she was viable, and the twice postponed launching was finally accomplished. *Anduril* was a "Thursday's child," promised "far to go."

When Don dented her bow with the champagne bottle, we saw only a minor repair job—annoying, but not serious. We were blissfully unaware that, like all boats, she would almost constantly have some minor "illness" needing attention. Like parents seeing their first child, we saw only the wonder and joy of the birth, not the pains and costs of the upkeep.

Why did we have this "baby"? (We certainly couldn't call her "an accident"!)

The chronicle of the *Anduril* actually began in the late forties and early fifties when a young boy read with fascination each month's issue of *National Geographic*. "Someday," he thought, "I'd like to take a boat and see Tahiti and Pitcairn and Easter Island."

A decade later he said to his bride, "Someday we ought to sail around the world." She smiled indulgently, for who doesn't dream of adventuring? But they had important things to plan—homes, babies, careers. "Maybe someday," I wrote in my diary that night. Later, to prepare for "someday," we bought a fifteen-foot Sea Spray catamaran and for five years enjoyed day sailing and racing within Los Angeles-Long Beach harbors. We read many books and decided on the boat we'd have when the right opportunity came.

Don's losing his job as personnel manager in some corporate conglomerating didn't seem like "opportunity" at first; but since I was teaching school again it wasn't a crisis; we could carefully consider what to do. Instead of taking another job, Don returned to the university to work on his Ph.D.; but he soon found the work too theoretical and the campus as "political" as the office. He was completing his course work and writing his proposal for his dissertation when his mother died, leaving him a small inheritance.

That decided us—not the money, but his mother's death. Nora was in her early fifties when she died, a dozen years from retiring and enjoying herself doing all the things she'd always planned. Her death reminded us of the others. My father had died at forty-eight, two years before he and my mother were to take a long-dreamed-of trip to Hawaii to celebrate their silver anniversary. The Falstaffian French teacher at Costa Mesa High School, where I was teaching, had had a fatal heart attack at a faculty party; he was in his early forties. A very good friend hadn't reached thirty before bone cancer killed him. "And at my back I always hear/ Time's wingéd chariot hurrying near." We felt the urgency of our own mortality.

Don quit school, and we celebrated New Year's Day 1973 by beginning work on our Cross 40 trimaran.

Behind a nursery, across from a new housing tract, next to the strawberry fields, lay the boatyard, birthplace and graveyard for the hopes of seventeen dreamers. The manager was building a boat and had sublet space to others to finance his project. Shortly after we moved in, Lee had a heart attack; his doctor told him he'd never sail anywhere. He spent his days visiting the yard—helping, watching, drinking. He never worked on his own boat again. Within a year he was dead.

Don began to spend sixty hours a week at the yard instead of fifty; the children and I worked three weekends a month. If a boat is a hole in the water, surrounded by wood, into which you throw money, a vacation is a hole in time during which you stay home from a forty-hour-a-week job to spend sixty hours a week on a "fun" project.

During this time only Don and one other dreamer were making progress. For the others the boat-building yard had become the boat-storage yard. Perhaps getting started had taken all their energy (and money). Perhaps the grubby reality of building didn't match the glamorous idea of "sailing away from it all." Perhaps the men (we were the only family there) only wanted an excuse to spend time away from home. Whatever the reasons, the situation stiffened our determination.

Then early in 1974 Don developed a tremor in his left arm. At first we blamed the fatigue caused by working overhead; but when the tremor grew worse, he went to see our doctor.

The doctor found a lump near the base of the brain. A tumor? He sent Don to a neurosurgeon. The lump wasn't a tumor, just an old calcium deposit, probably from some long-forgotten childhood injury. It was no problem. Swedes are thick-headed. Then what was causing the tremor? Don was in the hospital for five days undergoing tests. The diagnosis came—Parkinson's disease. Don shouldn't have it: he was too young; but there it was. Medication could control the tremor; degeneration should be slow; with luck he'd die of something else before the disease disabled him.

That's why we sold house and cars and sailed away.

Down to the Sea

Long Beach, California
July 25, 1975

Dear Friends,

It was late afternoon on launching day, but instead of feeling "salty" I felt like Alice at the Mad Hatter's tea party.

"No room, no room; you'll have to take your boat out of this harbor," said the man behind the desk in the marina office.

"What do you mean, 'no room'? I see ten empty guest slips. You told us last week that they can't be reserved, so they must be available. Surely we could have one of them if we can't stay where we are near the boatyard."

"No room, no room; you'll have to leave."

"But the boat was launched just this morning. She's not rigged yet; we can't raise sail. Besides, the wiring isn't completed; we'd have to run without lights. And it's getting dark," I wailed.

"No room, no room; if you won't move your boat we'll have to tow it out of the harbor."

With that, the official back of the Long Beach marina was, literally, turned.

I stumbled out of the office, tears of frustration and fatigue clouding my eyes. I'd been unable to find *Anduril* a berth on her birthday. (You see how tired I was, thinking such a dreadful pun.) It seemed an inevitable conclusion to a very trying twenty-four hours.

Wilmington Boat Movers had arrived at Trimaran City on Wednesday afternoon at five (1700 to us now nautical folks). Two and a half hours later *Anduril* was sitting on their trailer. Loren and Linda, who have just begun building their dream, helped us finish painting the bottom of ours. After a fashionably late dinner (the only thing fashionable about boat building), while the boys and Linda and I slept aboard, Don and Loren set up winches, completed some wiring connections, and attended to other last minute chores, finally crawling into bed (a literal phrase on a boat) around 0300. At 0345 Wilmington blasted their air horn. By 0450 we were out of Trimaran City, through the gates of Wampler's Superb Decor Nursery, and on our way to the sea. *Anduril* moved gracefully through the predawn quiet of Fountain Valley, Santa Ana, Westminster, and Long Beach. By 0600 we had reached launch site, the Long Beach marina boat yard. By 0700 *Anduril* was in the sling, ready for the crane to lift her into the water—a fifteen-minute operation. Instead, the labor was a long one. The yard didn't have all the necessary equipment ready and tried to "make do." On the first attempt all the "make do" blocks and bars slipped. On the second attempt a bar jumped loose and crashed onto the cabin roof, leaving two cracks in our new boat. At this point Don was called into the office to sign a waiver of liability—or no launch. After readjusting bars and blocks, Don and Loren jumped off the boat, refusing to "hold down" the back spreader bar, and a third attempt was made, this one successful. *Anduril* began her sea life at 0915 on Thursday, July 17, 1975. Don released his tension when he christened her so thoroughly that he took a chunk out of her bow. (Why didn't someone tell me to crack the champagne bottle first? Or tell him to smash it on a metal fitting instead of the fine wooden bow?) After toasting our new life, we went out for breakfast.

That afternoon the mast was stepped, after which we were told that we'd have to leave the boat yard slip immediately—but not before paying twice the estimated cost of launching. Wearily, we motored to W-2, the nearest guest slip in the marina, and tied up. I trudged to the office to sign in and pay; instead, I went through that incredible Wonderland scene that begins this letter.

Tired and upset, I returned to the boat and told the story to Don, who was even more tired and became not upset but angry. After stewing for several minutes he went to make some phone calls; he came back announcing that we were going to Newport Beach. Marina authorities had told him the same story—no room, no room. In desperation he'd called a friend who works for the harbor department in Newport Beach. Charlie found us a mooring and told a friend in the Coast Guard that we'd soon be underway. He said he'd drive up and help maneuver *Anduril* to the friendlier port of Newport Beach.

Meanwhile, Loren had borrowed a key to the heads; and after a revitalizing shower and shave, Don decided that *Anduril* would not move until her captain decided that she was sea-ready. Her crew was ordered to "Repel all boarders." Charlie good-naturedly rode back to Newport Beach.

"Early to bed" was followed by "early to rise." Marina police knocked on the hull at 0445 Friday. Seems we had not paid our dock fee! As Don sputtered, low key Loren calmly dressed and went to the office. We're here for a month.

July 27, 1975

We've been lazily busy, working to shorten our long list of things still to do. This morning we went out to test the engine. *Anduril* handles beautifully. She turns in her own length, responds quickly, doesn't oversteer. But she's so big! I'm used to my VW, not a Buick.

This afternoon Bigfoot (yes, the seven-toed tomcat is with us) ate his first fresh (caught by Erik) raw fish, but not before he had stared and pawed in great perplexity. Then crunch! went the head, eyeball crushed and oozing. From that first delectable morsel it was feast.

Newport Beach, California
August 4, 1975

Ah, the joys of the maiden voyage! Talk about up a creek without a paddle. The fourteen-mile trip from Long Beach to Newport, one month after launching and one week after raising sails for the first time, proved uneventful. But the landing! We thought that we'd have dock space for at least a few days. Instead, we had to pick up a mooring. That took four passes around the buoy. On the third pass we dropped the boat hook (recovered). Now here we bob on can #7 in the cove, surrounded by water. We didn't install the head and holding tank, planning to use the toilet on the dock. We didn't get oars for the dinghy, planning to step ashore. Fortunately, we're close to shore and have a six- by thirty-inch piece of plywood—a possible paddle. Also fortunately, a harbor official motored by, and Don went ashore with him. If all goes as planned, Martha will be home when Don calls, pick him up, and take him to Long Beach to get our car. On the way back he'll buy oars somewhere. Not an auspicious beginning, but we're committed. I mailed my request for leave today.

August 8, 1975

I started reading *Logbook for Grace,* a nonfiction sea story, but switched to *Dune,* Frank Herbert's sci fi story of a desert society. I enjoyed it very much, just as last week I enjoyed Colin Fletcher's *1000 Mile Summer,* the account of his backpacking trip through the desert. Is this preference in reading matter significant?

August 23, 1975

We sit in a circle of sunshine, unable to see through the fog to the Balboa Pavilion or to the end of the breakwater. An endless procession of boats parades by, hurrying to get settled before dark, then get on with the Saturday night parties. Instead of having our usual practice today—we set out buoys, practice turning, stopping, changing sails, picking up a "man" overboard—we stayed in to work. Don has finished the head and begun the mast lights.

On Tuesday a friend came for lunch and a sail. We didn't get back until 1900. It began as a warm, pleasant sail, during which I painted some forward and aft trim; the wind then freshened to twenty-five knots. We took down the drifter—the first time we've had to shorten sail at sea—and enjoyed a marvelous ride. The head, though, not yet bolted in place, slid forward and crashed through a locker door. Water seeped down the sail track bolts and through the dorade boxes (we hadn't finished the caulking), making damp bedspreads. But the nylon backing kept most of the water from seeping through, so the beds stayed dry.

That evening Erik baked our first cake aboard, a two-layer chocolate tower for Don's birthday on Wednesday. The hardest part of baking in the pressure cooker on the kerosene stove is getting the cake pan out of the cooker without burning your fingers. There's not much clearance between pan and pot.

en route to Catalina
August 25, 1975

Sailing is not my sport. Too much sitting. I have a crying need for large muscle exercise. At least at the island we'll be able to swim.

Newport Beach
August 28, 1975

After a short, pleasant trip to Catalina we're back in Newport. For some reason we couldn't moor in the cove, so we're in mid-channel, watching the Balboa ferry plow by. Going ashore here gets complicated; there's no public property where we can leave the dinghy, and beach-front residents don't take kindly to us transients parking in their front sand.

Last night we rowed the small dinghy ashore, deflated it, stowed it and the foot pump in the trunk, and drove off to Marina del Rey for our Windjammers Yacht Club meeting. At 0115 we were again at Art's Landing, this time inflating said dinghy. Now I have my leg muscle exercise for the trip; pumping up the big dinghy must be the equivalent of walking several miles.

We'll join ORCA (Ocean Racing Catamaran Association) on a cruise to Catalina over Labor Day, then go to San Francisco for sea trials. The next letter you receive will be from a seasoned (and I hope sea-sunned) sailor.

                         Until then,
                         Joanne

                                        San Francisco, California
                                        September 28, 1975

Dear Friends,

I'm sitting in the cold, damp main cabin—having taken off yellow "oilskins" (plastic these days) and orange float coat but still wearing wool socks, long underwear, and balaklava—writing to you of the joys of cruising. It has been a good trip, but *cold.* Remember these complaints when I later complain about the heat and humidity in the South Pacific.

Tonight we swing, very gently, at anchor in Aquatic Park, San Francisco, in front of Ghirardelli Square. Fog has given the City back its old skyline; not one of the new skyscrapers pokes through, but Coit Tower shines ivory on its dark hill. Tomorrow will be our last day in the Bay Area, our last chance to store up impressions of "home." Then we'll return to Southern California for about six weeks before going off to form new impressions of new places.

To bring you up to date——

After talking with friends at the outing on Catalina, we altered our plans. Instead of returning to the mainland and heading up the coast, we decided to visit Santa Cruz Island, relax a day in a beautiful, wild spot, and get a better heading on Point Conception.

Leaving Catalina at 0630 on Monday, we saw only fog. The haze and clouds carried no wind; we motored the seventy miles to Pelican Bay on Santa Cruz Island. Finally, the sun came out, giving us an enjoyable two hours ashore before dinner. How good it felt to walk on trails again! We landed the dinghy near a grove of eucalyptus, my favorite trees. The pungent aroma washed diesel fumes and chemical marine head smells from *my* head. We climbed to the point, past hotel ruins, fig orchards, and Santa Cruz pines, watching crows and sea gulls soar, catching the bright flash of surprisingly silent blue jays. Donald and I carried eucalyptus branches back to the boat, where their fragrance will, I hope, overpower the chemical toilet smells in the head.

Then, while you eagerly greeted eager students on that first day of school, we sat off the coast near Morro Bay, eagerly awaiting a wind that never came. It took us ten hours to travel eighteen miles.

The trip had been maddeningly windless. In frustration (and anxious gratitude) we'd motored through the flat water and dead air of Point Conception, California's mini–Cape Horn (not everything here is bigger and better). Then, running a little low on fuel and wanting practice at *sailing,* we put up the sails and began—drifting. Not until after we left Morro Bay did we get any good wind—and then it really blew. We learned a lot about storm management and became proficient at reducing sail. Reversing its normal pattern, the wind picked up at night, when seas seem bigger and freighters more menacing. Time and distance lose their daylight relationships; motion seems illusory; seas move, but the ship does not. We did, however, and got so far offshore in our first "big blow" (thirty to thirty-five knot winds) that we spent two days sailing back, tacking uphill in light air.

Those gray days and nights—gray water, gray sky, gray land to the east—were brightened by playful company. Groups of dolphins came to sport around our bows, gliding barely beneath the hull, corkscrewing down, then breaking the surface in long, graceful curves. We even saw some tailwalking. It was better than a show at Marineland, especially at night, when all these antics glowed with phosphorescence.

At Carmel, Erik, who wanders off in the dinghy as soon as we make port, discovered sea otters. We never saw them eating abalone—as fishermen complain they do—but we did see them lying on their backs, munching seaweed.

At Santa Cruz the anchorage teemed with life, none of it quiet. Gulls' cries pierced the air and our ears, especially when the gulls attacked some poor pelican, trying to steal its fish. Sea lions sported, nipping flippers, rubbing noses, basking in (finally!) sunshine. One bull bellowed at fishermen on the pier, barking thanks for treats thrown. Donald and Erik and I, rowing hard against a strong current as we went ashore to buy groceries, passed within two feet of a group of six, lounging. Never have we been so close to real wildlife as we were to those sea lions; most of them were longer than our eight-foot dinghy, and each of them certainly outweighed each of us. They were in their element, we were only using it; and the difference is real and great.

Bigfoot also noticed some real and great differences. He had never seen so many birds—and all bigger than he. King Tom of Cornell Avenue stayed below for several days.

Santa Cruz had shore-side pleasures as well. We visited the amusement park, grabbing for brass rings on the merry-go-round and riding the roller coaster. Let Don make his mark in sailing; if ever I make the *Guinness Book of World Records* it will be for roller-coaster riding longer than anyone else.

We had an eventful stop at Half Moon Bay, laundering and showering (these simple activities are events—and welcome ones—when you live aboard a sailboat), then sailed under the Golden Gate Bridge at 1130 on Friday, September 19. Fog and clouds lifted for us, and we came into a sun sparkling Bay. We have since spent time in Berkeley and Sausalito, seeing old friends and visiting old haunts. Fog allowing, we shall sail out in the kind of golden sunset we had last week. We expect to run straight to Long Beach, should arrive October 4 or 5.

                        Until then,
                        Joanne

                                        en route to Long Beach
                                        October 2, 1975

Dear Friends,

Steering the night watch is soporific. The slowly rocking compass needle hypnotizes; I want to sleep. To keep myself awake I sing off-key—grandpa's songs, school songs, adolescent ballads. After a night of one hour on, one off, my eyes are the same red as the night-lighted compass.

On our first night out from San Francisco I sat at the helm, concentrating on steering a straight course. The world hung before me in the globe of the compass. Quickly, I glanced ahead, then from side to side, relieved to see no lights of other boats. Then, as the pole draws the compass needle, the compass drew my eyes, and I again entered that glowing red world with its stark white numbers, uncomfortably aware that only I was awake, and responsible for the safety of boat and crew.

Though the night was calm, my hands clawed the steering wheel, and I hoped that I wouldn't meet any of the "things that go 'bump' in the night.'' Then I heard it behind me—an explosive breath, a swimmer out of air, forced to the surface, stealthy no longer.

I couldn't believe my ears. Imagination, hallucination, tricks—then I heard it again. Are there sea monsters outside of Loch Ness? If only it were Burt Lancaster, practicing for a sequel to his role in *The Swimmer!* No, it must be one of those crazy members of the Dolphin Club. They swam in the Bay daily; maybe one was swimming an endurance test beyond the Golden Gate.

Apprehensively—how could I steer a straight course if I didn't stare at the compass?—I turned my head to see it leap in a graceful arc, moonlight shimmering on its back. No Dolphin, but a dolphin; and not one, but dozens. The mariner's friend and good omen put on another great show. I relaxed.

Love,
Joanne

Interlude: The Whole Truth

Some things you won't tell even your best friends—how unpleasant your idyllic cruising life can be, for instance, or how stupid you were.

Boats are often damp, and ours was no exception. No clothing or bedding was really dry. Postage stamps stuck together unless folded with the glue outward. My hat rusted where I used bobby pins to hold it on. How I missed washer and dryer and central heating! But if I wouldn't mention these unidyllic realities, I was even more loath to confess the unseamanlike stupidities.

When we decided not to return to the coast after the Catalina trip, we gave no thought to fuel or water. "A little low on fuel" was an understatement; we had about half a gallon. That was enough for—twenty minutes? sixty minutes? We didn't know. We sat off Morro Bay for ten hours not because we "wanted practice at *sailing,*" but because we were saving the last of the fuel in case we needed the engine getting into the harbor.

Though I never mentioned it my letters, we also ran low on water—had but two cups left when we entered Morro Bay. Empty fuel tanks can cost you time; empty water tanks can cost your life. Allowing ourselves to run so low on both showed imprudent behavior, which sailors can't afford very often—sometimes not even once.

The anchorage at Stillwater, near Carmel, was lovely—but we thought we'd reached Half Moon Bay, even though we couldn't match what we saw with what we read on our chart. Not until after we'd anchored did we puzzle things out and pinpoint our position.

Returning to Southern California, we wound up several hundred miles farther offshore than we'd planned. We knew that because of variations in the earth's magnetic field a compass does not always point true north. We knew that the navigator has to account for this deviation when plotting a course, adding or subtracting degrees to make up for the magnetic variation as shown on the charts. Don subtracted when he should have added. We moved southwest as the California coastline fell away to the southeast. When he took his first sight about thirty-six hours after leaving San Francisco, he didn't believe it. When a second sight confirmed the first, he realized the mistake.

Well, the shakedown cruise was supposed to be a learning experience.

In Southern California I was razzed by my sailing friends. Tacking "uphill" indeed; "upwind" you mean. If anything, the geography teacher informed me, San Francisco is downhill from Los Angeles. I tried to explain that going north always seems "up" to me because north is at the top of the map. He shook his head, threw up his hands, and said he'd pray for us.

The Well-Traveled Sea

Magdalena Bay, Baja Calif., Mex.
January 4, 1976

Dear Friends,

Except for the inevitable problems involved in having Cain and Abel aboard and except for living in close proximity to a teenager, we are doing fine. The times of four captains and no crew have decreased, though the "old" man and the "incipient" man often clash. Reminds me of the bull seals in that Disney movie, though there's been no bloodshed. At such stressful times Erik, of course, becomes the model child. "See how much nicer I am than my brother." The joys of parenthood! Remember, these boys may be rented on a long- or short-term lease.

We're traveling more slowly than we'd thought, not because the boat won't move, but because we've stayed in ports longer than originally planned. There's so much to see and do!

We left Dana Point at 0715 on December 14, sailing at eight to ten knots on a fresh beam wind. By later that afternoon the wind had died, however, and we sat off Point Loma for nearly eight hours. By 0330 the wind was up again and waves thumped the underwings. We took down the #2 genny, and I fell soundly asleep as the sun rose on a clear, crisp morning.

An urgent call from Don sent me topside, without the pants I couldn't find, with float coat unzipped. For a shivering hour I held the wheel while Don struggled with a mainsail that should have been reefed earlier. A block on the reefing system blew apart, our first gear failure. Talk about a Nantucket sleigh ride! Oh, for a spray-blocking dodger and a self-steering system!

By 1015 the wind had died again; we had to motor into Ensenada—our first foreign port—to clear in before siesta.

During our few days in Ensenada we enjoyed the company of Marion and Howard, a retired couple from Ventura, and Marion's mother, Gladys, who are sailing south to warmer weather aboard the *Mariana*. As we were leaving Ensenada, Marion shouted, "If we're in the same harbor,

you're invited for Christmas dinner. I have a turkey in the freezer."
What a thing to tell two growing boys who are sailing on a boat without
even an ice chest! Of course we met up with *Mariana*. Donald spotted
her two orange dinghies as we weighed anchor at Cedros Island, the stop
after Ensenada.

"There goes *Mariana!* I'll bet she's going to Turtle Bay, too!
Hurry!"

We did—had a beautiful sail, making eight knots, caught and passed
Mariana. We were the first anchored, but by Christmas Day six other
boats had joined us.

Turtle Bay provides a well-protected anchorage, but the landscape is
bleak. Not even cactus grows. On those days before Christmas,
amphibious craft made uncounted trips back and forth from town to the
boat from Cedros. *Everything* in Turtle Bay has to be brought from
somewhere else—even water.

On Christmas Eve Don and I rowed along a path of moonlight to the
church for midnight mass. It was crowded with women and children but
only two local men—one newly married, one recently engaged. A radiant
nun sang "Silent Night" in the clearest, truest voice we've heard. We
understood only three words during the evening, but all the spirit.

Christmas Day was supposed to start with a wedding reception on
our boat; but since the groom was a self-proclaimed "Buddhist Jew," the
bride a Protestant, and both they and their five-year-old son Americans,
the local Italian Catholic priest declined to perform the ceremony. Since
we couldn't let the chocolate wedding cake that Erik had baked go to
waste, we had a "cake party" and put it to waist instead. That evening we
enjoyed a traditional Christmas dinner aboard *Mariana*. This butcher's
granddaughter especially enjoyed the turkey, my traditionalist husband the
plum pudding; Donald and Erik devoured Gladys' fudge.

Two days later the quiet harbor was whitecapping in twenty knot
winds. We tried to row to the beach across the harbor to do some shelling
but couldn't make it. Instead we stopped aboard *Intermezzo* and visited
with the Dashews, who were on a short cruise with their daughters, ages
three and five, to see if they liked cruising, family style. Leaving there we
tried again to row upwind but gave it up for drifting downwind to cocktails
aboard *Mariana*. Local fishermen came by, and Don bought ten lobsters
for a third of a fifth of vodka and a *Playboy*. (Try that currency at
Safeway!) Marion cooked those and four more that had been given to us
earlier. No hard tack and bully beef on this ship.

We arrived here doing six knots under all but bare poles. A nice
breeze built to thirty knots. Waves were breaking out from our bows,
dolphins skipping from crest to crest. We dropped the main and staysail

and put up the storm jib. What a handkerchief! Still, with only one-fourth our usual sail area we were making twice our frequent speed.

We anchored in six feet of clear water above a white, sandy bottom, only to have to reanchor when the tide went out. Row ashore at high tide and you have to drag the dinghy a quarter mile to the water at low. But it's a lovely spot—white sand dunes sparkling with polished bits of shells, hills abloom with cactus, clear blue water, a labyrinth of a lagoon. And of course, land smells. Never before have I enjoyed the smell of desert or the sight of buzzards.

We spent the day shell collecting, bone collecting (we're going to construct a fantastic creature for a biology lesson), and creature collecting. Erik and Donald came home with two clams, one crab, and two octopi. No more octopi until we really learn how to prepare them! Tasty, but tough, and we had trouble skinning them.

Mariana, who left Turtle Bay about six hours after we did, arrived on New Year's Eve, a day behind us. We took our ham and plum pudding to share with their abalone and baked potatoes—also polished off a magnum of champagne; no one stayed up to welcome 1976.

Three more boats arrived on New Year's Day, when we hosted a lobster feast for fourteen. The cost? Thirty-five .22 shells per half dozen lobsters. Everyone ate until full and we still had leftovers. I don't think anyone missed not seeing the bowl games. In spite of dirty dishes we were glad to be the ones "at home." The others had trouble even getting into their dinghies when they left, wind and wave were so bad. No one got home dry. Still, it was better than facing freeway hazards.

When the following day dawned clear and almost flat, we went to the lagoon, drifting in and out among the mangroves on the tide. Snowy egrets showed themselves plainly, while blue herons sought invisibility on dead branches. We walked the dunes, collecting shells, delighted with each new vista of sea and sand. I could grow addicted to this idyllic life.

Cabo San Lucas
January 8, 1976

After another wild night sail (twelve knots under double-reefed main and staysail), we're at Cabo San Lucas, again ahead of the rest of the "fleet." Finally, the water's warm enough for comfortable instead of invigorating swimming. Yesterday we even went in before breakfast. And the local panaderia has the best baked goods so far. The big negative about Cabo is that it's on the tourist track; two cruise ships have steamed in during the past three days; but since we're not interested in buying cheap plastic knickknacks in town, we never meet the crowds.

All along the way we've been surrounded by sea life. Dolphins accompany us everywhere, racing alongside, leaping in front, playing "chicken," seeing who can get closest to the hull. They are amazing creatures, supremely graceful. At night they are even more special, weaving phosphorescent ribbons around the boat. We've sailed among seals and schools of tuna. On the way into this bay we saw three gray whales heading north. One even stood on his (her?) tail before crashing into the sea. What a belly-flop!

January 23, 1976

If you could find it, one and three-quarter miles farther southwest than shown on the charts, "in a position that cannot be reconciled with existing hydrography," Isla Isabela would fascinate you. If you could visit when the fish camp wasn't polluting the aquarium around the rocks, the island would delight you.

You'd notice the birds first—more than thousands, the frigates apparently predominant, certainly dominating as they dive on the hapless booby and steal its fish. Every tree on this jungle-thick island is topped with three or four frigate nests. Males sometimes sit on a nest but are more obvious when they puff out their scarlet pouches and preen. Talk about vanity! Poor drab females, of course, have nothing to preen about.

Wanting to see all of this more closely, we set off to circumnavigate on foot. Walking under the trees full of nesting frigates was quite an experience. Nests often were no more than two feet above our heads, and we raised some commotion as we thrashed through the underbrush. (For joyful hiking, give me the Sierra instead.) Four-foot wings beat rhythmically, creating the only breeze; and frigate voices, clacking like the rhythm sticks used by young children, accompanied our steps. We saw only three young frigates and assume that the other nests had only eggs, not fledglings.

We had walked about half way around the island, seeing, hearing, and smelling only frigates, when a new sound stopped us. The trees had thinned a little (so we didn't need the machete we didn't have), and we could easily see what at first sounded like, walked like, and almost looked like geese. These ground-nesting birds covered the area, their nests no more than three or four feet apart. As we zigzagged downhill, we couldn't help but closely approach several of the nests. Some of the mothers left when we were five or six feet away. So much for maternal instinct. Others defended, getting off an ineffectual whistle and regurgitating a fish that they apparently hoped we'd take instead of the eggs. These were the hapless boobies, which the frigates terrorized. Here under the trees the boobies were safe from the frigates, whose wings couldn't fit below the tree tops and whose talons prevented them from walking on land. But we posed a new threat, dealt with in the instinctive manner.

Actually, I liked the boobies better than the frigates. They look gentler, with a pointed rather than a hooked beak and gray and white feathers that look softer than the glossy black of the frigates. Even their eyes look kinder. And the feet! Not the rapacious talons of the frigates, but webbed feet—in shades of bright blue, green, and yellow. Don said they looked as if they were wearing cheap plastic boots. We saw no booby young, but every nest had one, two, or three eggs.

Almost back to the boat, on a cliff overlooking the anchorage, we saw another kind of bird. Similar in shape to the booby but smaller, with less bright feet, they remain nameless until we get a book about sea birds. The boys call them diving ducks because of their webbed feet and the way they go after their food. We saw more young of this kind than of the others—newly-hatched, fledgling, and "teenage." The featherless newborns in their ugliness resemble every newly-hatched bird I've ever seen. The fledglings look soft, soft, soft—nothing but down and air. The "teenagers" look, typically, awkward. Part down, part feather, they stumble over gray-brown webbed feet, looking clumsy, not cute. These birds never left their nests at our approach. Even dad stayed put if he was sitting on the eggs.

The birds provide the fascination at Isabela, sometimes called "a miniature Galapagos." What the place will sound like when those eggs become birds boggles my mind. It's noisy enough now, sounding like a tropical movie, but without, thank heavens, the hum of insects.

If the birds fascinate, some of Isabela's other attractions delight. We walked through stands of banana trees, rows of pineapple plants (well-picked by the fishermen), and past a coconut tree, which Donald climbed to get us our first "wild" coconuts. They were small and green, the "milk" tasting more like quinine water. Better luck next time. We rowed back to the boat past the rocks that house zebra-striped and orange-tailed and bright blue fish. We could see them from the surface, even through the film of diesel from fishing boat engines. We would have enjoyed swimming, but between the diesel from the engines and the sharks attracted by all the fish debris we decided against it. Almost as disappointing was the lake that fills the crater of the volcano. Visions of Crater Lake danced through our heads. Then we came upon a khaki-colored sump (I was told that this is too charitable a description).

As for the people, we were one of two pleasure boats in a group of forty to fifty boats. Twenty or so were small pongas with outboard engines, belonging to the shoreside fishing camp. The people were either shy or hostile, at least not friendly. Their main activity seemed to be drying shark meat and fishing around the trawlers when these came in. The men on the trawlers were quite friendly. The boats would leave about 1900, returning by 0700. By then Erik was out in the dinghy, nosing around, finding out what there was to find out. Within minutes he would be aboard *Oceano Antarctico,* dropping hand lines with the Mexican fishermen on their busman's holiday. He and Donald spent two days fishing with them, catching more tuna and rock cod than we could possibly eat. At these times one wishes for refrigeration. Instead, *Antarctico* kept most of our fish in their freezer. It was little enough return for all the enjoyment they gave the boys and the good fish we got—tuna steaks two nights for dinner, lunches of rock cod fillets, of ceviche, of tuna salad. It sure beats chicken-flavored soy protein.

January 29, 1976

San Blas appeared on the horizon, our first tropical-looking port. We arrived at sunset, red sky feathered by coconut palms. It would have been quite impressive, except for the no-no flies, the first we've experienced. Fortunately, they weren't too numerous and were out for only about an hour each dusk—at cocktail time. Our 1966 Army surplus jungle juice effectively repelled them—or maybe it was the gin.

At San Blas we met again some friends from Mazatlan and through them some local families. José at sixteen has his own boat and outboard, which he takes forty miles across open ocean to Isabela for fishing. These pongas are sixteen to twenty feet long, high in the bow to make dry landing through surf possible. They carry fishing equipment and men, only a few supplies, and no life-saving gear. But José is lucky because he has the boat and can work it. It represents a tremendous financial investment, but with only our friend Barbara's halting Spanish and José's nonexistent English we couldn't learn how he got it.

Armenio, at thirteen or fourteen, was the kind of irrepressible mischief-maker who makes teachers laugh while driving them crazy. Apparently he goes to school every other year, this one being his year to work. We visited with his family—mother, father, and six siblings. In addition to one room with a dirt floor and some overstuffed furniture, they had a lean-to addition that served as kitchen and patio. "Prosperous" from father's shark fishing at Isabela, they had chairs enough to seat everyone and expensive tequila to down by the tumblerfuls. We spent a very enjoyable time with these people, even if our conversation was halting. Father, of course, did most of the talking. Everyone felt sorry for Barbara, who at twenty-three had "no esposa, no niños." She explained women's liberation (in terms of women working at paying jobs), which they had heard of and was fine for norteamericanos but not for Mexican women, who "don't work"—except at cooking, cleaning, marketing, childbearing, laundering, truck farming, etc.

The attraction at San Blas is a "jungle cruise" that leaves from about seven miles out of town. We thought we had asked the right questions; still, I felt uncomfortable when we were herded into a Greyhound-like scenicruiser that said "Tepic." Sure enough, it wasn't the local bus. When we finally made ourselves understood, we were let off—only about a mile and a half past our destination. Oh, well, we saved ten pesos.

The river cruise was almost as good as the one at Disneyland, except that there were no hippopotami with wiggly ears. The delight of the trip was swimming in a freshwater pool at the end of the river. (You can't swim at the beach in San Blas. Sewage turns the water brown; one can only imagine what it does to people.) Still, the whole thing was less than the spectacular we'd been led to believe. And the town doesn't even have a good panaderia.

Chacala, which we left a few hours ago, was something else—my favorite stop since Cabo San Lucas. A small village at one end of the bay houses maybe two dozen people, three cantinas, and a jukebox. The beach front is occupied by rows of coconut palms—and campers (only about half a dozen at this time of year). The water is warm and clear. But most spectacular, there are *trees*—real, live, hardwood trees—madrone, banyan, acacia.

Puerto Vallarta
January 31, 1976

Too bad Dick and Liz ever got here. Maybe it was nice once. Bandaras Bay certainly has everything a bay should have (except a Golden Gate), but Puerto Vallarta harbor, like Mazatlan harbor, has nothing—except dirty water and crowds of boats. We come to the cities expecting—what? Whatever, we don't find it, and are only too glad to leave. If only we could find a laundromat *not* in the cities! That and fresh eggs are our main reasons for visiting population centers. Even the laundromat is becoming less of an attraction; the washing costs more than the clothes are worth. I had thoughts of going down to the river here and laundering native style; but when I saw the dead dog? pig? and smelled the dead smells, I knew we'd have to find a laundry. (Had I known, I'd have used the river at Chacala. I'll bet it was fine.)

We did find an American-style meat market in town and bought hamburger and Mennonite-made cheese. (Apparently there's a Mennonite colony of 5,000 or so some few miles inland.) Together with Fritos and pickles we had a real home-style cheeseburger feast—our first. We really never missed it, because the local food has been so good. We've bought at the central mercados, eaten from street vendors, and enjoyed it all. But I haven't been able to bring myself to buy meat at the central mercados—not with all the flies and dogs in, on, and around the meat. It's not enough to make me a vegetarian, just enough to make me seek a cleaner sales place. And we found one here. There are also fast-food franchises in town. But since we never frequented the big bucket at home and since we've seen how chickens are raised (or not) here, we probably won't here, either.

We did stop ashore—unintentionally—yesterday when we sailed in. We found a sandbar in Puerto Vallarta harbor and rested there for seven hours, awaiting high tide. How fortunate we are not to have a monohull! I couldn't imagine living and moving at the angle we were on yesterday.

The buses are great—un peso, una persona. They begin somewhere, where people get in and sit down. So far we haven't found that spot. Talk about jammed New York subways! Today, though, I had a great spot—the rear doorstep. It was just like San Francisco cable cars, at four times the speed. Cool, man. Literally the only cool spot on the bus. I loved it, was sorry when the crowd thinned and señora had to take the seat so graciously offered.

We leave here next Wednesday, stopping at four Chacala-like (we hope) coves before Manzanillo, which we may avoid altogether. (Who needs another San Pedro?) Our next mail stop is Zihuatenejo, which I read about five years ago when it was beginning to be discovered. Here's hoping it hasn't become another P.V.

Should any of you come to meet us in some port, bring: Sebastiani (or any other good California jug wine), Skippy peanut butter (preferably chunky), Hershey's cocoa, Hershey's chocolate bars (with or without almonds), hard salami, and, if you're coming from San Francisco, Larraburu extra sour French bread.

Until then,
Joanne

P.S. Sometimes, to keep awake on night watches, we turn on the radio. Best station so far is KOB from Albuquerque, the station "for the man who makes his livin' drivin' a truck." Best songs: "Hank Williams, You Wrote My Life" and "My Truckin' Luck." Listen some 3 A.M.

February 1, 1976

Just some things I forgot, and since we didn't get to town to mail this, will add.

The front-running candidate for the ugliest tri of the year is here in P.V. Three stories high, she sports three squared-off hulls and a bowsprit on her main hull. Talk about obese, clumsy, and all those other adjectives about homemade boats! But sadder than her looks is that her builder-owner hates life at sea. The ocean scares him—after dreams, and years, and money invested.

With the sometimes light winds we have, we've started swimming while under way. We tie the small inflatable off the aft end on a hundred-foot line, dive off the front end, and swim back. Of course, that's possible only when we're moving *very* slowly.

We're also making Bigfoot available on long- or short-term lease. Poor incognito Martian, he's never dry. That long fur just soaks up seawater. And now that we're in warmer climes he's shedding. Everything is full of gray fur. But at least he doesn't argue.

Thankful for small favors,
Joanne

Zihuatenejo
March 1, 1976

Dear Friends,

If there's one bit of philosophy I've learned on this trip it's "faster horses, younger women, older whiskey, and more money." We hear it nightly on the truckin' station out of Houston.

I've also learned "If you can't stand the heat, get out of the galley." Try the head instead. With the forward hatch open, that's our coolest spot. And the cool air coming up from the underwings through the drain in the head sink cools our wine and our lettuce. Makes brushing teeth a bit awkward, but never mind.

Although we haven't seen really clear skies since we left the desert landscape of Baja, I'd have to vote for this section of coastline (Puerto Vallarta to Zihuatenejo) as my favorite.

Yelapa exists in the same bay as Puerto Vallarta, but not in the same world. Transportation in is by a six-day burro ride—or a two-hour boat ride from P.V. One lovely hotel of six or seven cottages nestles in a corner of the beach. Disembarking from the water taxi, you carry your own luggage ashore through the surf. The beach is no more than a mile long, but of fine, white sand. Near the hotel are three or four open air cantinas. Here the *Sombrero* disgorges about a hundred passengers four or five times a week. Virtually all of them stay in the shade of the cantinas, leaving the beach deserted. At the other end of the bay a river sends fresh water into the sea. Those tired of tropical settings and salty water can hike the trail along the river. Here native women gather, especially on Mondays, to do their laundry in the old-fashioned way. (Enough bleach is used that I'm sure the water is fit to drink!) Well-tended palapa houses dot the trail. Bougainvillea drips over everything, shattering both sun and shade with brilliant colors. Coconut palms and orange trees are confined by fences, but chickens and pigs are not.

Soon, however, you pass the last house, and with it the last sights and sounds of civilization. Now you hear only the river, gurgling its way down its rocky bed. Though sandy beaches invite a stop, the real treat comes near the end of the trail. Here it winds through shaded, *ferny* glens, ending at a waterfall and large pool. Shades of the lower Sierra! You understand why I liked Yelapa. (The town, up another trail in another direction, houses freaked out, out-of-date hippies and some of the most surly—understandably—Mexicans we've seen. Altogether a bad trip. Stick to the waterfall hike.)

The other beautiful bays are more accessible from land. Those of you with campers and sick leave should visit Bahia Chamela or Bahia Tenecatita. You could enjoy being sick at either place for a long time.

When we were in town, we saw the traveling department store—a man with the trunk of his car full of clothing. He'd stop and honk, and women from four or five houses would run out to finger the merchandise, taking home to try on any that had more shape than mumus, returning with either money or the dress.

Another lovely bay suffering for lack of tourists is Bahia de Navidad. A hotel of more than a hundred rooms had only six rented. This was great for us; we paid a small fee and used the tub and shower in one of the vacant rooms. All other places seemed equally empty. It's been a bad tourist year—the time to come south.

Awards for our favorite (so far) coastal city in Mexico go to Manzanillo. When we sailed in Don said, "We're back in San Francisco; what did they do with the Gate?" What a beautiful bay—hills ringing it, mountains farther in the background, even a white tower resembling Coit (if you're nearsighted)! We didn't take the boat into Manzanillo itself because we didn't know if we wanted to stay (and because entering a "real" port means a lot of paperwork). Instead, we spent a week at Santiago, at the other end of the bay, where we met some old friends and made some new ones. Among the former was the *Mary K,* whom we'd met on the day she left Morro Bay last September. Carol and Jack are sailors who have interests in and talk about things other than boats. They even read real books, not just murder mysteries and Gothic novels.

Unfortunately in some ways, Santiago is developing into an American retirement community. But it *is* nice to hear *our* native language again, and all the people we met, Mexican and otherwise, were more than friendly. The Robertsons came out when we landed our dinghy on the beach in front of their home, gave us English-language newspapers, and told us to take as much water as we needed from their faucet.

We visited Manzanillo twice, taking the bus once and motoring over once with *Mary K.* The central mercado proved the most varied and interesting of any so far. Many of the Indians come in from the hinterlands, bringing handicrafts and who knows what kinds of seeds and grasses. Supermercados had both brown and powdered sugar, so we could have frosted cakes again. Even the officials were friendly and helpful.

Between Manzanillo itself (a dirty, diesely, working harbor) and Santiago lies a smaller bay fronted by a hotel that "you have to see"—Las Hadas. Since we'd heard, however, of the treatment (highly inflated prices) they'd given the San Diego-Manzanillo racers and since we've seen Disneyland and therefore know fake Moorish architecture, we didn't stop, even for a drink.

Next stop was Isla Grande. Only one day there convinced me that we'd have to spend a week, so we're going back on Wednesday. We came here to see *carneval* festivities. Nothing like the Rose Parade, but interesting—a flatbed truck with queen and court, King Neptune and seahorses, a triceratops led by a caveman, and the cerveza jeep with its cervezad crew, which included a ten-foot-long dead snake and several dead lizards. All this after dark, down a cobblestoned street with no street lights. The square, however, is well-lighted. That's where the dances and basketball games are held, both very well and loudly attended. Weddings, too, are big business during this pre-Lenten season—at all times of the day and night.

Someone is pouring money into this town. New building and paving are everywhere. Still, except for here at the main harbor, the waters are clean enough for swimming and the people kind enough for relaxing. Although two dozen boats were here over the weekend, we haven't had the misfortune to see the cruise ships come in.

As for us, Erik remains our cat food fisherman and Donald our people food fisherman. He got a swordfish on a lure and line that shouldn't have attracted anything that big. Three magnificent jumps and he (the fish, not Donald) had lure and half the line. We couldn't land him, though; we had to cut him loose. When anyone does catch Erik cleans. He enjoys it, and who am I to argue?

Cain and Abel are getting along better, but David and Absalom are often at it. (I leave it to the "educated"? among you to interpret these allusions for the rest of the "yahoos." [But don't explain that last allusion.] {Is this what's known as a Chinese puzzle?}]) Donald is now (objectively) taller than his mother and (subjectively) smarter than his father. We have no conflict over the former, but much over the latter. Add to that that "nobody understands" our teenager and you have almost the whole picture. The whole picture includes a mere forty feet of boat. When Donald and Erik both are teenagers, we're signing them over to the Chilean navy.

Two things have bothered us about Mexico—the military everywhere, patrolling with automatic rifles, and the bars over all windows, homes as well as stores. We didn't live this way in the "violent" U.S.A.

Another three-hulled "apartment house" came in yesterday. Ugly as sin. (How did that become a saying, sin being as attractive as it is?)

And to all a good night,
Joanne

Zihuatenejo
March 2, 1976

Dear Friends,

What does a pregnant dachshund look like? This question was prompted by seeing a pregnant sow that cleared the ground by barely an inch. Poor thing looked really uncomfortable.

We walked into town this afternoon to mail a letter and found "them" tearing up the main street with jackhammers. I felt right at home, started an American lit class then and there.

Everything we've seen in Mexico belies the "lazy Mexican" stereotype. Quite the contrary, everyone here seems to be hustling—not in the sense of selling shoddy goods to unsuspecting foreigners, but in the sense of making the most of every opportunity—and creating opportunities where they don't exist. I don't understand, though, these small businesses. Everyone's home seems to be a semi-store; some specialize in lemonade and other fruit drinks, others in candy, still others in dusty canned goods and overripe produce. And each one patronizes the other's store. The same money just goes round the village.

Acapulco
March 9, 1976

Hot showers!

March 10, 1976

Salami!

March 13, 1976

Talk about "the life"! We're anchored outside the Acapulco Yacht Club, enjoying hot showers, warm swimming pool, and cold margaritas—all without paying exorbitant fees. Business is so bad this year that graciousness has returned. As long as we maintain a semblance of decorum and spend some money at the bar, we're welcome. If it wasn't for the dozen U.S. boats here, the place would be empty.

Still, I don't like the big cities. Invariably the anchorages are dirty, sometimes filthy. Raw sewage, for instance, is dumped here every morning. Just as at home, if we want to swim we have to travel to a suitable beach—no jumping off the boat. For that, we could return to our last stop, Isla Grande, where the bottom is visible through thirty feet of water. Vibrant-hued fish, some almost irridescent, dart by. We were one day too late for the big party, when seventeen boats were in the small anchorage (would have been too crowded for my taste); but we enjoyed the ice cream social with four other boats—homemade fresh pineapple ice cream, enjoyed against the background of a tropical sunset and followed by rounds of terrible puns and old jokes.

Yesterday morning we went into town to shop and ran into a strike. Stores were shut down all morning to protest high taxes and import duties. And three cruise ships were in! All us poor tourists wandered around looking through closed doors; nobody could spend money.

One thing here is noticeable by its absence—graffiti. Only the government writes on walls. This being an election year, slogans cover all possible surfaces. Solidarity, liberty, education, responsibility, José Lopez Portillo, who has the total solution—reminds me of *Animal Farm*. The opposition party sports infinitesimal posters, most of them peeling off lampposts. Democracy, Mexican style.

We met a San Francisco boat with a sailmaker captain, and now have the sun awnings we didn't have time to get before we left. They make a delightfully cool difference. And Barry gave us a delightfully cheap price. Glad we waited.

It's Sunday at the yacht club, and more of the people who belong are here. Working in a place like this I think I'd become very radical very quickly: moving chairs, serving drinks, handing towels while the beautiful people—no better or handsomer, only richer, usually only because of better choice of ancestors—drink, swim, lounge. Strange that we're part of b.p. activities now. Most of us sailboating (cruising, not racing) Americans have more in common with the waiters than with the waited on.

March 16, 1976

If you begin to green with envy (or cheap gold), remember that I do laundry for four in cold water in plastic buckets with a plumber's helper for an agitator, then wring out by hand and hang up to *almost* dry in the humidity.

Red-handedly,
Joanne

Salina Cruz
April 12, 1976

Dear Friends,

Of all the cities so far, Oaxaca proved the most interesting and most enjoyable—also probably the poorest. The states of Oaxaca and Chiapas are Indian country, and Indians seem to be the nonpeople of Mexico. Government spending, of which we saw much evidence in and around Puerto Vallarta, Acapulco, and points north, seemed almost nonexistent as we traveled from Puerto Angel to Oaxaca. Nevertheless, we're enjoying our stay in these southern parts (except here in Salina Cruz, about which more later).

You who know geography and/or have looked at a map know that the city of Oaxaca has no seacoast. How did we get there? With some apprehension we left *Anduril* and Bigfoot in the care of three other boats at Puerto Angel and took the bus to Oaxaca—167 miles over a two-lane, dirt, mountain road on a second-class Mexican bus. Since we got on at the beginning of the route, we got a seat. Some poor souls stood the whole way—including the girl with the kid (literal meaning) in her pocket. (The three goats rode atop the bus with the luggage and the chickens.) At every stop we seemed to take on more than we unloaded, until we exceeded posted capacity by almost 100 percent. Did we ever welcome the popsicle vendors! Hand two pesos out the window and get four popsicles, more cooling and thirst quenching than any drink. Though I never liked them at home, I've become addicted to popsicles in Mexico. They're made with real fruit and fruit juices, and those made with milk taste much better and are much cheaper than the Mexican ice cream.

The bus took us (for nine and a half hours) through "homeland"—mountains 4,000–5,000 feet high, covered with pines and eucalyptus. Even through the dust we could smell the trees. I still prefer it to saltwater and fish smells. Getting off the bus in a terminal scuzzier than any central valley Greyhound station, we shouldered our packs and took off to find a hotel before dark. Our native dress, which includes but is not totally represented by bermuda shorts, tennis shoes, and backpacks, again gave the locals something to stare at and giggle about.

We found a hotel, complete with continental breakfast delivered to the room on a tray (one of the highlights of the three days, let me tell you), and spent the next three days playing tourist. We explored the ancient Zapotec ruins at both Mitla and Monte Alban. At Mitla, which is still a living town, we followed a five-piece brass band leading a funeral procession to the church. We stayed to examine the church, which had been built on the site of and using many of the materials of the ancient buildings, then examined some of the tombs and living quarters. Some intricate stone work had been done—mosaic patterns laid up without any kind of glue on vertical surfaces. But if Mitla was interesting, Monte Alban was impressive. The whole site covers hundreds of acres on the top of a mountain, chosen, apparently, for reasons of defense, although I like to think that some of the ancients thought the spectacular view just as important. We saw carvings, tombs, observatory, living quarters, ball court—all of them built up on or carved into the mountain. As we took the bus back down the hill we could see dozens of still uncovered tells.

Unfortunately, to my way of thinking, the treasures of Monte Alban were not left on the site but were taken to the museum in Oaxaca. Splendid gold and silver jewelry (I bought a replica and shot April's budget before April began), skulls inlaid with turquoise, intricate stone carvings—all look impressive behind glass and on pedestals, but just once I'd like to see magnificent artifacts either at the site or displayed in a reasonable facsimile.

For on-site splendors we had to visit the churches. Oaxaca boasts (yes, the brochures boast) twenty-nine, but we visited only half a dozen, all featuring lots of statuary and gold leaf. Talk about conspicuous consumption! I don't know how the city could ever have supported so many cathedrals. Most of them are crumbling now, and only Santo Domingo is being repaired, primarily because of its drawing power as a tourist attraction. It has the most gold leaf; a museum is housed in its monastery. Though I am impressed and awed by these structures, I am impressed and dismayed by the contrast between them and the condition of many of the people. Two or three such edifices may be justifiable, providing food for the spirit, but twenty-nine?

Of course we visited the open air market, but as an ex–movie star once said (untruthfully) about a redwood tree, when you've seen one, you've seen them all. (Strangely, that statement is truthful if made about coconut palms.) But we did find sesame seeds; in fact, we bought out the woman's whole supply, a kilo and a half. Crazy gringos. Who wants that many sesame seeds? We also bought a few pieces of Oaxaca's famous black pottery.

Perhaps the best part of the trip was the three days with no chores to do (not even beds to make), breakfast brought (including freshly squeezed orange juice), and all meals eaten out. I've been told how awful such living out of a suitcase is. Just let me try it for a while.

We returned on the night bus, first class. That meant we each paid forty cents more and had a reserved seat. We came back to waves the likes of which stupefied us. The surf was running eight to ten feet, and what had been a pond when we'd left looked like San Francisco Bay's potato patch on a very bad day. We'd never have left the boat had we known the bay could get like that. Ignorance is bliss.

Between Puerto Angel and here we visited a little cove inhabited by twenty or so families. We made friends with half a dozen of the children and a third of the marine base (three marines). We gave the kids paper and pencils, and they brought us clams and taught us to eat them raw. The marines just wanted to talk—until the next day, when four other boats came in and the lieutenant was gone. Then "get the gringo" became the game and drove one boat, frightened, out of the anchorage. A drunk young marine (maybe seventeen) swam out to the new arrival in his uniform shirt and underwear and began talking very loudly in Spanish, demanding papers, money, who knows what else. Evidently the people aboard the boat knew *no* Spanish and were convinced that this drunk kid in his BVDs was somebody both official and important. Don was about to go over when drunk and friends left the sloop and came to our boat. Now, Erik had gone off with the dinghy, and we have not yet made a boarding ladder, so Enrique tried to scramble up the side of the boat, all the time yelling "marinero" and "dinero." Don finally helped him aboard (a drowned Mexican marinero would have been a problem) and began shouting back, calling him a drunk and some other terms he learned years ago when he had a summer job pear picking with a crew of Mexican laborers in Northern California. Then he insisted on name, rank, and serial number, and Enrique began to calm down—and throw up all over the aft end of the boat. Suddenly, profuse apologies and we're all "amigos." By this time the marines we'd met the previous day had swum out to see what was happening, and after more "amigo" talk they towed Enrique home. But by then the sloop had upped anchor and left, and we haven't seen her since.

We left the marines, the children (who could do all the cat's cradle and other string games; where do kids learn these things?), the clams and lobsters to come here, our last Mexican port. Normally the winds blow twenty-five knots here in the harbor. We're having some unaverage but not unusual thirty-five to fifty-five knot winds, complete with blowing sand and grit. These wretched winds come from Texas, one more black mark against a state I never liked. It is not pleasant, and the water, of course, is like any commercial harbor—ugh.

April 16, 1976

"In unity there is strength," so when Don and ten other skippers went to check out, they decided not to pay the *mordida* that several boats paid last week. There was some unpleasantness and some talk of "typing fees"; but when Lou sat down at a typewriter and began to fill out forms and Don mentioned "Tourist Bureau," problems dissolved.

April 18, 1976 (Easter Sunday)

Friday night we had our first storm at sea—rain, hail, and wind enough to get four of us up to reduce sail. Between the rain and my steamed-up glasses I couldn't see a thing. We caught some water, enough for baths today and a small load of laundry, but things were too hectic for real water catching. That's been the story of this trip—hectic. Good afternoon winds have almost invariably increased to on-the-nose chop, necessitating reduced sail. At least we've learned a lot. I understand now why boats require so much maintenance. What punishment they take! No house ever had it like this.

Radio contact with several of the other boats in the "pack" shows our good fortune. Throughout the worst of the weather and most rolly anchorages, we've been comfortable. And we haven't had any losses. One of our group lost all internal rigging last night, and another lost a new headsail overboard.

April 19, 1976

Donald and Erik colored eggs yesterday, after the Easter bunny's arrival, since Saturday chop and headwinds had prevented such activity. After the Friday night storm our DR (dead reckoning) was way off. We spent last night hove-to off what Don decided was Acajutla (El Salvador), even though Donald and I said there weren't enough lights. We came the twenty-plus miles to Acajutla this morning.

Erik is being more conscientious about his studying (under pressure).

We still irritate Don by telling him how to handle the boat coming into an anchorage.

I have hay fever or a head cold.

The *#!&%* stove is worse than ever.

Acajutla, El Salvador
April 21, 1976

People here are courteous—and poor. Dirt poor, poorer than anything we saw in Mexico. Vendors are unaggressive, officials and townspeople polite. It is impossible to practice our Spanish. All the people here want to practice English. It's their ticket out to someplace with a future—preferably the United States.

The eleven of us went to Sonsanate yesterday and attracted quite a crowd of children and adults alike. We were followed around town by nearly thirty people. They watched us eat slices of watermelon. Lew, skipper off another boat, taught some of the children closest to him how to play hot hands, and the game spread through the crowd like an epidemic. Females of all ages fingered my hair to see if something of such a strange color was real. Provisioning was impossible; there isn't much to buy in the markets, except cheap avocados and cabbage. The bread is *terrible,* and we never did learn what they do with the beautiful beef on the hoof that we saw grazing in rich pastures as we rode inland on the bus. There was an overabundance of cheap harmonicas imported from mainland China. Also, Foremost is here—and Fudgsicles.

April 23, 1976

Hove-to off the coast of Nicaragua (it better be!), reading *Walden.* It's an enjoyable way to spend my watch. I just hope we're in the right place. All the lights that said "Corinto" when we arrived have gone off.

May 3, 1976

It wasn't Corinto, but at least we were above the harbor; most of the group landed below and had to beat back. Three went on instead. Counting elapsed time we "beat" the two boats we travel most closely with by eight and twelve hours.

We hadn't planned to stop in Corinto, and I wish we hadn't. The harbor at the mouth of the river is quite dirty, the whistle blows at any time of day or night when there may be work available (it sounds a lot, but only for one or two jobs; there's massive unemployment), we dragged anchor three times (so did every other boat except the one whose anchor was wrapped around a submerged cable; they couldn't raise their anchor), and we had to pay $20 for the "privilege" of being in Nicaragua.

The epidemic of anchor-dragging was caused by the opposition of wind, tide, and currentts. We started out with floating anchor line, which wrapped around our prop and rudder. We unsnarled it and set out a second anchor. Apparently they pulled each other loose. Then we put two anchors on one rode. They tangled and undid each other. Finally, we put out one anchor on a buoyed nylon line; the buoy pulled up the anchor. I was glad to leave.

The trip to here (Bahia Elena) took three days. We had head winds all the way, usually above twenty knots. Then Saturday morning as we approached the entrance to the bay, winds hit forty and clouds hid our destination. We turned and ran for eight hours, averaged six plus knots under storm jib alone. We finally arrived here Sunday around 1600; the gear shift went out as we were anchoring; Don spent forty-five minutes fixing it.

We had a spectacular lightning show last night, then some rain. We didn't catch much water.

We saw more sea life coming into this bay than anywhere else—literally hundreds of dolphins, all cavorting, leaping extraordinarily high, swimming extraordinarily fast. The boys counted two dozen turtles, several marlin or swordfish.

The bay is pretty, but still dry. Today we had wind gusting to more than forty knots. The morning was pretty, with fast-moving clouds playing light and shadow on the gold hills. The coolness was welcome. Now if only we could *walk* somewhere and see real trees!

May 8, 1976

Yesterday we saw our first wild monkeys—spiders, we think. Also birds of bright colors—woodpeckers, orioles, what-have-yous—but no parrots.

Winds have been bad every day—apparently "normal," judging from our experience and that of other boats here during the last two weeks. Yesterday the wind bounced a hatch cover across the deck; it dented the cabin side and Don's knee.

May 11, 1976
Playa del Cocos, Costa Rica

Now I know why pioneer women hated the prairies. Will the wind never stop? We left Elena Saturday for Salinas, decided not to fight into the wind, rode to the next bay over from Elena, found even more wind and less protection, returned to Elena. We left Sunday at 0530, downwind in front of forty-five knot winds, going nine to fifteen under double-reefed main and staysail. We turned into it, replaced the staysail with the stormjib, and did six knots for the next five hours, into Culebra, "the best harbor in Central America—safe, secure, and easy of access." Whitecaps were hitting the shore, so we came here, where they stop ten yards offshore. We can't swim in the wind and the chop; and it's too much of a chore to row ashore to explore. Off to Puntarenas.

As ever,
Joanne

P.S. I can't get used to traveling east to get to South America, or to the sun rising over water and setting over land. Who topsy-turvied the world?

Puntarenas, Costa Rica
June 11, 1976

Dear Friends,

Ah, the hazards of traveling. According to our guidebook, "Chagas' Disease (South American Trypanosomiasis) is another disease not often seen in Great Britain [or the U.S., I'll wager]. It is a chronic illness, incurable, transmitted by a large insect which lives in rural districts on dirt floors frequented by opossums. It bites at night so avoid sleeping in such conditions." We shall.

June 12, 1976

The boys and I (Is that as catchy as *The Egg and I* or *The Bears and I*?) are on our way to Cartago and the Irazu volcano, from where, on a clear day, you can see both Atlantic and Pacific oceans. Don has stayed aboard the boat in Puntarenas because the afternoons have not been clear. Some days there is little or no rain; but often a big storm blows up, and we didn't feel we could leave the boat unattended, even in the harbor. Things got pretty wild one evening last week; sailboats playing bumper cars in a shallow channel is no one's idea of fun. So the snake in every paradise strikes again.

June 12, 1976

We sit in our rain-proof sanctuary—the local movie theater. Unless more customers arrive in the next ten minutes, Peter Sellers will perform for a dozen of us. And in quiet, for there is no popcorn or candy concession.

The trip from San Jose to Cartago, like the one from Puerto Angel to Oaxaca, Mexico, was like coming home. We're in high country (4,000 feet or more) again, among pines and eucalyptus. The land scent evokes more homesickness and nostalgia than anything else. As in Washington state, everything here is green—varying shades, but no blue-black, forest green. And as in Washington it's obvious why everything is green. Rain by any other name—even liquid sunshine—is just as wet.

On the whole, then, Costa Rica pleases, except that there are too many cigarette smokers. Haven't seen so many—at social gatherings, here in the theater, in restaurants—since the English department office (and office parties) at Costa Mesa High School in 1969. And since we've been living pure for so long and have even become used to clean air, it's more annoying than ever.

It's no wonder that norteamericanos like Costa Rica, even aside from the climate, scenery, and relatively low cost of living. Even though Spanish is the national language, the culture and people are not Spanish but Western European. You see a heterogeneous crowd on the streets, just as at home. Even a blonde or redhead who learns to speak Spanish like a native can pass for one (a "Tico"). And there are bald heads, too, something we haven't seen (except on yachties) for months.

June 13, 1976

Today we visited Irazú, the volcano that last erupted in 1963, blanketing San Jose in inches of ashes for two years. On a clear day you can seen both Atlantic and Pacific oceans, but there are no clear days during the rainy season. We saw only clouds, mists, and the crater, smelled only the sulphur rising from the green water at the bottom. And was it cold! A change, and a welcome one at that. My first time above 10,000 feet in two years! That's too long. One of the disappointments of ocean sailing is that it all takes place at sea level. Now if *I* were arranging things...

You people back home are not on your toes taking care of things. Mother just sent a newspaper article noting that Larraburu, makers of *the finest* of San Francisco's sourdough breads, has gone out of business. If you'd really been thinking, you'd have bought the Giants and Larraburu and replaced the styrofoam hotdog buns with sourdough rolls. In that way you'd have saved two S.F. institutions (I know the Giants came from N.Y., but do you remember how long ago *that* was?) and created a conglomerate that surely could have created jobs for two world travelers about three years from now.

More of life's little ironies, or what the big guy would be excoriated for is praiseworthy in the little guy. The Costa Rican legislature, in its infinite wisdom, has passed a law making it illegal for a business to have a name not Spanish or "one of the aboriginal tongues." Businesses already licensed will not be affected, but there will be no new McDonald'ses, Pizza Huts, etc. (although the same pseudo-food will undoubtedly be served under Spanish titles, more's the pity). (Some critics are wondering whether or not the ten thousand Chinese restaurants can be categorized "aboriginal.") Can you imagine the world outcry if the U.S. pulled such a stunt? And this happening when beleaguered U.S. schools are being pushed to sometimes absurd lengths to provide multilingual education and when counties are being forced to print multilingual ballots. Do public schools in Mexico or Costa Rica or China provide multilingual classes for English-speaking minorities? Do their governments print ballots in English as well as the national language? Does anyone think they should or raise a fuss if they don't? No—but people sneer at Americans who don't learn the language of a country they visit for two weeks.

July 27, 1976

It's almost time to leave Costa Rica. Our three months are up on August 17, and the timing is right for arriving in the southern hemisphere during their summer. So next week we head for the Canal Zone, taking about a month to explore the islands along the way. We won't be sorry to leave this particular anchorage. It is, as someone said, the nicest sewer we've anchored in.

For most of the trip to Panama we hope to be in company with a Canadian boat with three children—boys eleven and thirteen and a girl fifteen. Both sets of parents are delighted that we've found each other. They think it's only too bad we're not going through the Canal. We think it's only too bad they're not going to Chile, then west. I don't know exactly how the meeting has changed things on *Komox,* but here it's meant that Donald washes his own clothes, also showers and washes his hair daily, of his own volition. It's also meant that we have some new music—Beatles and Bay City Rollers and Paul McCartney and Wings. I thought (devoutly hoped) I'd left all this behind. I guess there's no escaping teenagerhood, not even three thousand miles from home.

We've just finished three weeks of painting, have about four days to go. We expected to have to paint the bottom (grubs grow fast in this warm water), likewise the interior (we never finished it before we left). But the *#! exterior paint...

How was the Bicentennial celebration? We missed the ambassador's do in San Jose, since we were hauled out at Joe's Hacienda Nicoyana, but the American colony there had its own celebration. Almost two dozen boats came in for the potluck, dinghy races, and just general roistering. Erik and Chris (from *Komox*) won the sailing dinghy race, and Don and I came in second in the George Washington—wife standing in the bow and husband rowing. One more potluck and then it's off for Panama.

As always,
Joanne

Balboa, Canal Zone
September 14, 1976

Dear Friends,

Greetings from the socialist capital of the world—the Panama Canal Zone. Ironic that this is what Reagan wants to keep "American." Those of you who have lived on a military base know something of what it's like—only here there are seven bases, and everything in between is owned and operated by Pan Canal, including the schools. Employees live in subsidized housing, buy at subsidized commissaries, get subsidized medical care. No private businesses are allowed in the Zone—and no non-Zone employees are allowed to buy there. Consequently, visitors often know more about Panama City than do "Zonians" who have lived here from five to twenty years. News in this ghetto is also controlled—both radio and newspaper. Only the official line is allowed. For the past three days we've heard of the "student riots" in Panama City. Radio broadcasts (Be thankful for commercials. We have to listen to public service announcements on this government subsidized radio.) and signs at most exits warn Americans against going into Panama. We've been in every day and saw our first "riot" yesterday. A cordon of police passed by, clearing the street. We were pulled into the safety of an ice cream shop. All the merchants along the street pulled down their iron grills to protect their windows. A stream of college students flowed down the street, carrying banners protesting increases in the prices of milk and flour. Next came a disorganized, disorderly (but not rowdy) bunch of high school students, glad to be out of classes on a nice day, emulating their elders. A phalanx of police followed—and then a horrendous traffic jam. Shutters were raised, and it was business as usual. Zone radio later reported violence, cars being set afire, etc., practically in front of our ice cream shop viewpoint. New Zonians look with a jaundiced eye, as we do, at the media. But "old hands" live in fear. Reminds me of the neighbors in Westminster buying guns after the Watts riot.

October 4, 1976

We spent our ten allotted days at the yacht club, returned to Panamanian waters and the Perlas Islands, and have returned to the yacht club to get the last of our "CARE" packages from home and to have the last work done on our stove and ham set.

We took a month sailing here from Costa Rica, stopping at many lovely islands along the way. Some were uninhabited; there we swam in clear waters teeming with tropical fish. At the inhabited islands the natives taught us and gifted us. While the boys and I were snorkeling, gathering a few scallops and missing two giant lobsters at Isla Brincanco, some local fishermen/lumberjacks visited Don on the boat. When he said he didn't know conch, they jumped off the boat, dove underneath her, and came up with three big ones (and a stray scallop) for dinner; they also showed Don how to prepare the things. Pounded and fried like abalone, they're delicious. The next day we got our own, this time grinding them up for spaghetti sauce.

At Isla Parida we met Jorgé and his family, who have a fairly large farm on a forty-five degree slope. He gave us two twelve-pound watermelons, vine ripened and juicy. He was delighted when we gave him a Polaroid picture of his family. They had been worried about us, not having firm land under us during the storm the previous night. We had been concerned that their palapa hut didn't keep them dry. Maybe it's perspective, not ripeness, that is all.

The Panamanians we met in the city proved just as friendly. On our first day here, before we knew the city, we had to take a bus somewhere way out on the main highway. When we boarded and gave the address to the driver, he insisted that we sit right behind him so he could be sure we got off at the right place. A policeman got up and gave me his seat. Another time Don and I were discussing whether or not we were on the right bus. The man sitting behind us made the driver stop to let us off and put us on the next bus, the correct one.

The buses themselves are an experience. They are the most colorfully decorated and cheapest (five cents) of five countries of colorful, cheap, and crowded buses. My only complaint is that every driver turns on his radio to maximum volume. Stores along Avenida Central do the same. With my low tolerance for noise it's painful to go downtown.

Canal Zone buses vividly point up the difference between Panama and the Zone. All CZ buses are painted the same—white tops, orange bottoms. No psychedelic designs, landscapes, "mod" stickers, or religious paintings adorn them as they do the Panamanian buses. No radios, either. No crowds. And the fare is four times as much.

We did have one unpleasant incident last week. Don was mugged—at 10 A.M. on a main street. Having taken to heart the advice given by some rape counselors, he grabbed one assailant by the throat, held on, fell down, and started screaming. He was immediately surrounded by help. One "muy mal hombre" got away, but empty-handed. Don and the crowd kept the other one until the police arrived (almost immediately). Don suffered an almost invisible knife scratch on his collarbone and excessive adrenalin production. We still think Panama a friendly place.

Even the Americans have welcomed us. We were on our way in from the Perlas Islands last month when we spotted five sailboats.

"We're having a barbecue. Free wine on the beach. Turn around." We did, and met some Balboa Yacht Club members who have been helpful ever since. During that first day at the island, I mentioned that we were anxious to get to Panama, since we were out of all fresh foods and shortening as well. People off one of the big tris presented us with a goodie bag—lettuce, tomatoes, cucumbers, fresh eggs, butter. What a delight after a month without! Later, when we asked if we could buy a propane stove somewhere (our Optimus kerosene stove has been trouble and frustration since we left home), these same people gave us the one they'd recently taken off their boat.

Since we've been here at the yacht club anchorage people have driven us around town, taken us out to dinner, bought us a few things at the PX (Skippy peanut butter, marshmallows, cat food, and cat litter—all unavailable or very expensive in Panama). After we crewed *Komox* through the Canal, we had to take the train back here (transcontinental fare—one dollar). We arrived at a place we didn't know, asked a nurse getting off duty where to catch the bus. "You can't get one from here. Hop in and I'll drive you to the yacht club." Taxis lined the street.

Last Sunday we were at Contadora, the developed island in the Perlas group. A Pan Canal pilot swam out to the boat and invited us home for dinner. He has a beautiful vacation/retirement home, extravagantly furnished, with a sweeping view of bays and islands. We had a delicious steak and fish dinner.

Our fishing has been good, but not super. We usually manage to catch mahi-mahi, Sierra, or tuna twice a week when we're under way. At anchor we go after shellfish (except at places like this). So far we've taken no lobster, except for what we catch from local fishermen, using *Playboy* and .22 shells for bait. Shrimp fishermen want just the magazines.

We still haven't heard whether or not Ecuador will permit us to visit the Galapagos. We had an introduction to a highly placed official in the defense ministry, which runs the islands; but there was a coup in Ecuador while we were sailing down the coast, and our man did not keep his job. So we have no name to drop, though we still hope to get permission. If so we'll go there, then to Peru. If not, straight to Peru and backpacking along the Inca trail. High country at last!

Elevatedly,
Joanne

The Sea Not Taken

en route to the Galapagos Islands
November 15, 1976

Dear Friends,

We're traveling through what is marked on the charts as the doldrums. The wind is blowing thirty to thirty-five knots, and we're headed into it. Ours may be the first boat to circumnavigate beating to windward the entire way. In unison now, everyone repeat that old Gaelic blessing: May the road rise to meet you; *may the wind be always at your back.*

We last stopped at Cocos Island, where Don, a new friend from Ft. Lauderdale, explained the enmity of old salts toward trimarans. "You got here in seven days. It took us thirteen. Then you sat rocking gently at anchor while we rolled from gunwale to gunwale in the swell. If you trimaraners want to be socially acceptable you'll just have to slow down and be uncomfortable with the rest of us."

Not that beating to weather feels especially comfortable, even in a tri. The wind whistles in the rigging, the shrouds shriek under tension, salty foam flies everywhere, and the wind whips your face redder than any sunburn. But what a sensation of motion! You know you must be flying along at eight or ten knots—until you look at your knotmeter or glance back at your wake and realize you're lucky if you're going three. The boat's working and the helmsman's working, but so much energy is being spent fighting wind and wave that not much remains for making way.

Down below, the pickle jar clinks against the honey jar, and you hope that neither breaks. Some books that weren't put away slide across the table and fall to the floor. On every other wave you lose your seat (and sometimes your stomach) just as on a roller coaster. You notice that the leaks you fixed at the last port aren't leaking, but some new ones are. Though the wind doesn't sound so loud, all the other noises and shudders are magnified, and you can feel the water thudding against that three-eighths inch plywood. The sensation of speed is even greater than it is outside. "Slow down! We're not racing! Oh. Two knots. Sorry."

At least on this trip we haven't been plagued by rain as we were five of the seven days between Balboa and Cocos Island. We would have enjoyed some of the beauty of a wind-whipped sea on that trip—seeing waves cresting and breaking, foam dancing in the sunlight on the crests before sliding down the face to dissolve slowly in the trough, shimmering patches of translucent turquoise hanging just below the foam, melting in rivers down the face of the breaking waves. We enjoyed nothing like that on the trip from Balboa to Cocos. It started placidly enough; the first afternoon we had so little wind that we trailed the dinghy and went swimming. But the wind came up faster than Don and Donald did, and we had a Chinese fire drill trying to slow the boat down and get them aboard. We broke a batten on the mainsail and lost a dinghy seat, oar, and sponge in the process. On subsequent stormy days we lost one of our watercatching buckets and broke the lifeline stanchion that the ham antenna was temporarily attached to. ("That is something up with which I will not put."—Winston Churchill) Fortunately, we didn't lose the antenna. Our worst casualty came when we hit a log one night while sailing along at seven or eight knots and crushed six inches of the bow. It looked terrible but didn't make a hole, so we had no real problems.

Cocos Island is noted for its pirate treasures and its sharks. We saw none of the former and few of the latter—happily, for that meant we would swim in the brilliantly clear, warm water. Don repaired the crushed bow with underwater epoxy.

Although we didn't search for treasure, many expeditions have. So far as recorded, nothing has ever been found. Each expedition, however (and subsequent visiting yachts), recorded itself on the rocks along the beach or main creek. Some of the carving looked very professional. Much of it dated from the 1800s. The oldest we saw read 1648–1651—no name, just a beautiful sailfish cut into dark red rock. I'm sure his bill at one time pointed to the treasure, but who knows where he stood more than three centuries ago?

Among cruising folk, Cocos Island has become noted for its pigs. Fresh meat! Donald, with assorted others of the family, went hunting six times, came back with tales of tracks, but no pigs. Finally, Juan, who lives most of the year there with his wife and daughter, got two pigs and a deer and shared them with us and *Svea*. That meant a longer stay, since some of our meat went into *Svea*'s freezer. It also meant pork roast five times in one week, since we couldn't leave it there indefinitely. I still like pork, but I prefer it grain-fed; and I absolutely abhor the smell of warm, freshly killed meat. Still not enough to turn me vegetarian, though.

Galapagos Islands
November 21, 1976

We crossed the equator, and it's *cold*. The Humboldt current does it. We've put away the bathing suits and taken out the wool socks. Bilge temperature beer would again be cool—if we had any.

We've come here even though we never received permission. If no one said "yes," no one said "no," either. Our request was simply ignored. We'll visit the outer islands first, winding up with an "emergency" stop at the entering port (to fix the "hole" in the bow).

We're anchored at Fernandina Island, a black volcano rising from a turquoise sea. (Actually, it looks more like middle blue-green, which used to be my favorite color but which Crayola has apparently stopped making.) What fascinating life ashore! The marine iguanas look like miniature dinosaurs, complete with grinning mouths and spiky heads. They spit when you approach too closely. When they swim they move only their tails, trailing their legs limply behind. Seals abound, almost tame, playful except during the hot sun times, when they wisely seek the shade. Flightless cormorants and the world's smallest penguins live here. They glide on top of the turquoise water, plunge smoothly down to fish. Erik says the penguins use their stubby wings like hands for climbing when ashore. They and the cormorants look a little silly ashore, with those useless wings. They are surely two of the funniest birds existing. And I can't get used to penguins on the equator. The pelicans look more than silly; they look ridiculous sitting in the tops of spindly mangrove trees. There are clouds of boobies, and after watching them we know why they're bird-brained. They crash into the water at full speed from heights up to a hundred feet. Ouch, my head! But all is not paradise and fascination. Flies irritate. They come by the hundreds. At least they move slowly, making them hand-killable—a good thing, since our Mexican fly swatter disintegrated in previous battles.

The islands themselves remind me of a cross between the California high desert and Death Valley—very arid with low shrubs struggling for a foothold in volcanic rock. Not being a fan of the desert, I don't especially like them. I'll take my hikes when we reach the Andes, thanks.

November 28, 1976

We've found "Turtle Bay." On the charts it's called "Isla Bartoleme," but only Turtle Bay seems appropriate. We've seen at least fifty of the creatures in the surf line, where they stay all day. Most of them are paired and mating; it looks like a difficult and tedious process. Those who come ashore just drop at water's edge, looking really fagged out. I don't think I would like leading a turtle's life.

The last few days when not ashore we've been making Christmas ornaments and writing Christmas cards. True to long established principles, we didn't begin until Thanksgiving. No pre-Halloween Christmas in this family!

en route to Lima, Peru
December 13, 1976

Call me Betsy Ross. I've spent the afternoon stitching up a Peruvian flag. We bought a Mexican flag; and in El Salvador, Nicaragua, and Costa Rica, we could make do with our "Charlie" flag. But Panama, Ecuador, now Peru, and next Chile require that we do stitchery. Panama, especially, was touchy. Woe betide anyone whose Panamanian flag was smaller than his American flag!

December 14, 1976

Today marks the first anniversary of our voyage. We're celebrating with a cake and a *very* slow day. At this rate we won't reach Lima until New Year's.

To conclude the Galapagos story——

Our visit was cut short when we met a cruise ship at one of our anchorages. We told them of our "emergency" and they gave us all the information we needed about getting into Academy Bay, where to shop there, etc. Since they also supposedly radioed that they'd encountered us, we thought it prudent to go to Academy Bay the next morning. There we were treated very courteously and allowed four days' stay. We actually did take the boat up the river and grounded her. Don removed the temporary patch on the bow and did a proper job.

People were unfailingly kind. Twice we were presented with freshly caught fish for dinner. Then on Friday morning we were taken inland. We'd met a local guide while waiting for fresh bread at the panaderia. Victor took us to his father's farm, where we picked avocados, bananas, oranges, grapefruit, lemons, and peppers—almost more than we could carry and all for no charge and with no expectation of favors. It was quite an enjoyable experience—capped by a new kind of public transportation. The route halfway up the mountain (you walk the rest of the way) is run by private cars, most of them old, small, pick-up trucks. We couldn't take the first one back from the farm because it was filled with potatoes and a cow going in to Saturday's market. We tried sitting on the trussed up cow, but the axles hit the red dirt road and the tires sank inches into it. So we waited an hour and got a ride with potatoes and coffee beans.

Just before leaving, we went out to the Darwin research station to see the most famous Galapagos inhabitants—the giant tortoises. These come in a dozen varieties, distinctions between them too small for most people to notice. Whalers, goats, rats, and wild dogs have seriously reduced the population (two or three races are extinct) so that few visitors see these creatures in the wild. In fact, the tortoises sometimes don't see each other. One island had but two males and thirteen females who never seemed to be in the right place at the right time. They were brought to the station and now there are scores of little ones living in pens for several years before being returned to their homes. Just call us cupid! (Is it just me, or is there really something ironic about these manipulations to "restore the original balance" of the islands?)

December 16, 1976

Pity the poor Peruvian bureaucrat. Government offices must stay open Monday through Friday, 9:30–11 and 3–5, and on Saturdays 9:30–11:30. During the summer (January–March), Saturday hours start at 9, but there are no afternoon hours on any days.

Suffragettes take heart from Uruguay. Not only do women have the boat—I mean vote (Freudian slip?)—but divorce is legal. Women may divorce without giving a reason; a proposal to extend this right to men met with vehement opposition. Down with equality; up with privilege.

off Lima, Peru
December 18, 1976

Here we sit, waiting for Monday. We arrived too late for Saturday morning office hours; had we gone in after hours we faced unknown overtime fees (in Ecuador they're double); had we anchored in some cove, waiting for Monday, we faced fines—$233 for a Chilean vessel that anchored in Peruvian waters before being cleared into Lima. So we are hove-to off the harbor, waiting for business hours, spending our time putting up Christmas decorations and cleaning house.

It's a good thing we're here. It's been two and a half months since the last real shopping, and we're again running out of things—eggs, jam, sugar. We've learned to substitute other ingredients for eggs in baking, but I can't bring myself to try scrambled gelatin and baking powder.

> Your travel substitute,
> Joanne

> Lima, Peru
> December 22, 1976

Dear Friends,

Because of the postal strike in Lima, this letter is coming to you from Sioux City, Iowa. A prize will be given for the most original explanation of how this came about. To be considered, each entry must be received.

> January 14, 1977

Almost everyone in Peru smokes. Otherwise we are (usually) enjoying ourselves. Today I'm indulging in a wash and dry—for the laundry, not for me. I've ridden about ten miles on the bus to the nearest laundromat with twenty pounds of laundry. Not the greatest fun, but it beats doing it in buckets on the boat and hanging it out to non-dry in the humid air. I don't even have to do it myself—can't, in fact, since only authorized persons are allowed to touch the machines. They're almost more precious than (and almost as expensive as) the remaining Inca gold. Now if only I could find a place that served innumerable cups of coffee while I sit and wait and write. Barring that, the local juice bar at the artisans market provides soft chairs and relative quiet—also the chance to watch fellow Americans speak English ever louder to make these "dumb Indians" understand. I've often been tempted to say I'm Canadian.

We've been here three weeks and have had our share of good and bad experiences. Don and I spent a week down with the flu. Packages sent from home have been taken before we received them—we suspect here at the yacht club. And all the mail we have received has been pre-opened. Then yesterday we experienced our first serious theft. The radio-cassette recorder needed repair, so we took it with us when we went to the bank. I set it down on the counter while I got out the passports, and it vanished. Hope the thief knows a good electronics man.

On the other hand——

Just before Christmas we were walking home from dinner at the *pollo a brasa* (local version of Colonel Sanders) when an English-speaking couple struck up a conversation. Cesár was born and raised in Lima but spent five years in the States going to school. His fiancée was down for the holidays. Since then we've been part of the Narvaez family. We spent Christmas with them and have seen them almost every day. Cesár commands a harem of three girls and two cars, so we often have other than bus transportation in the afternoons, when most offices are closed during the summer. Our boys have a house on shore to go to where they can play records, watch "The Munsters" dubbed in Spanish, get teased by grandpa and fussed over by the girls. We have a friend and very helpful translator.

Yacht club members and boat boys (unlike yacht club managers) have also been helpful. When Señor Morales, owner of the luxury motor yacht on the next mooring, learned that we were trying to find out how to get diesel, he gave us forty-five gallons from the several hundred he was getting the next day. We have not been allowed to pay for it.

So we forget the radio and remember Cesár and Sr. Morales.

Though we haven't yet left the Lima area, I think we have a feel for the country. More than half (I think) of the people live here, many in hovels such as we have not seen since El Salvador. Even in these areas, though, the streets are swept—though the piles of garbage so swept are heaped around the outer wall of the community. Roof tops (low, because short people don't need tall houses) sprout TV antennas, which are sold by street vendors, just as avocados and oranges are.

Thousands of new houses are being built, most by cooperatives (somewhat similar to unions). In their squat boxiness they remind me very much of Daly City. "Ticky-tacky" they may be, but an immeasurable improvement over the squatter towns. And they blossom in vivid violet, garish green, and outrageous orange. We've been unable to find out how much these cost, but I suspect that, as at home, the current slum dwellers can't afford this redevelopment.

Most appalling of all are the "new towns" that spring up like mushrooms overnight. Hundreds of (mostly) Indians come down from the hills at a time and raise tents or shacks on any available land. One of the downtown parks in Callao (Lima's port) looks like a Boy Scout Jamboree. Every public restroom is inhabited, as are the backstage rooms at the open air theater. And there seems no way that the government or the social structure can cope as quickly as the squatters move in.

Attempting to cope, the government has imposed a curfew on Lima and its suburbs. No one is allowed on the streets between 1 and 5 A.M. Restaurants and bars start closing at 11 P.M. so that employees have plenty of time to clean up before going home. Buses on the longer runs stop running by 11, and most of the others are finished by midnight. Taxis make a killing between 11 and 12:30. Television commercials throughout the day explain these rules. Police supposedly will assist anyone who has an emergency during curfew. (I don't know whether or not labor is an emergency.) If a private citizen must be out during curfew he must walk down the center of the street waving a large, white flag. A person driving a car must also fly a large, white flag as well as have his car windows rolled down and his interior lights on. Woe betide anyone on the streets under any other conditions. César says it's shoot first, question later. And the military (all branches) patrol the streets all day long, automatic weapons at hand, making believers of us all—not a very comfortable or relaxing atmosphere. And Chile's supposed to be worse, especially with the threat of a Peru-Chile border war. On to the South Pacific!

(I thought that my Spanish pronunciation was getting better, but I just got *chicha morada* [a Kool-aid–like drink made from boiled corn] instead of *un vaso de agua* [a glass of water]. Maybe it's just that no one drinks water here.)

Peruvian officialdom is extremely officious. We should have known better, but we had a few packages sent down. The first came air freight. That meant airport customs. We spent two days running papers from hither to yon to be shuffled, stapled, and torn apart. And we had César with us to translate! The customs man felt terrible because he was ready to charge us a large fee when we pointed out the "yacht in transit" address (supposedly free from duty), whereupon we had to move back three spaces and miss our next turn. At the end of the second day we had to go to three different offices to complete the forms to pay fifteen soles (twenty-two cents). But since our total costs came to only $3.50 and we didn't have to pay an agent (we saw agents getting the same run around), we didn't feel too bad.

When Don and I went for a small package at the post office customs, we had less luck. We spent only two and a half hours there but got a *real* run around. "Go over there." "Get out of here." "I said, go over there." "I said, get out of here." Don finally got angry and we got some action. They found and opened our package and got the forms ready. Again "yacht in transit" caused problems that we finally resolved. However, charges were to be $4.25 on $2.50 worth of merchandise. It wasn't worth an ulcer or a jail cell (Don was really angry by then). I hope they choke on the herb tea.

Having gone through customs only at the Canadian and Mexican borders, I can't say what our people are like. But these officials are petty tyrants. They pull *everything* apart, go through all the pockets on all the clothing. We saw several inspectors at the post office open and use after-shave lotion and hand creams that came their way. I suspect that everything does not always get back into the box. In fact, I wouldn't be surprised if half the merchandise sold by the street vendors came from customs offices.

Because of currency problems, import duties are constantly being raised. A VW costs nearly three times what we pay; a 79-cent jar of cold cream costs five dollars. Two-bedroom apartments with indoor plumbing rent for $150–$250 a month; teachers, bank clerks, etc., make $175–$300 a month. Food costs as much as in the States and clothing half again as much. The only things we found that cost less are movies (72 cents to a dollar) and buses (11 cents). I don't know how the people afford to live.

Many would like to leave, but the government is making it increasingly difficult. Plane tickets (for Peruvians) bear a 30 percent surcharge, as do monetary transactions. (Tourists outside Peru cannot use soles; they must use hard currencies.) Each vacation day out of the country costs a Peruvian 1,000 soles ($15) to his government—in addition, of course, to whatever he spends abroad. The family (Cesár says the mother) of a student studying abroad must post a bond assuring the student's return. If he doesn't return, mom goes to jail; when he does return, he pays the government an amount equal to what he spent abroad.

The old U.S.A. may be sick, even dying, as her critics claim, but you can't find better in any part of the world we've visited so far—a "fact" that frequently makes me despair. Is this really the best mankind can do? (We saw *All the President's Men* last night and have been catching up on election news. It's a despairing day.) We heard all the Carter-Ford "debates," even saw the second (first?), and the only person I was tempted to vote for was the reporter who kept repeating her questions when they weren't answered. I'm glad I didn't get my absentee ballot until last week. How many votes did "none of the above" get in New Mexico? (Or was it Nevada? According to *Time,* one of the states actually gave that as a choice.) In the Canal Zone we applauded Hayakawa's statement on the canal: "We stole it fair and square in the first place." Now we hear that Jimmy didn't mean he'd cut the defense budget when he promised to trim $7 billion from it. Give me fair and square theft. Or does the emperor really have new clothes that we just can't see from so far away? Tune in tomorrow. We shall be leaving for Cuzco and Machu Picchu, and I will leave off philosophizing and return to vivid description of glorious landscapes and the wonders of the ancients. (Speaking of that, we've visited several museums, thus spoiling my desire for buying anything new. What I want sits behind glass in museums; nothing on shelves in stores is so good. I never knew Don to be so interested in museums.)

The laundry's not done, so you get stuck with more of the same. Corner grocery stores, surprisingly to me, charge less than supermarkets. And you can get small quantities. Want a pound of flour? We'll open a kilo sack and sell you half. Want three cigarettes? Winstons or Salems? Napkins are single-ply and cut into fourths or smaller pieces for restaurant service. Every tourist who ventures outside the Sheraton learns to carry toilet paper. Cold drinks and hot showers are almost the same temperature. Apparently all the red dye # whatever that can't be used in the States has come to Peru, where four times as much is used in the hot dogs. The first fifteen days of the month are beefless—even meatless, unless you get to the market by 6 A.M. (no mean feat with curfew until 5). "Milk" means evaporated, and it's usually unavailable. Seemingly no one uses the available powdered whole milk, and the little fresh milk apparently goes to restaurants. Drivers, while perhaps not in infancy, have not left adolescence. The horn is the most important item on the car. Some people have decided to drive on the left, British-style. Give me the safety of the seas!

en route to Cuzco, Peru
January 19, 1977

Finally into my loved high country (12,000 feet) and how are we doing? Headaches and general altitude sickness, but getting better every day. Sea legs don't prepare you for high altitude hiking.

We started the trip—Lima to Arequipa—on a first-class Peruvian bus—equal to about a twenty-year-old Greyhound. The ride wasn't unpleasant—until the bus broke down in the middle of the desert. Six hours later all the five gringos aboard and four of the locals were rescued by the repair bus. Other locals, used to this, I suppose, crowded onto the first two buses that stopped. I think we got the better deal. Instead of standing room only on a hot, crowded bus, we got to spread out in comfort. Still, it was not an auspicious beginning, since we missed our train connection.

That missed connection proved a mixed blessing, giving us several hours in Arequipa. I much prefer it to Lima: hills, instead of that dreadful flatness, and water. The city, being only half the size of Lima, is much cleaner. Arequipa also considers itself an independent republic, belonging to Peru only "temporarily"—rather like the two Californias. Communist literature and posters adorn all bookstalls and many walls.

Before dinner we visited the beautiful Convent of Santa Catalina: flowers everywhere, brightly colored exterior walls, frescos, brick vaulted ceilings. I think I could have lived there happily, surrounded by sunshine, beauty, and quiet. Even the laundry facilities (water piped to huge, earthenware wine jugs), though outside, were lovely, surrounded by a lovely garden. In its heyday the convent covered 250 hectares, housed 50 Dominican sisters, 15 novitiates, and 200 servants. No wonder the nuns had time for embroidering the beautiful altar cloths and vestments.

Our next experience in Arequipa was horrifying. We had to get on the train. Thousands of people, mostly Indians, crushed to get through a five-foot-wide gate and board the train. People were almost trampled; I thought I was going to lose my right arm. Erik got separated from us and panicked. Don was fighting the crowd to get to him when they both were swept inside the gate with the crowd. I've never felt so frightened and helpless. Then, just when we thought we were safely aboard the train and settled, Don had to move one of the backpacks from one overhead rack to another. Arms up, he was hit—lost his wallet containing his credit cards, half our money (I had the other half), and our train tickets. There was no way, of course, to catch the thief. And the money was in cash, because travelers' checks are so damnably hard to cash here. Police were sympathetic, but no help—except that they got Don to the head of the line to buy more tickets. We spent the night cramped into two facing double seats, low-backed, no more than three feet apart. People under five feet tall might find them almost not uncomfortable, but for us it proved a wretched, sleepless night—especially since the lights stayed on all night (to deter theft?). And it got *cold,* though our down sleeping bags kept us warm enough. These contraptions amazed the Indians, who carry half a dozen blankets and just keep adding on as the temperature drops. Their eyes grew bigger and bigger as they saw the blue thing we had grow from its stuff bag size to something big enough to cover four of us.

This is real Indian country. The women have not succumbed even to plaid, pleated skirts, much less to pants. They still wear their heavy wool stockings, several wool skirts, sweaters, wool blanket shawls, and various styles of hats, depending on what village they're from. Slung on the back and around the shoulders and neck is the multicolored shawl, usually holding a baby, often holding potatoes or oranges as well. They are formidable women, all right. The men, wearing fewer clothes and carrying nothing, appear half their size—and not one-tenth so formidable. One of them sympathized with Don for having but two children, suggested that a doctor could probably help him to be a "real man."

(Right now the train is stopped, and the vendors are streaming through, selling candy, cigarettes, stew, fruits, cheese, hot chocolate, drinks, sandwiches—even a lamb quarter!)

Except for Erik, we top these people by at least a head, though many of the women outweigh me. And now I know where all those crinolines went after the style died in the States. It's not just that the women *seem* to be wearing them. They're for sale in the market stalls—a few taffeta, mostly nylon net, all dyed bright pink, blue, or green.

We spent last night in Puno, almost the end of the world. It borders Lake Titicaca, which we visited afoot but didn't go out on, thanks to the theft of Don's wallet. Actually, we probably wouldn't have gone anyway. We're a month behind "schedule" now, and boat rides are no novelty. Now it's on to Cuzco and Machu Picchu. (We learned from our earlier experience. We managed to get and hold three double seats. All the other gringos are in first class.) César gave us an introduction to his uncle and godfather, the archbishop of Cuzco, so we're hoping to find free lodging there. If not, it's another "economy hotel" complete with toilets that don't flush and cold running (sometimes) water. Still, if it's as clean and has as comfortable beds as last night's, we won't complain—much.

en route to Machu Picchu
January 21, 1977

Hit again! This time me, at the mercado. A wad of bills (worth 50–75 cents) was taken from my front pocket; the toilet paper that was in the same pocket was left. And I didn't know I'd been hit. I realized that I'd been separated from Don and the boys, like a calf cut out of the herd for branding, and I put my hands back to keep hold of the pack (I didn't have anything in my back pockets). Not until I went to pay for some coffee we drank a half hour later did I know I'd been robbed and realized when it happened. The thieves were right out of *Oliver Twist.* We've taken to carrying money in shoes and in my bra. It's a little hard to get at in a crowded bus, and the money from the shoe gets more than a bit smelly, but it's secure. We've had too much stolen to be able to afford a money belt.

What beautiful country this is! The Incas knew what they were doing when they made this their center. Traces of their terraced hillsides still remain, some of them currently farmed. The land seems very fertile, probably yielding two crops a year, at least of corn. There's also much cabbage, some alfalfa, marigolds, fat pigs, and some cattle. Though above 10,000 feet we're in the Cordillera Negre (more "verde" than "negre" to me)—no snow at any time of the year, except perhaps scatterings on the highest peaks. Across the way (hundreds of miles) we can see the Cordillera Blanca, always snow covered.

The vegetation here sends me schizophrenic. Cactus, which we did not see along the coastal desert, thrives here, alongside some kind of fir or pine. Lombardy poplars take me back to my Chicago childhood. Eucalyptus trees take me home to where I left my heart. Here the trees are cropped. Primitive sawmills produce building lumber; leftover wood provides fuel. Eucalyptus being what they are, the crop is constant, stumps of felled trees yielding saplings. And all the while the roots hold the soil. I wonder if these, like those in the Bay Area, were brought from Australia, and when, and by whom.

We enjoyed our economy hotel in Cuzco—hot showers, warm blankets, and clean, clean, clean. It was run by an Italian woman and her children. The boy found us walking up the main street, waited while we rejected two awful holes that had been listed in our guidebook, and assured us we'd like his. We did. (The archbishop is in Lima.)

Much of modern Cuzco has been built on the remains of the Inca city. The old walls attest to the skill of the ancient builders. One stone with twelve angles fits perfectly into its wall. And, of course, the Incas used no mortar—just perfect cuts and perfect fits.

en route to Lima
January 24, 1977

Our car on this train is a musical one. A troupe of singers and dancers is apparently traveling to Lima for some of the folklore contests/exhibitions. They're not dancing in the aisle, but they are singing and strumming. A blind vendor has come aboard, selling songs. The sun is shining brightly, sparkling the river, shimmering the eucalyptus leaves, sliding between pine branches. Mist shrouds the highest peaks; lower peaks stand grandly green against the blue sky and white clouds—not breathtaking scenery, but serenely, majestically beautiful.

Machu Picchu was breathtaking—literally, too. We walked the five miles along the Inca trail from the train station to the ruins, climbing about fifteen hundred feet. It was drizzling slightly when we started; as we climbed the mists receded, unveiling more and more of the green mountains and canyons. Unfortunately, when we came to the end of the trail we did not see the ancient city in all of its grandeur. We came out at the hotel parking lot, full of buses getting ready to go down the hill to pick up the first of the tourists. Then, of course, we had to go through the ticket gate. What a sight awaited! You could feel the presence of Inca ghosts. The place looks just at it does in magazine ads, only more so. While the temples contain the largest stones and the finest work, the agricultural terraces impressed us more—mile upon mile of intricately crafted stone walls stepping up the mountainside. Terraces were only five to ten feet wide, and all the soil for them had to be brought up from the valley. Even now, in "ruin," they are productive, producing dahlias, gladiolas, lillies, and sweet wild strawberries. We exhausted ourselves on ancient walks and stairways, then scrambled down the hill to catch the Indian train just as the place was filling up with "regular" (i.e., high-paying) tourists. Some day we'll have to spend at least a week there—but at the top of the hill. I couldn't face that climb every day. What you can't face at the top of the hill, though, are the prices. Everything is geared to the big spenders—nothing for us campers.

We're taking the first-class Indian train back to Lima. (We always promised ourselves that some day we'd go first class.) I've written about the second-class Mexican bus. It was luxurious compared to this first-class Peruvian train. We *did* push our way on first and get seats for four, which we've usually been able to hold to no more than five. College students on vacation happily crowded half the car; Indians stoically crowded the other. The pregnant woman behind us has been nursing a two- or three-year-old boy almost the whole trip—except when she went to the head to wash out his dirty clothes, which she hung out on the back of our seat. Of course, the aisle is jammed and the seats so close together that our knees touch the opposite seat. Real red carpet service!

The air in this car is unbelievable; it smells of pungent onions, spicy pork and peppers, fragrant dahlias, daisies, roses, lillies. The vendors today have been worth the discomfort of riding for twenty-four hours in seats designed for people four feet tall.

Later

You wouldn't believe this now! It's about six stations later, and I've never seen such a crowd, not even lining Colorado Boulevard for the Rose

Parade. We've held our small four seats to three people (Donald is crammed in elsewhere) and a load of baggage (not all ours); but the aisle is overfull of people and baggage, and most of the seats hold five or six people. We have our feet on the floor under us, and people keep asking to put their baggage there. Since we have to *sleep* this way tonight, the answer is no. We're not making points as friendly Americans. Talk about the territorial imperative! Give an inch and you lose six. And with this touching culture, people will drape themselves all over you if there's nothing inanimate available. The vendors now have to play leapfrog to get down the aisle, but it doesn't stop them.

January 31, 1976

From six until midnight the train sat in darkness in Juliaca while military police searched it. All lights in the station and on the train were turned off. We could hear the slap of bare feet running along the platform, the heavy thud of booted feet following, the thunk of nightstick on flesh, see the grotesque shadows cast by the flashlights and lanterns the military police carried. Two men were taken from our car and returned a few minutes later, bloodied about the head, but whole. Then, like a magnet, our car attracted a continuing stream of people and produce. People were stacked two levels deep, and things at least four levels. No one would talk to us except to say that our car was "safe" since outsiders (we; the others had disembarked several stations before) were there. I thought we were in the midst of a revolution. Not until the train left Juliaca after midnight did we learn that the police were making a routine check for contraband—food, especially meat.

We got back to find a hole in the side of the boat. Something had hit it, denting the quarter inch stainless steel chainplate and cracking a frame. It was done by a hit and run who ran. So we can't; we have to repair first. Take me away from this city life.

Donald just got over being sick, and Don's down again. I've decided that Lima has bad air (it's not the water). And well it might, since every third person smokes, every second one spits, and almost every one uses any corner for a toilet. Do I sound bitter? At this point, I am. Even the beer is terrible, and there's no decent chocolate. If we didn't want to visit Easter Island we'd not go to Chile. Tahiti, here we come.

Depressedly yours,
Joanne

P.S. Thoughts while stocking up—— How do you get in the meat line, the potato line, the sugar line, and the milk line all at the same time? Beer costs twenty-five soles; the bottle costs twenty. You can't buy the beer (or anything else) unless you have a bottle to turn in. A guest left us a full bottle of 7-Up, but only after we found an empty for her. The environmentalists would love it here. Also, no BHT or other chemicals are used to "preserve freshness." Instead, we have stale bread and bugs—in cereals, flours, pastas, everything. Are the bugs really better than the chemicals?

en route to Chile
February 15, 1977

Dear Friends,

Our guidebook promises us abalone, apples, walnuts, and wine in Chile. If we ever get there, we may not leave. The wind has been non-existent the past two days, the current pushing us backwards. At least when the wind stopped the sun came out, giving us pleasantly warm days. Before that, sailing to Chile was mighty chilly work, calling for long undies and wool hats. And to think that we left a heat wave in Lima, the thermometer hitting a record-breaking twenty-nine degrees (think metric).

I read the February 7 issue of *Time* and became outraged by "The Sexes." I hope all of you were, too. To use brutality to sell shoes, undies, magazines, or whatever seems to me the height of obscenity. And while we "protect" our children from scenes of nudity or loving sex in movies—the country has gone mad. Stop it. Write letters. (I did.) Boycott products. March.

The *in situ* museum of the Inquisition in Lima affected me the same way. I almost vomited, did weep. Man's inhumanity to man, all in the name of God. I can understand war and murder, but I'll never understand torture. At least the Church did it to save souls and Hitler to create his version of a perfect world. But to make a buck? I realize that the advertising is only faked, not real, and so is of a different order from the Inquisition and the Holocaust; but we live by our symbols, by our semantic environment. What we say, so shall we reap.

Stepping down from the lectern (or out of the pulpit), I'd like to take you on a tour of the Larco Herrara Museum. Here we have enough Inca and other South American Indian ceramic ware to stock a dozen museums. A small room in a separate building houses what used to be the "underground" collection, known only to scholars. Now guidebooks and signs in the museum invite visitors to see the "Erotic Room"—pornography in pottery. Apparently the Incas didn't have the *Playboy* mammary mentality, though they had almost everything else, including Gargantuan overstatement. There was no brutality, though—just ribald, overt sex. Dinner must have been an interesting affair with these pieces on the table. Makes you wonder if there's a similar "back room" to every museum.

February 16, 1977

The wind has picked up a little. I'd say it's ruffling the surface of the water because that seems like an apt (if overused) metaphor. But I wonder if it isn't dated. How many of you remember the days of skirts worn over numerous petticoats, occasional glimpses of white lace ruffles? A prize for the best metaphors about pants suits or Levi's.

Well, the wee crawlin' beasties are back. I suppose I should view those bugs as simply more protein (after all, I like snails), but somehow I can't. Give me BHT and other nasty preservatives. I may die sooner, but at least I won't have to face my cereal bowl walking away first thing in the morning. I read somewhere that fully ninety percent of the grain crop in many underdeveloped countries goes to the bugs. I didn't believe it—but now I'm not so sure.

Packaging is bad here, too. Many U.S. goods are over-packaged; but a lot is lost here because bags and boxes are so flimsy. It's impossible to get a load of groceries home without losing at least part of one bag of sugar, rice, flour, etc. And I don't think that the flimsy plastic is less ecologically damaging than the better kind.

I'd heard that life begins at forty. Apparently that's premature. Item: Hulda Crooks, whom we met when we hiked the John Muir Trail in 1971, hiked to the top of Mt. Whitney again last August, her fifteenth ascent in fifteen years. Hulda was eighty in 1976. Item: Nellie Brown has won twenty gold medals, eleven blue ribbons, and thirteen trophies in eighteen months of competitive swimming. A polio victim since childhood who broke her back ten years ago, Nellie is eighty-three. Item: Also eighty-three, Mae West is playing her first starring film role in thirty-three years. And what would you like to do when you grow up?

Light winds have kept our speed down to two to four knots, and there's a two knot current running against us. This is proving to be one long trip—fifteen days instead of six.

We're also slowed down because we can't fly our big headsails; the headstay broke. One of its nineteen twisted strands broke, and it began to unravel. When we hauled down the genny, that piece snarled. Looks like a ball of yarn a cat's had for an hour. Actually, we couldn't get the genny down past the snarl. We had to hoist Donald up in the bosun's chair where he sat swaying in the wind twenty-five feet above the deck in the black of night, unhanking the sail clip by clip. It would have made a very exciting picture except that we were all too busy to get the camera. It seems always to be that way. We have only placid pictures.

Antofagasta to Valparaiso, Chile
March 16, 1977

Those of you who are "into touching"—either for sound psychological reasons or because you're dirty old men/women—ought to visit Peru. You can't enter or leave a room without hugging and kissing everyone there. And if you have to walk around a knot of people in the market or on the street, it's not a fight—just a greeting or farewell. Chile hasn't shown itself quite so demonstrative, but we've had incredibly warm welcomes everywhere so far.

We arrived in Arica, our first port of entry, at 1700, wondering how much such a late arrival would cost us. Our first pleasant surprise—no cost. Our second—no "after hours." The navy runs Chile's coast, and naval offices are open twenty-four hours a day. The commander insisted we stay for tea (instant coffee), then sent us on a tour of the town in the navy jeep. Next morning the same jeep and driver took us, our headstay, and some self-steering parts to the shipyard. Within two days Señor Gomez had everything fixed for us—no charge. All he asked was that we move the boat from the commercial basin to the yacht club, which we did. There we repaid our hosts by being "on display." (I'll never feel comfortable visiting a zoo again.) Our timing was perfect. It was Tourist Week in Arica, and dozens of yacht club members came to see the norteamericanos and their strange boat. One woman brought us tank tops printed with the Chilean flag; another (seventy-two years young and the best swimmer in the club, by her admission and my observation) gave us twenty English paperbacks. Children climbed aboard during all daylight hours (not, however, before we were awake in the morning). We had planned to leave on Saturday morning, but since Sunday was the culmination of tourist week, with festivities climaxing at the yacht club, we stayed until Monday. Hang gliders and parachutes sailed down into the bay, not quite on our decks. Waterskiers and beauty queens buzzed alongside. It was a really good show.

Arica is a charming town, clean, well-tended, and surprisingly full of gardens—surprisingly because it's desert, at least ten times more stark than the Mojave. There's no cactus, no sagebrush, nothing. The church on the main square was designed by Eiffel: understated, chaste—a more than pleasant change from the gaudy gold works of the Spaniards. The intense green, blue, red, and yellow windows look tacky from the outside, but they provide a pleasing glow inside.

From Arica we sailed to Iquique to pick up our mail. It was there because a fellow teacher from Costa Mesa High School has a niece teaching at the Methodist-run English College in Iquique. We spent four enjoyable days with Joan and Bob, meeting some of their teachers (American and Chilean), using their washing machine, viewing slides of central and southern Chile, and eating—meat again, fish, fresh fruit.

To encourage tourism in a town that has really nothing to offer (except hospitable people like the Johnsons), the government has declared Iquique a free port. We bought a cassette recorder to replace the one stolen in Lima.

We did have some trouble with officialdom in Iquique. When it came time to leave, the navy captain would not approve our traveling straight to Valparaiso—too far (where he thought we stopped en route to and from the Galapagos, I don't know). So we had to stop in Antofagasta. It turned out that the captain had a friend in Antofagasta who was interested in buying a trimaran, even though he had never seen or sailed on one; that, and not safety, was the reason for our stop. And it was another enjoyable one.

As we entered the commercial harbor a sailboat came after us, frantically waving. It came very close and Roberto stepped aboard, directing us to the yacht club. We were their first visiting yacht in several years and their first trimaran ever. Though we'd made the papers in both Arica and Iquique, we didn't make the front page until Antofagasta, the largest of the three cities. We were taken home for hot showers and baths, dined and well-wined for two days. The boat was always full of visitors. Again, we had to go to sea to get some rest.

If this sounds as if we're enjoying Chile, you're right. Though being "on exhibit" has its drawbacks, it's ego-rewarding to have the biggest and best boat at the yacht club. (Arica had a dozen yachts, Iquique two, Antofagasta three yachts and half a dozen Lightnings; all the clubs had many social members). And the food—new tastes intrigue, but old ones delight. No fruit tastes as good as a crisp apple—unless it's a seedless grape. And to have walnuts again, and raisins, also good abalone (sometimes served with lobster sauce, for an embarrassment of riches), and passable to good wine!

As for the political situation, we have seen fewer military in evidence here than anywhere else except Costa Rica. That we can't find anyone with nasty things to say about the government is suspect; but we've talked to people from businessmen to professionals to janitors, from "Norman Thomas socialists" to Mormon missionaries, from immigrants to natives. All say that the Allende government was incorrectly glorified and the present one is incorrectly villified in the foreign press. Human rights have been violated under the present military government; apparently the same was true under Allende, but involving different groups of humans. The economic chaos under Allende created such social chaos that no one benefited. And the Cubans and Russians were waiting on the borders. Or so we're told. No one mentions the CIA—another suspect omission. Now the economy is recuperating and inflation is being managed. Everyone is better off—except those in jails. What is Truth? Certainly I can't tell you; but it seems to me that "freedom" doesn't mean much when your property can be confiscated on the whim of the government, when only Party members can get jobs, when inflation runs 300 percent and more per month, and when food is unavailable.

We saw *Three Days of the Condor* in Arica. Why didn't my high school guidance counsellor tell me that my own government pays people for reading novels? My one real talent, and all these years it's been just an avocation.

March 21, 1977

"Write of what you know." Well, then, books, having rummaged the paperback shelves at Iquique English College and being too cold when coming in from a steering stint to do ought but curl up with a (good?) book.

First we take *Letters of James Agee to Father Flye*. Judging from this book, those of you who have some of my adolescent and postadolescent letters should be able to make a few bucks. I, too, complained of having too much that I had to do (required courses and baby tending, however, instead of assignments for *Time* and *Fortune*) so that I didn't have time for my "real work." I also complained that I was too weary to write a decent letter and apologized for that and for not having written sooner. Frequently I recommended books or movies I had enjoyed or denounced others I thought overrated. Occasionally I propounded my not very profound political views. And although I didn't have galloping alcoholism to berate myself for, I did touch on perhaps the beginnings of such problems among our suburban ghetto clique. Of course I wrote of suicide. All in all, I think the letters would hold up well when placed between the Agee letters and *Memoirs of a High-School Prom Queen*—especially if you include the notes passed between Sheila and me during our first college history class.

The Pooh Perplex, by F. C. Crews, we should have discovered long ago (maybe some of you did). Wickedly witty essays satirizing literary criticism. And to think that the man was at Berkeley when I was, yet I never studied under him.

In a less literary vein I learned in Frank Slaughter's *Divine Mistress* that a relative of Amerigo Vespucci was the model for Boticelli's "Birth of Venus." Donald had this information confirmed by Samuel Eliot Morison's *The European Discovery of America.* He also learned that if Vespucci had really made one of the journeys he faked, he would have landed in Antofagasta, our last port, which he never saw.

Ernest K. Gann, during his career as pilot, flew an unpressurized plane through the Andean passes at Arequipa and Lake Titicaca, Peru, where we traveled by train (at a slightly lower altitude). His account of his career in *Fate Is the Hunter,* though sometimes "too much of a muchness," is usually interesting and well written. We especially enjoyed the chapter about the icing of an airplane—real fear vividly conveyed.

Robert Pirsig's *Zen and the Art of Motorcycle Maintenance* crowns the stack we got at Iquique. Read it if you haven't; reread it if you have. When we get back I'd like to talk to you about it. Right now I have only excited first impressions, most of them favorable.

March 22, 1977

Look! Up in the sky! It's a bird! It's a plane! It's supersun! After seven gunmetal gray days (four of them so dark we couldn't take a sight) we have a change. A well-washed denim sky meets a brand-new denim sea. The clouds have been swept away, leaving only wisps, and the sun shines over all. A beautiful day for a bath—except that the wind is blowing thirty-five knots plus, has been for fifteen or so hours, and shows no sign of letting up. (Or is it "dying down"? Try to explain those phrases to someone learning English.)

My father, rest him, had a schtick that went so: He'd have someone repeat "What am I doing?" four times, each time stressing the next word in the sentence. After "What am I *doing*?" he'd answer, "Making a darn fool of yourself." Now, then, "What are we *doing* here?"

2115

We're hove-to, waiting out this gale. I don't know whether it's half or full gale, but it's more than good enough for me. Don says it would be "fun" (!) to turn and run with it; but then it would probably take us three weeks to get back to the coast.

Foul weather gear and damp towels hang everywhere; nothing is dry. Only one of us is officially awake during each two-hour watch, but I suspect not much sleeping will be done by the others. If only the wind didn't *howl* so! Let me tell you, I am scared. But it's so clear and starry and beautiful out there. Just hope and pray it's blown out by morning.

Valparaiso, Chile
April 3, 1977

Of course, it did blow out. We had another day of wind and nice weather. After that we were swearing at the calms.

I wonder what effect this is having on the children. After the real responsibility of handling the boat in bad weather, how will they feel about the sand-box student government? They'll probably accept it with as good/bad grace as they've accepted everything else that "authority" has foisted on them—like sailing around the world.

We've been real celebrities here in Valparaiso—television coverage as well as newspaper front page. Too bad we didn't see our electronic debut, but we were in Santiago. We were reminded unfavorably of Los Angeles. Mountains surround the city, on which the smog settles. Ugh and double ugh.

Valpo, on the other hand, reminds us of San Francisco—and that's a favorable resemblance. We travel the world to see new and exotic places and like best those that remind us of home.

Those of you coming to Tahiti, please bring a little home with you—Nestle's chocolate chips, Skippy peanut butter, etc.

April 4, 1977

I keep buying *Time,* thinking I want to know what's happening at home. Maybe I shouldn't; it creates too much anger. A cover story yet on Marabel Morgan and "total exploitation and manipulation of husbands" (aka *Total Woman*). She brags about using one-syllable words, *pastes* together a "book," and earns $1.5 million. Crass materialist that I am, I'm jealous as hell.

Then there's child porn. How sick is U.S. society? Have we been away too long?

More cheerfully—talk about conservation. Oregon bottle laws have nothing on Chile. *Everything* in a bottle (even wine and liquor) has a deposit. Cooking oil is dispensed at the supermarkets. Bring your own bottles. Bakery prices do not include wrapping. Bring your own paper, bags, and string. No egg cartons—unless you buy three hundred eggs; then you get the flats and the wooden box. Needless to say, you don't see much trash lying around. Of course, raw sewage is pumped into the bay, and that's where we were told to dump our garbage.

en route to Robinson Crusoe/
Alexander Selkirk islands
April 9, 1977

"Don't look back; somethin' might be gainin' on ya." Satchel Paige's good advice applies particularly when you're running before a gale. The waves in front look big enough, but you see only their back sides, moving away from you; turn around and see them rearing, cresting, certain to crash down on the boat—WOW! Eyes front.

Yes, we're at it again—we were running before the gale all day, are fore-reaching tonight. It's not *that* bad, except it's so cold. Those waves don't crash down on us but send us surfing before them, even with only the storm jib up. Too bad we're not sailing in the right direction. We're destined to beat wherever we want to go. We sailed hard on the wind due south from Antofagasta to Valparaiso. We turned due west to Selkirk and Crusoe and never eased the sails. No wonder Alexander Selkirk, the real-life Robinson Crusoe, asked to be put ashore even if it was on an uninhabited island four hundred miles from anywhere!

During our last few days in anywhere (Valparaiso, Chile) we were entertained in widely differing styles.

The "supermarket king" of Chile, whom we'd met at the yacht club, invited Don and me for lunch. Though he lives in Santiago, he keeps an apartment in Valpo. His son, a university student, lives there, looked after by the daily maid-housekeeper-cook. When we accepted the invitation, he phoned and told her to fix a "light" meal (since he was going riding after lunch): sea urchins on crackers, poached fish, fried cheese empañadas, salad, bread, wine, fresh fruit. The apartment itself is ordinary, though comfortable. But it has a spectacular view of gardens, hills, and the bay. And it's in the one section of the hill (the president has vacation quarters there) with no public transportation. Residents have cars; employees walk.

The next night we dined "informally" with the directors of the yacht club at the club—no evening clothes, but all the men wore ties, most with suits, a few with sport coats. Since our boat has a woman aboard, directors' wives were allowed to attend—apparently a rare treat. We had an enjoyable time—lots of pisco sours (we'll introduce you to this one when we return) and good Chilean wine (the first good wine since we left California sixteen months ago); conversation in English, Spanish, German. We can now say "cheers" in Spanish, German, and Tahitian.

When we finished dinner we found Oscar and his friend waiting, suited and tied, for us to visit them. Oscar lives across the street from the club, had seen us in the anchorage and on the evening news, and had come down to talk to us. After visiting the boat, he insisted that we visit his home. We "maybe'd" for several days; but when we learned that he and his friend had been waiting outside in the cold for an hour while we finished dinner at the club, we felt obliged. So we were introduced to a small part of the gay community of Recreo (an area of Valparaiso).

The apartment was a Berkeley bohemian pad of the fifties (not a hippy pad of the sixties)—peeling wallpaper, chipped plaster, high ceilings. Pictures and posters adorned the multi-colored, multi-papered walls; prominent was a half-life size poster of *David*—as sculpted by Michelangelo, not with the fig leaf that the copy at Forest Lawn wears. On an easel stood an unfinished oil of Don Quixote—Oscar's project for the past fifteen years. We were introduced to Victor, Oscar's roommate;

then Juan, Oscar's friend, played the piano—Chopin, show tunes, and Sinatra's "My Way." Oscar sang a song. We ate grapes. Before we left each of them presented us with a gift: a miniature flower arrangement, made of bread dough; a little pot (ceramic); and a picture of a vase of daffodils, made from split straw.

Donald prefers the life style with the maid.

April 11, 1977

We kept the mainsail up about thirty seconds too long the day before yesterday—got a yard long tear in it. Donald and I spent 43,200 seconds patching it. A what in when saves how much?

Robinson Crusoe Island
April 18, 1977

I've found my Pacific island. You can have palm trees, bananas, and breadfruit—also insects and poisonous fish. Here are *real* trees—acacia, cypress, pine, eucalyptus. Of historical and literary interest—the pirate caves and lookout of Alexander Selkirk, whose solitary four years and four months on the island gave Defoe the idea for *Robinson Crusoe*. Of gustatory interest—decent beef, some lamb (mutton, I suspect), good tuna, enormous and tasty lobsters, thicket upon thicket of wild blackberries. Hills (the entire island) invite hiking. We've seen no clearer or cleaner water anywhere; though I'd prefer it ten degrees warmer, I could get used to it. Trouble is, eight hundred already inhabit this paradise, and the locals are pushing tourism. By the time I return it will probably be Disneyland.

en route to Easter Island
April 20, 1977

Having seen my island from its bleak and barren west side, I may have to reconsider. Yet it has a virtue surpassing those I've stated. On Robinson Crusoe Island you could have a genuine Christmas tree.

People there work, even if they don't live, communally. Boats are owned by the fish cooperative, and practically everyone fishes for a living—lobster, cod, and bass. The cod and bass are salted on the island, then shipped to the mainland. The lobsters, trapped at eighty feet or more, travel alive to fine restaurants in Chile and Argentina. When we left, more than twelve thousand were in the holding traps, awaiting the boat from the mainland.

Apparently the cows, like the boats, are owned in common. They live on the uninhabited side of the island. When the community wants beef, several of the men get into a boat, go to the other side of the island, kill a cow, and bring it home. A "butcher boat" visited us on the first day, but as I didn't want a whole side or the job of butchering, we said no. Nevertheless, that night we had barbecued beef.

Don and I were walking down the hill from Selkirk's lookout when we were hailed by the day's butchers. Nothing would do but to stop and have a glass of *vino bueno*. Two chairs were set out on the front "lawn" where we sat and sipped and talked. On the front porch half a dozen men were butchering the kill, separating bony from boneless cuts, trimming off every scrap of fat (rendered for cooking, since imported shortening is *very* expensive). Inside, as many women were cooking. More than as many dogs and chickens waited patiently for scraps. After we'd drunk two glasses of wine, Eduardo insisted that we eat "a little" *carne asado*. Out came two plates heaped with slabs of barbecued beef—as well as fresh salad and homemade bread. Eduardo and Herman (pronounced Air-mon´) hovered over us, urging more wine, more bread, more meat. We felt awkward at first, especially since no one else was eating. But talk about "finger-lickin' good"! We were given knives and forks, but the meat could be attacked only by hand. And so we won praise for eating "Chilean style" instead of like fussy norteamericanos. By the time we had almost finished, practically everyone else had greasy fingers and satisfied smiles, too—and we returned to the boat for the lobster dinner the kids had waiting.

Today we're experiencing a new sensation. We're not beating into the wind! We hope that most of the 1,600 miles to Easter Island will be this way. According to our pilot charts it should be—and we certainly deserve it.

Between us and Easter Island at least four rocks/reefs have been reported. No one's seen them again, but as the U.S. *Sailing Directions* says, "The fact that these islets and rocks have been seen and described is considered more convincing than the fact that they have not been seen subsequently." I really don't like this book. It warns that Easter Island never has good weather and has no good anchorages. It advises boats never to go there. I much prefer the British Admiralty book, which claims that there are always safe anchorages on a lee side of the island.

April 21, 1977

Supercalifragilisticexpialidocious! The sun is shining and it's warm. Off with the long underwear, dig out the shorts. Laundry. Baths. Of course, with sun comes no wind; at this rate, come Bastille Day we won't even be at Easter Island, much less in Tahiti.

April 22, 1977

If only we'd had today's wind with yesterday's bright, warm day! Today we're bundled up again in long underwear and foul weather gear, reefing down sails and riding out rain squalls.

"Star-tling" night last night. So many stars appeared that the sky looked more like the northern than the southern hemisphere. There was no moon to spread a wide swath on the water, but stars flung ribbon paths on all sides. The sea lay so flat that stars touched it on all horizons. The wind began; ribbons became shreds, shreds broke into flashing, silvery sequins. We slid along, skimming the sea, a breathtakingly beautiful ride. Then clouds began to form, and by sunrise we had a white-gray, windy world, only occasionally shattered by shards of gold and blue.

We idled away yesterday's calm with various projects. I read Durant on the rise of the Roman Empire. Don sawed and sanded. Donald baked French bread, spice cake, and pizza. Erik stirred up popcorn and chocolate-oatmeal fudgies.

I've given the galley over to them, especially when it comes to baking. I hunger not for sweet but for meat. I even dream about it—thin slices of rare roast beef, pastrami, salami; pork chops, lamb chops, T-bone steaks; roast turkey and fried chicken. In my meat hunger I've taken to snitching the canned fish we bought for Bigfoot. It's labeled salmon-type sardines (?) but seems like scrap tuna. Maybe Caesar's army marched on vegetarian fare and maybe world hunger makes meat eating immoral; but if President Carter can frankly confess to a national magazine his lust for women he can't have, surely I can confess to you my lust for filet.

Later

We sailed through a rainbow this afternoon, each Roy G. Biv color distinct, the whole glowing vibrantly. This rainbow did not stop with an arch but continued into almost a complete circle, the colors slicing the dull green sea. We found, however, no gold.

April 24, 1977

Last night we had it all—rain (our first since November), wind, and waves. We spent the night fore-reaching again; it's no way to get anywhere but the only reasonably comfortable course to take. At least the north wind brought warm air with the rain. Today we have bright sun and a south wind, and in this hemisphere that's all the way from the Antarctic, and it's *cold.*

April 28, 1977

Sailing, sailing, over the bounding main—and it's bounding, all right, just like a fool buckin' bronco. The sea reminds me of Texas in another way, too. Wherever you look you see only miles and miles of monotonous miles and miles. We relieve the monotony by reefing down. We've done a lot of that recently, having experienced the month's gales for this part of the ocean (according to our charts) during the past week.

Today Donald baked a cake to commemorate the mutiny on the *Bounty.* Much more of this rotten weather and I'll mutiny.

May 2, 1977

We had a real fright this afternoon—a mind-numbing, stomach-churning, mouth-drying fright. For the past seventy-two hours we've been sitting out high winds. Flying only the storm jib, our smallest sail, we lock the steering wheel and plow into the wind, making about two knots—not very exciting, but prudent and comfortable in thirty-five plus winds and big seas. This afternoon, just like *that,* the wind piped up until it was whistling sixty. No time to put on foul weather gear and shoes. We had to turn the boat immediately and get wind and waves behind us. Of course, during that maneuver we were for several seconds broadside to the waves, the most dangerous position (a broach). I was sure that we would have to learn to sail this boat upside down. But Don turned us all right, and while he kneeled facing aft (and those waves!) to steer, Donald and I played the sail. Within an hour things had "quieted" back to "normal"—our thirty-five plus winds. We're back on course, poking along at two knots (trimarans are fast boats, right?), getting damper every day, and telling ourselves it can't last forever.

May 5, 1977

Yesterday dawned (and remained) clear and bright—and windless. We did our "sunny day things"—bathing, laundry, airing out, painting, varnishing. Last night the almost full moon dimmed the stars and glowed the night. We sailed down a broad path of moonbeams, then followed the moon even after sunrise. What a change from what we've been experiencing!

Only at sea, I think, does a day truly sparkle. The sun shines on miles of water, all of it reflecting the light. Wherever you look lie pinpoints or patches of brilliance. Of course, we wish for a *little* more wind, but here it seems all or nothing, feast or famine, and we are content with our half loaf. Soon enough, judging from barometer and clouds, we shall again have more than we bargained for.

Friday, May 13, 1977

Who says Friday the thirteenth is unlucky? Land ho! What a beautiful and welcome sight it is on this bright, clear day. Although the wind's died now, we've had two days of what sailing ought to be—a smooth sea, a clear sky, a beam wind—a pleasant end to an often unpleasant journey. The books tell us it should be this way all the way to Tahiti. I'll let you know when we see you there.

Love,
Joanne

en route to Pitcairn Island
May 23, 1977

Dear Friends,

"We would never travel on the sea if we had no hope of telling about it later" (Blaise Pascal). Here's hoping.

Though "the weather is never good for more than a few days at a time at Isla de Pascua [Easter Island]" (U.S. *Sailing Directions*), we managed five good and one tolerable day—but not until after we'd hurriedly weighed anchor one night and spent three days at sea riding out the storm. Easter Island has no real bays, only open roadsteads; and although one side or another of the triangular island should always provide shelter, this storm was so bad that we preferred to seek shelter at sea.

We returned to blue skies broken by white clouds and to the clearest water anywhere. We could see the bottom at depths of more than sixty feet. Since the water has also warmed up, we spent hours cleaning six months' growth off the bottom of the boat. We could have lived for weeks on the barnacles and grass growing there. Although it's only comparatively clean, we can travel about a knot and a half faster. Don't worry about keeping your powder dry; just keep your bottom clean.

If you visit Easter Island, it should definitely be by air and in the company of some knowledgeable archaeologist. We saw and marveled at most of the major statuary groups; but unless you know more than we did, it's a case of "if you've seen one, you've seen them all."

The quarry was the most interesting. Several dozen incomplete statues remain there, miles from where they would have been erected. Donald and I hiked the two and a half miles from the anchorage late in the afternoon, walked round the quarry at dusk. Talk about brooding silences! Both the brooding and the silence were palpable. We felt almost as if the statues had carved each other. Surely no human hand was responsible.

Twilight doesn't last long here, especially when clouds blot out both moon and stars, so Donald and I walked home in the dark. Robert Frost wrote about the "Something there is that does not love a wall,/ That wants it down." I always agreed before, but that night I was thankful for the stone wall. If we'd had to go cross-country instead of walking beside it, we'd never have found our way—at least, not without breaking a leg in the rocky pastures. As it was, we had to find the side "road" off the main "road" solely by foot feel.

"I think we turn off here. Oops, no; too brushy."

"Here. No, too rocky."

"Here. Yes, a smooth dirt path going in the right direction. Should take us to the cove where we beached the dinghy."

Fishermen on the beach had a lantern, and the masthead light on *Anduril* shone, the only star in the clouded sky. I now appreciate the light-in-the-window devotion.

After three days the wind shifted enough that we could again anchor at Hanga-Roa, the only real settlement on the island. There we were ushered into several beachfront shacks (the homes and workshops of native craftsmen) to "looky-looky" at carvings, shell necklaces, etc. We saw poverty second only to what we had seen in El Salvador—proud, clean, neat poverty.

At Nancy's home/workshop we were served tea and spaghetti. My tea came in a thermos bottle cup with a handle, on a saucer; Donald's came in a similar cup but without a handle, on a soup bowl; Nancy's husband's tea came in a glass, on a metal baking tray. Donald got the only spoon—a big serving spoon—for sugar; the husband got a broad-handled fork, which he first used for stirring his sugared tea, then brandished at a rat that ran across the dirt floor. We immediately won favor with this family because Nancy could tell at a glance that I, too, was "protestante," not "catolica." I didn't tell her that I was free of makeup because of laziness, not religious conviction.

We left in overcast, motored an hour to charge the batteries, then picked up a pleasantly brisk wind that's been with us since—and not on the nose. For the past twenty-four hours we've sailed seven to ten knots through star-spangled night and cloudy day. But we saw a red sky this morning and are ready to take warning, though hoping we won't have to.

May 30, 1977

Wishful hoping didn't work. Of course we had a storm—two days of it, complete with heavy rains. At least we caught enough water that we didn't have to tap our full tanks. We actually got more water than we wanted—pouring down chainplates and leaking through ports until we had wet beds and damp clothes. Because the boat "works" under the stresses of wind and wave, no seal lasts indefinitely. And since we gave away our last tube of caulking compound in a fit of generosity last November and couldn't find a suitable replacement in Peru or Chile, we're stuck with wetness until we get to drier climes and friends whose suitcases will carry such goodies to us in Tahiti.

Yesterday also dawned red, but only slightly so. We had sun all day but clouds and drizzle drip by dinner, rain before nightfall. The extensive clouding gave us good radio reception; we picked up five minutes of U.S. news and learned that A. J. Foyt won the "Indy 500," that the Russians are disagreeing, that the First Lady is going on a "diplomatic mission" to Latin America, and that the First Family went deep sea fishing. As the prophet said, "There is nothing new under the sun."

"What about under the moon?" you ask. "What profound thoughts do you have as you sit in darkness, steering a small, fragile craft over endless miles of ocean, alone in what must seem infinite space?"

Two such thoughts——

Since we have no self-steering system, someone has to be on the helm at all times, even in rainy weather. As Donald said while steering through the drizzle last night, "Now, this is what I call a driving rain."

My gem: History, as usual, got the story wrong. It was not Nathan Hale but his spouse who was an American spy during the Revolutionary War. When she was hanged by the British, Hale apologized for not being a polygamist with his famous statement, usually misquoted, "I only regret that I have but one wife to give for my country."

Enough said?

June 2, 1977

The boys, lacking anything else to do, are reading Dickens. Erik liked this metaphor from *Oliver Twist*: "But tears were not the things to find their way to Mr. Bumble's soul; his heart was waterproof." Wish we were.

June 5, 1977

What a different sensation, sailing off the wind! Surfing down waves, wind abaft or abeam, no rocking, no swaying, no splashing, a comfortable seven to twelve knots (at fifteen I chicken out and want to reduce sail). We sailed three days like this; then this morning, when we came in sight of Pitcairn Island, the wind shifted. Bounty Bay, really only an open anchorage, not a bay, is somewhat protected from all but the north and northeast. Guess from whence the wind blows now? So we're hove-to off the island, waiting for better weather tomorrow.

June 8, 1977

After two days of standing off in bad weather, we finally met living history—Pitcairn Island and the descendants of the mutineers of the *Bounty.*

The island certainly suited Fletcher Christian's purposes. I thought that Puno, Peru, lay at the end of the world, but Pitcairn beats it by more than a mile—1,300 miles from Tahiti, the same from Easter Island, and more than 4,000 miles from a continental land mass. Today, with the increase in air transportation and the decrease in ocean travel, it's more isolated than ever.

Nevertheless, the remaining islanders (about sixty-four) have a reasonably good if restricted life. Wild goats provide fresh meat; fish abound in the waters around the island; and the fertile soil yields lettuce, tomatoes, onions, radishes, oranges, grapefruit, lemons, limes, corn, pineapple, breadfruit, coconut, papaya, sugar cane, taro—and probably more that I didn't see. The island is supported by its stamp revenue—more than $200,000 last year, we were told. No trading for old shoes or *Playboy*s here; it's a cash economy—all currencies (except francs—the Pacific nuclear tests are not approved) accepted. Additional money comes from selling baskets and wood carvings through mail orders or to the few passing ships. Although the island could be entirely self-sufficient (and was for its first generation), it imports staples and manufactured goods. Sometimes the islanders can buy from ships' stores. We saw a fair amount of expensive radio, stereo, and camera equipment.

The people are Polynesian friendly, not British reserved. As noted in our navigational books, islanders came out in their boat to pick us up—although now they use an inflatable rescue boat with an outboard engine instead of the oared long boats. There aren't enough able-bodied men to handle the heavy, wooden boats. Since it still wasn't calm enough to anchor, Donald stayed aboard and sailed circles while the rest of us went ashore. (Erik and Don traded places with him later.) It took expert seamanship to get us ashore dry in the surf that was running.

After dragging the boat ashore and into the boat shed (no boat is ever left on the beach), we started up the hill. Woe to seafarers! I was chagrined to be puffing after only a dozen steps and embarrassed—but relieved—when they sent a tractor to pick us up.

Ivan Christian, the magistrate, first took us to his home, where we enjoyed tea, cakes, biscuits, and conversation, and met Tom Christian, world's busiest ham radio operator and Fletcher's direct descendent. Then onto motorbikes for a tour of the island—two miles by one and hardly a level spot on it. We stopped at the school so the teacher could get our names for the next issue of the *Pitcairn Miscellany*. He has nine students; one is fourteen, the others eleven or younger; it's a nice teacher-pupil ratio, but it means seven lesson plans—individualized instruction to the *n*th degree.

Two hours later we were back at Ivan's for lunch—hot dogs, corned beef, goat, fish, potatoes, corn, bread sticks, salad, and ICE CREAM. And yes, many of the people look as if they eat that way every day. After lunch we walked, picked oranges, and visited with other families. It's pleasant, small-town life, but it's dying. Only the old and the young marrieds with primary-school-age children remain. The only teenage girl has no friends her own age. Even Tom Christian, concerned about the education of his four children, talks of leaving. Unlike the others, who usually move to New Zealand, he'd probably move to the States—to Glendale, in fact, or La Cañada. He lived there in the sixties, working for "The Voice of Prophecy." Now when you talk about what a small world it is, mention Tom and Joanne, who met on the speck of Pacific called Pitcairn Island and shared reminiscences of Glendale, California.

We would have enjoyed staying for the community dinner celebrating the Queen's Silver Jubilee, but it was still impossible to anchor (without worrying), and none of us wanted to be the one to sail circles while the others feasted. So our new friends took us out to *Anduril* just before dinner—but not before loading us with oranges, bananas, tea, two boxes of food for the son of an island family who is in Tahiti as crew on another yacht, and a hot jubilee dinner for four. God save the Queen!

Later

I guess we're going the right way; it's right into the wind.

June 15, 1977

I'm writing this by the light of the kerosene lantern as I sit on the cockpit sole and the boat more or less steers herself. We've reduced sail because, as usual, we're headed into the wind, and more sail was too uncomfortable.

This afternoon we had the makings of a real one. Rain and wind came up with startling speed and great force. The rain stung like sleet and whipped the waves into froth. The wind piled wave upon wave.

Fortunately, it was over almost as quickly as it had begun, and it brought one benefit—showers. We had no time to put on foul weather gear as Don called for help getting the sails down. Instead, we shed clothes as we ran, and with the force of that rain we didn't need to scrub to get rid of a week's accumulation of dirt.

I'm calling this "the long underwear route to Tahiti." We haven't shed it yet, though we have taken the extra blanket off the bed. There's hope—not much life, but hope.

June 17, 1977

The joys of cruising, item # ???. Donald and I just figured out that we haven't enjoyed a night of uninterrupted sleep for two months. And our last hot shower was on March 12. It's a good thing we're godly (?), because we sure aren't cleanly.

We've been beating for so long that Donald is convinced that the trade winds are a myth—probably found only along the Mythythyppi. (You see what being cooped up is doing to us.)

June 19, 1977

Land ho! ETA Tahiti—June 20, between 0400 and 1200.

June 20, 1977

Landfall, 1100. Long underwear shed 1102.

Nakedly happy,
Joanne

Interlude: The Whole Truth

Not everything is idyllic, but you don't write home about the family problems you're having. The first of these centered on school.

Donald was thirteen, Erik eleven when we started the trip. When friends and family realized that we were actually going to do this crazy thing instead of just talk about it, they were dismayed.

"But what about the boys' schooling? Look at what they'll miss."

At this point I usually climbed on my soapbox and lectured about the differences between "schooling" and "education." Then from the point of view of a disillusioned California public high school teacher I listed what they'd miss—drugs, booze, promiscuity; overcrowded classes, busy work, two more repetitions of U.S. history.

"Even if they don't study at all," I said, "they'll learn more on this trip than they would sitting in a classroom."

Of course, we didn't intend that they should not study at all. Although we had examined several correspondence courses, we had quickly discarded them. Don and I had both taught. Surely we could devise better lessons calling for less busy work, and it wouldn't cost us anything and we wouldn't have to wait for mail.

We loaded aboard all the boys' school books, supplemented by teaching aids I'd received at conferences and a wide selection of "just reading" books—highbrow, middlebrow, lowbrow, and nobrow.

Then we set up a watch schedule that gave ample time for study. During my three daytime hours on the helm (0900–1200) the boys would work on math and science, getting help and instruction from Don. They would also read their assignments. During the afternoon (1200–1800), while they alternated hours at the helm, the one off watch would work with me on literature and composition and the social sciences. While in port we'd fit all the schooling into the morning hours, leaving the afternoons free for education.

It was a splendid scheme; we just had trouble making it work. Perhaps some parents can be their children's teachers as well, but we found it very difficult. A child in school has a parent as an ally if he falls out with the teacher. A teacher in school has administrative support if (s)he falls out with a student. But when son is also student and parent is also teacher-administrator, all the lines blur.

Then add the fact of being on a boat. While our tri is so stable and comfortable that we've never been unable to read, the ride has sometimes been so bumpy that we've been unable to write legibly. When we're in port and everything is calm, writing school lessons is the least attractive of hundreds of activities.

The fact of being on a boat also meant confinement. Not always affectionately, Don sometimes referred to *Anduril* as "our forty-foot box." While we were underway or kept inside by bad weather, we couldn't get away from one another—no slamming doors and taking a long walk or getting into the car to drive down to the beach and brood; no running to the gym to shoot baskets or work out with the punching bag; no telephoning a sympathetic friend or relative and swearing or crying out the anger and hurt. Come hell or high water (and we had both, figuratively and literally), we had to work things out where we were and with our own resources. Since those resources included four loud voices, there was a lot of shouting. Too often we tried to ignore a problem, thus fanning the fire of anger rather than extinguishing it. Even in port we were often confined. Since we had only one dinghy aboard, anyone who wanted to go off "alone" had to be rowed ashore or at least had to watch the clock and come back at an appointed hour so that the others weren't stranded. (Being tied to the dock in a dingy port was therefore sometimes more idyllic than being anchored in an idyllic lagoon.) We had many thorny problems along with the rosy sunsets.

As for being freed of the restrictions of school and jobs, school and jobs don't only restrict; they also enlarge, and provide more than education and money. Friends, for one, or at least associates and acquaintances, a wider circle than the family. On a boat you take your friends where you find them—and leave them soon afterwards, only to repeat the process in each port. Friendships can be carried on via mail or ham radio, but neither is a satisfying substitute for a friend's being there in a crisis—or a situation that feels like one.

So while the "idyllic life" I wrote home about was true, so also was the life I noted in my diary:

1/7/77—Yesterday and last night we had a horrible hassle. Both children resent being here, away from all their friends. They also apparently hate each other and us. They can't/won't take directions, don't want to do any chores. Don responds in authoritarian and sarcastic ways, which I, of course, point out. Then we're estranged, too. I don't like the thought of packing up and taking the boys back to California, but I don't see any alternative. Three years of this would be unbearable. But so would three years of being sole parent to teenage boys in Southern California. Maybe I'll just swim over the horizon.

Bath time (off shore, February 1976)

Bask time (Galapagos, November 1976)

Inquisitive visitor, laundry time (Galapagos, November 1976)

Inquisitive crew cat, fileting time (off shore, February 1977)

High country (seas, Easter–Pitcairn, April–June 1977)

High country (Machu Picchu, January 1977)

High country (Mt. Hagen, May 1978)

Peace on earth? (Bethlehem, December 1978)

Peace on earth (Kapingamarangi, April 1978)

Pacific Paradises

Tahiti
June 25, 1977

Dear Friends,

Welcome to paradise—cold showers, warm drinking water; local tomatoes $1 a pound, local bananas 12 cents each, soft drinks at the cafeteria 78 cents, beer $1.10; movies $4.50; traffic roaring by on the highway; and the jets that bring the tourists and their money thundering overhead, most often between 0600 and 0900. Our neighbors live no more than ten feet away; boats are even closer in the "high rent" district—but then, they have electricity. At least we're out of our long underwear—and not yet complaining about the heat.

We've had a show every afternoon—from about four until sundown the canoes have been out practicing for the races on the fourteenth. Paddlers come in two sexes but only one size—big. And can they move those boats! The double canoes are not only the biggest but the fastest. Seen against the silhouette of Moorea and the setting sun, they make a spectacular sight. Today the sailings canoes were out. They move gracefully, but our Sea Spray (and maybe even a Hobie Cat) could outrun them. But who's in a hurry here?

Taha'a
August 29, 1977

Today I became the mother of two teenage boys. Can't say that I believe it, but Erik assures me that it's so. Strange how the children grow older but we don't.

"Bastille Day" (Féte) lasted more than two weeks in Papeete, two months in Bora Bora. We began it by crashing the governor's reception the night of the thirteenth. Don and I and his brother and wife had hurried into town to see the torchlight parade, which ended at the governor's residence. When we saw the reception line, we knew that something else was going on; and since no money was changing hands and no invitations being collected, we decided to join in. Back at a run to the boat, Wilma uncurling her hair on the way. Into long dresses, slacks and good sport shirts, and shoes all around. Then back to the governor's, no more than twenty minutes later, just in time for the entertainment. We had a ball—lots of free booze, canapes, and French pastries. Wilma took pictures of everything. Charlie danced with Miss Tahiti. And since we were among the last dozen diehards, the governor himself graciously shooed us out. It had been a long time since we'd crashed a party; this was a great reentry.

All kinds of events went on for the next two weeks, and for the best of them—the canoe races—we had front row seats. Although the practices had been impressive, the races were that and more. People and canoes came from all over Tahiti and the outer islands as well—hundreds of boats and thousands of people, all wearing colorful pareaus and flower crowns. One day the weather turned nasty, with high winds and heavy rains; but except for the women's singles race, which was cancelled *after* the women had paddled against wind and current to the starting line, the races went on—for three days. Men, women, boys, girls, singles, teams—everyone paddled a course at least four miles long. Most spectacular, of course, were the double canoes—fifty feet long, some of them, carrying twelve or sixteen people. The men's race drew sixty or more of these boats—nearly a thousand men. They left the starting line as one, paddling furiously, faster than any of us could have powered our boats out of the harbor. As Earl, our neighbor, said, "I'm sure glad those guys ain't carrying clubs." No wonder the Europeans were amazed when they came upon these islands and their people.

Canoe and sailing races were one big event. The other was the dance contest. Again, groups came from all the islands for five nights of competition. Eight or nine groups performed each night, dancing for almost half an hour. Talk about exercise—and of every muscle, too! It did my heart good to see those hip-swaying dances done by women with hips. This is Polynesia; no *Vogue* models need apply.

Another evening we strolled up to Pomare Boulevard for the fruit carriers' race. Each man carried thirty kilos of bananas, oranges, breadfruit, etc., on a pole balanced on his shoulder around a half mile course. I enjoy backpacking, but really!

We didn't stick around for the speedboat races—three to four hours of deafening noise around Papeete harbor. Instead, we rented a car and drove around the island. Although Papeete is the population center, people live everywhere along the perimeter of the island—hardly an empty lot on either side of the road. And except in Papeete, that's all it is—one road along the coastline. Unfortunately, we didn't get into the interior. But there has to be something to come back for.

Two noises we couldn't avoid. The carnival barkers screamed into their microphones from 4 P.M. until at least 2 A.M. daily, exhorting people to gamble. Their voices carried shrilly across the still harbor, especially from 10 P.M. on, when there were few other sounds. When we visited one night, we saw that they were doing a good business—keno, roulette, wheel of fortune. The usual scene was Tahitians gambling, Chinese running the games. And *money* changed hands; no poor natives here.

A more pleasant sound came from the Protestant church. We were anchored right in front of it, and before Fête there was choir practice several times a week—pure, sweet tones and wave-making volume, all without instrumental accompaniment. We stopped everything to listen to these free "concerts," sung simply by the faithful. No professional choirs here. Each little community has its church, and each church a joyous, sweet-singing congregation. They put to shame every church I've been a member of or visited, except the Mormon Tabernacle Choir, hardly your local, amateur group.

Speaking of Mormons, there are lots of them here, all readily recognizable. No one else wears slacks, white shirts, and ties.

After Fête we took Charlie and Wilma to Moorea to more "unspoiled" territory—and for all its commercialism and the numerous interisland flights that come in daily, it is still largely unspoiled. We swam and snorkeled in beautiful clear water, both deep and shallow. It seemed a little cool to us, but our Alaskan in-laws found it just right. (They also thought prices in Tahiti "not high.") Wilma hadn't learned to swim in Alaska, but she made a great start here and loved it. She enjoyed the chickens that run loose almost more, never having seen a live one before. Seals and whales, yes, but no chickens.

Just before Charlie and Wilma left my mother and stepfather joined us at Moorea. After a week of using the hot shower in their room and eating hotel food with them, we did the same with Martha and Larry when they arrived after Mom and Jim left. Martha and Larry's trip, however, took them from Moorea out to the leeward islands, where we joined them at Huahine. Since they left ten days ago we've been back to cold water sponge baths and home cooking—not nice.

Bora Bora was nice. Once all our guests went home the weather, which had been fitful, turned balmy. We spent four days in a beautiful lagoon on the north side of Bora Bora. (We had the whole lagoon and its miles of beaches to ourselves because it's so shallow. Even with our shallow draft, we had to "walk" the boat through coral in places.)

Turquoise ripples lapped gently on the sand of the palm-covered motu, while on the other side sapphire waves became white foam as they crashed on the reef. White terns circled overhead, their bellies milky green from the reflection of the water. We lazed and loafed, repaired and mended, scrubbed the &*!# bottom. We've spent the last several days here at Taha'a in similar lagoons doing similar things. Tomorrow we return to Bora Bora to look for some new old friends before we set off for Tonga.

Reactions? Well, after all the fuss made about us in Chile it was a letdown to arrive in Tahiti and find that nobody cared. We'd sailed five thousand miles from the mainland over some rough seas, but nobody was interested. There were seventy boats in Papeete harbor when we arrived. What's one more?

Probably because of these large numbers of visitors, we've found the locals less friendly and less interested than in other places. Everywhere else we've been visited by the locals in their pongas, motorboats, whatever. Here, not one, not even on the outer islands. Not only are we not a novelty, we don't have anything these people need or want. They buy in town. Don did meet a friendly cab driver while going to the airport to pick up Charlie and Wilma. He and the boys had decided to walk the two or three miles since the buses weren't running at 0400 and the plane was late. (We knew that because we'd not heard it. You *know* when planes arrive and depart in Papeete.) A taxi stopped and wouldn't be waved on. Yes, the driver understood that they weren't looking for a cab, but he insisted on giving them a ride—no charge. Try that in L.A.!

In one way things are much worse here than in L.A. People drive like maniacs. Whether it's a car, bus, motorscooter, or moped, it never moves except at top speed. We saw four bad accidents in front of the church during a ten day period. The high seas are much safer.

Since our guests left we've been devouring the books and magazines they left. Did you know that you can now buy low calorie, low fat dog food? It's no wonder foreigners get funny ideas about the U.S., what with movies and advertising. What next?

Well, television has come to the islands—"Little House on the Prairie" dubbed in French. Don and I went for a walk one night on Huahine. No one else was about; every house we passed was dark, except for the tell-tale blue-gray glow (only black and white TV). We felt like characters out of Bradbury's "The Pedestrian." Surely some day we'll be picked up for the crime of walking outside after dark.

Laundry still is a nuisance. Having it done by low-paid labor or by machines costs a lot. In Papeete at least there was a laundry facility in the "Sanitaires Publics"—a half circle of a tub, maybe six feet in diameter, three feet deep, and with a cement ledge an inch and a half wide, sloping inward. You vaulted into the tub, turned on the tap, and washed your laundry. If it needed scrubbing, you did that on the cement ledge. If it needed agitating, you pretended you were pressing grapes, the difference being that you came out with clean instead of stained feet. For this I gave up my Kenmore? Oh, well, as we all know, "Sailing is the most expensive way to travel third class." On that note, which I can't claim as my own, having overheard it at the Bali Hai bar on Huahine, I take leave for now.

Again red-handedly,
Joanne

P.S. "Sailing is the expensive way to travel no class." That's not mine, either, but I like it.

Not everything costs too much in the French Societies. New Zealand cheeses and meats are cheap. And fresh New Zealand butter costs about a dollar a pound, canned butter a few cents less. Canned margarine costs thirty cents *more* per pound than the butter, and Crisco fifteen cents more than the margarine. You figure it out. We'll just eat butter.

en route to Tonga
September 4, 1977

Dear Friends,

"Roll on, thou deep and dark blue ocean, roll!" It certainly did last night, wave after giant wave. Whether the sea gods were angry because we'd begun this part of our voyage on a Friday or whether it was just our "usual" second-day-out storm matters little. It was a lulu. The wind not only whistled in the rigging, it shrieked and moaned. The building wave sounded like a muffled drum roll. Raindrops ping-ed on the water like short cymbal clashes—quite an orchestra, playing ominous, threatening notes. The seas grew bigger than we've seen. Bad judge of distance though I am, I know some of the waves topped thirty feet. We'd be lifted as one rose, poised on the top as it broke under the bow; then a slide down until the next one caught us, lifted us, and sent us rushing forward. The rain became intermittent drizzle, but for ten hours the wind never let up. Don and I traded off two-hour turns at the helm; we wouldn't let

Donald or Erik steer. Once we "played submarine," as Don calls it: a
wave crashed on the foredeck, sending tons of water across the
bows—only the second time we've had blue water on deck. Inside,
everything shuddered, but our only "casualty" was the bowl of leftover
rice, which slid across the countertop and spread itself on the galley
carpet. After ten minutes of picking up sticky grain after grain, I was back
in bed—not sleeping, but wondering what in the &%#* we were doing.
But not to worry. As long as we "stay cool" the boat will see us through.
She suffers physical fatigue, as we do, but fortunately doesn't know
psychological stress. We haven't decided whether that's greater when you
can see the monsters bearing down on you or just hear them in the
blackness of night. By 0200 the moon was up; by 0400 the wind was
down. We turned the boat over to the boys and turned in for some real
sleep.

All of this came after our three most tranquil, enjoyable days in the
outer islands. After enjoying several anchorages in Bora Bora, we'd sailed
to Taha'a and Raiatea, about thirty miles away. As we left Bora Bora we
saw friends sailing to the island. Knowing that they usually stay put for a
long time, we continued on our way, spending a quiet week loafing, filling
up water tanks, doing laundry, and mowing (with pancake turner) the
grass off the bottom. Then we went out of our way back to Bora Bora to
see *Endless III*—and also finally to meet three other boats we'd seen
around for the past several months, one from New Zealand, one from San
Francisco, one from Fort Bragg. The second evening we all went ashore
for a beach party, complete with guitars, singing, dancing, and bonfire.
Eats, however, were not the traditional steaks, hot dogs, or
hamburgers—not for refrigerator-less cruisers six thousand miles from
home. Casseroles, instead, and wonder of wonders, desserts. Usually
we're the only ones to bring dessert, but on Bora Bora everyone did.

We spent much of our days in the water, finally warm enough for
me to get into and stay in. We snorkeled around the coral reefs, dove for
marlinspike augers in the soft sand near the reefs. Among the five boats
there we must have pulled them up by the dozens—and left them by the
hundreds. Once you know what track to look for you could see them
everywhere. The sea floor looked liked a veritable freeway, complete with
complex interchanges. In my inimitable graceful fashion I wounded
myself with these beautifully marked spiral shells. I dropped one on deck
as I was picking it up to show to Erik; the edge of the mouth sliced my
knee and the point drove into my big toe. The knee was a deep, clean,
bloody cut; it probably will scar. The toe felt quite painful, maybe
broken, so we splinted it with wooden ice cream spoons left over from
Costa Rica before I limped to the party. By the next day it felt fine, so off

came the splint and on went the fins. This time I drove the point of a shell into my thumb as I was digging for it under water. We're told that the natives used to use these shells for chisels; they must have made excellent ones.

By the time Donald's birthday came (we'd celebrated Erik's quietly by ourselves at Taha'a), only *Endless, Puff* (a tri from S.F.), and we were left, so we had a birthday (Donald's, Erik's belated, Don's and my un-) party aboard. Although the cake was so tender that it fell apart and we had to glue it together with frosting and although I was so busy drinking wine and talking that I almost forgot to make the spaghetti sauce, a good time was had by all—tinged with a little sadness, for *Puff* was soon to return to Tahiti, thence the Tuamotus, *Endless* to set out for Japan via Samoa, and we to move southwest to Tonga. And who knew when we would meet again?

The next morning, "One last swim before we leave," I said, and was rewarded by swimming right over the manta ray that inhabited "our" lagoon and had entertained us all for days, gliding just below the surface, sailing with its flippers cutting the surface, and sometimes somersaulting out of the water. This time, as it gracefully swam north, Don and I swam south to the boat to haul up the anchor and be on our way.

September 5, 1977

On that day eighteen years ago I never dreamed I'd be spending an anniversary this way.

Rereading the letters, I see I've left out a lot. Backing up——

The French are very protective about their Pacific islands. No hippies or deadbeats need apply. All visitors have to prove that they have a way out (try buying a one-way ticket to Tahiti) and sufficient money to support them while they're there. That means that boat captains have to post bond for their crews, and sometimes——

Some days after we arrived in Papeete a boat from Ukiah lost her crew. They rowed off in the dinghy, never to be found (although the dinghy was). French officials would not let the boat leave until the crew was aboard or shipped home some other way. Many days later someone reported having seen the crew at the airport, apparently homeward bound. The gendarmes checked with the airlines, verified the information, and finally let the yacht leave.

When we were about to leave Papeete we ran into the young sailmaker who'd made our sun shades in Acapulco. Actually, he ran into us when he rowed out to say hello—with an ulterior motive. He'd taken on a female crew member somewhere between Hawaii and Papeete. He was ready to leave Tahiti, but she wanted to stay. Trouble was, her money hadn't arrived from France; and until she could show it, our sailmaker friend was stuck with her. She put on what Don called her "for sale" costume (fish-net bikini top and long gauze skirt) and they made the rounds, trying to transfer her to someone else—anyone else. It took more than a week (still no money from France), by which time most of his bananas had spoiled—bad news for a vegetarian.

As a family owning the boat we came under slightly different regulations—exactly what, we don't know. (The French port officials have copies of Fijian regulations, but none of their own.) We refused to lose interest on four thousand dollars by having it sent to Tahiti just to prove we had it. Instead, I cried and Don argued. Finally, the obnoxiously officious official said O.K. *to me.* He'd give us our visas, "but," shaking his finger at us, "don't get into any trouble!" Another couple got their money out of the bank in one-dollar bills—fourteen hundred of them. It could just as well have been three hundred; the officials certainly weren't going to count. Ah, French charm!

The natives have as little to do with the French and their "charm" as possible. I wouldn't be surprised to hear of a Tahitian independence movement before the end of the century. Though they like their television sets and motor scooters, the Tahitians otherwise live much as they did a hundred years ago, except in Papeete. They have, to their detriment, become fond of sweetened condensed milk. Mothers feed it to babies and everyone stirs it into coffee and tea. Almost everyone over fifteen has lost at least four teeth. The smiles you see on the hotel help are real, but the teeth aren't. And public relations calls for porcelain, not the usual metal caps.

You think *we're* crazy. In Papeete we met a couple from Australia who were just completing their circumnavigation. They'd started out with a thirty-three foot boat, but as Jan said, it was too big for her to handle alone should something happen to Ian, so they got a twenty-three foot boat instead—not quite as long as we are wide. Jamie was born in South Africa about sixteen months ago and has sailed with his parents ever since—usually clad only in saltwater-washed nappies. When they left Papeete in July, Jan was several months pregnant, cheerily suffering morning sickness *in the harbor.* You don't have to be crazy to be cruising, but what else would you call it?

Too bad, says Erik, that we can't pick up T-bone steaks off the bottom as easily as augers. I agree.

September 7, 1977

Reading an article about backpacking in one of the magazines someone left almost reduced me to tears. There's just too much sea level in sailing, too much monotony and sitting still while under way. In short, I miss my mountains! Take good care of the Sierra until we get back.

Palmerston atoll
September 9, 1977

Do you know where we are? I'm not sure, but our navigation was right on, and after floating along windless for two days we got close enough this morning to motor in.

Since the reef encircles the five islands without a passage big enough to get through, we're anchored outside, right off a broken up Korean fishing boat that slammed aground about eighteen months ago—not a comforting sight. But the islanders know their waters well, and as at Pitcairn Island come out in their boats to take us ashore. In such a chancy anchorage we wouldn't leave the boat alone, so today only Donald and I went ashore. When we were just entering the narrow passage in the reef, seas crashing around and behind us, and the outboard engine died, I thought we were in the imperiled boat. But a little deft paddling on one side and pushing off the reef with a pole on the other and we were through—just as the engine caught and a breaker lifted our stern to give us a good push. The lagoon, of course, was calm, though coral-dotted; and again, the colors of the water were spectacular—unreal turquoise, milky jade, and that Crayola middle blue-green. Naturally, I'd left the camera on the boat so couldn't record all this on film. Maybe tomorrow. (Actually, today. It's about 0200 and I'm on watch. This is not the kind of anchorage where everybody gets to go to bed at night.)

Like Pitcairn, Palmerston has an inbred British-native population, only more so. Instead of six or seven mutineers, all the people here can trace paternity to one Englishman, John (?) Marsters. He arrived sometime in the 1850s, planted coconuts, and eventually took three wives—simultaneously, not in succession. Before he died, he divided the island they lived on into thirds, and to this day the different branches of the family have kept the same shares.

The population now numbers only fifty-six, about half what it was at its largest. Though Palmerston was granted "forever" to the Marsters family by Queen Elizabeth II, it is governed by the Cook Islands, themselves now independent but still with close ties to New Zealand. The government sends a teacher for the primary school (seventeen students, aged five to twelve, plus six preschool; apparently there's less other diversion here than on Pitcairn with its nine students); from talking to her I gathered that it's considered compulsory service in the boondocks, rather than a choice assignment. But she said she enjoys the peaceful life and enjoys even more being so far away from the school administration. She runs *her* school the way *she* wants. (Think of having your boss more than three hundred slow boat miles away!) Anyone who wants a high school education has to go to Raratonga, and for schooling beyond that to New Zealand. The present John Marsters said that the population declines every time a supply boat comes in. And as we walked the island today we saw many closed and boarded up homes. Unless tourism "rescues" this island—an improbability, with its lack of resources—it won't last out a generation. Talk about vanishing species—outer islands ought to be on someone's "protected" list.

Palmerston is not a garden spot like Pitcairn. Practically nothing except coconuts and breadfruit will grow in the poor coral soil. The inhabitants have dug out and cultivated a taro patch and have been able to coax along some sweet potatoes, but that's it. Chickens run everywhere, feeding on the coconuts, but they're for eggs, not meat. The Palmerstonians might kill a few chickens for a festival, but Colonel Sanders couldn't open up here. We saw only two pigs. The people live mostly on fish and coconuts, with an occasional turtle and, in season, crayfish. They seem very concerned about husbanding their resources. The "season" on crayfish is their own doing, yet even without the force of any "law" the people respect it. Each of the families also has a "turtle obligation." They watch for the eggs to hatch, and before the young get to the sea (where most of them die) they catch them and take them home, feed them until they measure four to five inches, then turn them loose. Each year (?) each family is responsible for two turtles per person—and I have no doubt they fulfill the responsibility.

Copra and fish provide the people with necessary cash—not nearly as much as Pitcairn's stamps provide. The coconuts have been over-planted, too close together, and the yields are decreasing. In addition, copra is not as much in demand as it once was. The fish, mostly parrotfish, goes to Raratonga on ice. While this fishing in the lagoon is apparently as good as ever, John said that fishing outside the reef isn't. They used to get twenty to thirty large tuna annually (record: 280 pounds), but no more. The Korean fishing fleet? Movement of food source? French atomic tests? All of the above? None? Palmerstonians accept and live with the situation. What else is there to do?

I enjoyed the day ashore and wouldn't mind a week, maybe even a month—if I were teaching, maybe even a whole school term. But a lifetime? I could envision a lifetime on Robinson Crusoe Island or Pitcairn. They, after all, have hills and valleys. Crusoe has Chilean wine and blackberries and beef. Pitcairn has oranges and goat and New Zealand cheese. (Too bad neither has a beautiful lagoon. If I'd been in charge of creation I'd have arranged it.) But a lifetime on flat land with only coconut trees swaying overhead—even though life is unpressured and the lagoon a swimmer's delight—isn't my idea of Eden.

en route to Tonga
September 12, 1977

It's long underwear time again. That south wind that blows in from Antarctica is COLD. Whether we somehow failed to communicate or whether Donald and I somehow offended, the islanders did not come out Saturday to pick us up and take us ashore. And since we were fixing our leaky dinghy we couldn't have taken it ashore if we'd had a mind to—which we didn't; we still have some brains left. We waited to see what Sunday would bring, and of course it brought a storm. So we upped anchor and headed out to sea, missing most of the worst, sailing through drizzle and drip. Then, waterspout! A waterspout looks like (is, actually) a miniature tornado, but over sea, rather than land. We watched the funnel shape grow from the bottom of a cloud until it reached the cloud of spray on the sea surface. We were enthralled—until we realized what we were seeing. Reduce sail to ease handling, but keep up speed and get out of the way! The spout followed along about half a mile behind us for a while; then, as we took off perpendicular to its track, we watched the cloud stretch, thin, and break. End of waterspout, after about ten to fifteen minutes. Nevertheless, some things I'd rather just read about.

Niue Island (where?)
September 14, 1977

Not only long underwear, but hot water bottles. Better too cold than too hot (you can always add more clothes, but there's a limit to what you can take off), but it's getting ridiculous.

There hadn't been a boat here for about ten days; yesterday three of us arrived. Since we were here first, we got the mooring buoy, didn't have to anchor in the coral. The Niue Island Blue Water Yacht Club's guest book talks of hot showers and washing machines. Tomorrow we search.

September 19, 1977

The hot showers, cold beer, and laundry facilities belong to the "old days," when a Canadian was running the yacht club. You can still get them, but only if you meet the right people and drop the right hints. We're still backward about that so are as dirty as ever.

Never again will I make nasty comments about "basket weaving." You should see the things they produce at Niue—beautiful, intricate, durable baskets, purses, mats, hats. All are hand woven from natural fibers and leaves, and there's not a bit of bad workmanship in the lot. Since we're not getting more money until Samoa and since they're not set up for personal checks or credit cards, we were limited in what we could buy, but we bought to the limit—even had visions of setting up as distributors in the States, but that position's long gone. A Hawaiian representative handles the whole West coast.

We left Niue on Saturday because the wind came up from the wrong direction (what else is new?), making it difficult to go ashore in the dinghy and increasing the possibility of *Anduril's* going aground. After about fifteen hours of sailing we hit a flat calm, went about fifteen miles in twenty hours. Why couldn't we have had that weather in the harbor? And it's said that *women* are perverse and fickle!

I always did like eucalyptus and pines more than palms, and now even more so—especially coconut palms. Not only do they have no fragrance (drying copra *stinks*), but they're downright dangerous. Those coconuts *fall off*—and from fifty feet they come down with great force. We met a guide at one of the hotels who was hit in the back by one as she bent over to pick one off the ground. She spent two months in the hospital. Truly, coconuts and palm trees are vastly overrated.

September 26, 1977
(September 25 to you)

If you're still looking for island paradises, try Tonga, "the Friendly Islands." They are—and cheap, too. We can eat fresh vegetables without having to mortgage the boat. Last night we had dinner (cook your own barbecue) at the hotel. It cost $3.80 for the four of us. It was so expensive because the kids' steaks were $1.50 each. Two sausage dinners made up the rest. We had reasonable amounts of meat and all we could eat of seven different kinds of vegetables and salads, plus watermelon. Drinks, of course, came extra—cost nearly double the dinner price for a dozen drinks (soft and otherwise).

More important is the "Friendly." Everyone says hello, and if you say more you can always get conversation. Young schoolchildren have three phrases that they practice incessantly—"Hello. Where are you going? Good-bye." Young girls are again fingering my blonde hair to see if it's real.

The poverty here is real. Everything is patched and mended—clothing, housing, people. There is a lot of clothing to patch and mend. I don't know what the islanders wore in Captain Cook's day, but since the missionaries it's been long dresses with at least medium-long sleeves. I've seen about ten women wearing pants—covered by long tunic tops. It's a lot of clothing for the warm, humid climate (it's only cold on the sea at night).

The place isn't exactly undiscovered—at least by yachties. Fifteen of us share the small anchorage in front of the hotel. We were more fortunate than the others. We made friends with some Kiwis staying at the hotel and developed a wonderful symbiotic relationship. We took Stan and Jean to the local points of interest on the outer islands and they let us use their shower and bath. It's been only six weeks, and I still remembered the bath in Tahiti, but it was nice nevertheless.

Swimming is good, the water greener than elsewhere. Though we've seen lots of fish, we've not caught any. We also swam into the underwater cave—a scary experience for me, as I get increasingly claustrophobic. But I'm a better person for having done it.(?)

en route to Fiji
September 30, 1977

We've rethought some of our thoughts about Tonga. The people are not nearly so poor as we'd thought—certainly not so poor as those we saw in El Salvador. They have very little money; but most of them live in homes adequate to comfortable, with electricity and indoor plumbing. The land is productive and local food very cheap (tomatoes and green peppers, for instance, cost about three cents each). Almost every home has a garden. And everyone—or at least every family—owns land. The king gives each male subject part of an acre (a sixth, I think) in town and more (eight acres, I think) in the outlying areas. When a Tongan says "my island" he usually means it literally. Generally, the people farm these acres—coconuts for copra and bananas being good crops—and the more astute gather the tourists for trips to "my island" for lobster-catching, Tongan feasts, etc. Those people who actually live on their outer islands are generally poorer. They still have plenty of food, but they have practically no money. The yachties are their store. They bring us shells, tapa cloth, and tourist gee-gaws (I could strangle whoever taught them this artsy-craftsy junk); and we gift them with powdered milk, needles and thread, and empty jars and plastic bottles. All of this is a gift exchange; nothing is bought or sold. But people remain on the boat until they are quite sure that no more gifts are forthcoming. After three families in a row have been aboard (they never come together), you get a little tired of the game and begin to lose patience. We've become the new "cargo cult."

Yachties sometimes have trouble getting permission to visit the outer islands. Seems that one of "us" planted some marijuana a few years ago (as did a Peace Corps worker; but he planted his in town), and the powers that be are *really* uptight about the weed. The newspapers are currently quoting U.S. Narcotics Bureau stuff from the thirties—pot smoking leads to violent crimes, leads to hard drugs, etc. Yet no one is concerned about kava drinking; that's traditional. Don went to a men's "kava club" last Saturday, and he said it reminded him of what he's seen and heard of pot parties—talking, music, people nodding off. Apparently kava isn't against anyone's religion.

(Don and Donald are getting the big genoa ready since we're "racing" to Suva. The other boats left yesterday and the day before and have had good winds. We're hoping for the same. For the first time Donald actually *wants* a lot of sail up; also for the first time he scrubbed the bottom without grumbling. Maybe we should race all the time.)

Almost everyone in Tonga wears some kind of girdle. Mourning girdles are woven of pandanus leaves. They vary in size from about one foot to three feet, depending on the closeness of the relationship to the deceased, and are worn for three to twelve months, also depending. By the end of the mourning period they are quite tattered. Other girdles denote status. Some are crocheted; others are woven waist bands with raffia or crocheted squares or some such hanging down. Apparently no one who isn't wearing a girdle can see the king, and those who do wear them in daily life, including those in mourning, are deferred to—first in line at the market, better cuts of meat, etc. Wish we had more time to study the culture.

Even children wear the girdles, though not to school. For that—uniforms. Each school has a different one, the Catholic girls wearing starched blue cotton jumpers (shades of Chicago, 1950). Church schools seem to outnumber government schools about four to one. Concession to custom allows Mormon men and boys to wear the traditional "skirt" (I forget what it's called) instead of Western pants with their white shirts and dark ties.

October 2, 1977

Finally, we're moving—trade wind sailing. We've made our best distances so far—180 and 168 nautical miles per day. (Sailing a multihull is a fast way to travel slowly.) The seas seem smooth, since we're going with them. But steering is difficult; following seas exert tremendous pressure on the rudder, and an aft wind means that unless you steer a *straight* course one of your sails collapses (we're running wing and wing; a sail on each side). The motion of the boat is quite different from what we get when beating into the wind, and we're so used to *that* that this makes Erik and me sick. I should have an apt quotation, but I don't.

Queasily,
Joanne

Suva, Fiji
October 13, 1977

Dear Friends,

"He who would go to sea for pleasure would go to hell for diversion." B. Franklin said that, I am told. If he didn't, he should have.

"The fleet" convened here for a week or so; then "Time and tide wait for no man" and "'The time has come,' the Walrus said." And some as yet undefined biological? chemical? stimulus in the brain? seat? itchy foot? of *marinus simpliticus* triggered an exodus. So this morning nearly a dozen boats, driven by who knows what urge, left the safe harbor, comfortable bar, invigorating swimming pool, and sybaritic hot showers of the Tradewinds Hotel and took to the sea. We, being a breed apart, sailed south instead of west. But in a week or so we will belatedly join the westward migration, meeting the rest of the flock? herd? pod? on Fiji's "sunny" coast. Any of you who like Portland or Seattle would love Suva. But don't get thrown into gaol (next to and across the road from the Royal Suva Yacht Club). Raincoats are issued only to guards.

Suva is certainly the most exotic and cosmopolitan city we've visited. Diminutive Indians (men wrapped in turbans, women in elegant, even when well-mended, saris) jostle the streets with strapping Fijians (Afros elaborately groomed) and impeccably proper Kiwis (short pants, long socks, and clipped accents). Everyone looks so exotic that I feel especially ordinary.

Buses show the signs of British control. The posted passenger limit *is not exceeded.* No Latin American packing and crowding. But as everywhere, the buses must have been built for the smallest among the population. They have uncomfortably small seats and little leg room for "Westerners." Native Fijians practically need to be contortionists to squeeze in.

October 19, 1977

Does the world seem as crazy to you at home as it does to me? We're "out of it" for weeks at a time, then come into a major port and "catch up" on the "real world"—hunter-killer satellites and hunter-killer satellites armed with lasers, to the tune of $58.7 million; possible foreign manipulation of the U.S. commodities market; Billy Carter (is he real, or some novelist's fiction?). This is man, the rational animal? I doubt even Jonathan Swift's view of the species as "capable of rationality." I feel like a Dickensian caricature in a subplot who doesn't know what's going on in the main plot. *Is* there a main plot? *King Kong* seemed more realistic than the real world. (It cost us fifty cents here, and I'm glad we didn't pay the four-fifty in Tahiti. The Empire State Building is still the tallest building in New York City, no matter how much taller the Twin Towers are. What happened to all the natives on the island—the Pacific one, not Manhattan?) If this paragraph confuses you, you haven't been reading current newspapers or magazines—or *Alice's Adventures in Wonderland.*

Mbengga, Fiji
October 22, 1977

We saw the famous Fijian firewalkers, right here on their home island. The *Lindblad Explorer* came in (a day late, according to the villagers); and we, having been invited by several of the villagers, joined the group. First, of course, there was time to buy—tapa, shells, pineapple, etc. The men sang and danced nearby; then we walked to the firepit. The fire was real and hot, but we were disappointed in the "ceremony." It was obviously hokied up for tourists, and one step in and out isn't my idea of fire *walking* (not that I'd have taken even one step on those hot rocks!). We're glad to have seen it and even gladder we didn't pay five dollars each at the hotels in Suva.

We talked to many people on the *Explorer*. They're on their way to Chile, reversing our route. It's a great itinerary, but they don't stay anywhere for long. We were invited out to the boat for lunch, but they were upping the anchor before serving—after only three hours here on Mbengga. They're scheduled for one day on Easter Island and one on Pitcairn. If they don't have good weather, they won't get ashore—no waiting around as we did.

Donald finally got the ham radio working today. We've been receiving for some time but couldn't transmit successfully. Now we're A-OK. If any of you have hams (baked, boiled, Polish, or otherwise) for friends, let us know their call signs and when they're usually on the air. Maybe we can give you a call.

Who wears the pants in your family? Around these islands no one does. The women wear calf-length dresses over long skirts, and the men wear a wrap-around skirt, variously called a sulu, vala, or lava-lava. (Think of the dress code arguments we'd have had if the football team had decided to wear skirts!) Europeans, of course, wear pants—usually bermuda shorts, but dressy, i.e., with long socks. Wow! all those sexy male kneecaps!

From the "Notice to Mariners" given to us at the hotel where we anchored in Suva: "You are invited to use [our] facilities...There are few rules and no discriminations except against poor behaviour, and that is behaviour that will annoy others, such as un-due noise, bad language or bad dress." Shirts and shoes to be worn in lobby, lounge, and restaurants. In the evening, shorts "must be accompanied by long socks." (If they accompany you, must you introduce them?) And they made it stick. Any school that wants to enforce a dress code ought to hire a few Fijian waiters/bartenders.

Another note on Fiji—— They grow and process their own sugar. It would make health food addicts happier to see the state of their "processed" sugar. But better for you or not, raw sugar doesn't make a good meringue, so we were delighted to find fine white sugar at one market and bought twelve pounds of it. I gave a friend six pounds of the salt for making play dough for her kids. Do you think we'll use the other six pounds of fine white salt in the next two years? Thank goodness Erik tastes when he puts things away.

November 5, 1977

Farewell to Fiji—a beautiful country, but sailing here gives me the fidgets. Reefs and isolated coral heads lie scattered all around, and charts are *very* inadequate—the U.S. doesn't make detailed charts of the area, and local charts have no soundings. So it's day sailing only and very often with someone up the ratlines—usually Erik because he has the best eyes. Yesterday he spotted something and shouted for us to "turn around!" Imminent disaster—"How We Lost Our Boat on a Coral Reef"—but it was only a chambered nautilus floating by. It was the first one we'd seen, and Erik wanted to pick it up! (We did.)

Donald's been having a lot of fun with the ham radio; if he keeps studying he may even get an American license when we reach Samoa. How he's getting out with the antenna the way it is I'll never know. I "fixed" it on the way from Tonga—knocked it down when I steered into an accidental gibe as we were reefing down one night. Don couldn't find the parts to fix it in Suva, so he and Donald jury-rigged it—works fine, but looks peculiar, like Dr. Seuss' cat in the hat. And the bamboo pole propping it up emits an eerie whistle.

If you discount the sea and imagine a road, you'd think you were driving the San Diego Freeway. While Suva is wet, this side of the islands is dry. Except for the coconut palms right at water's edge, you could be at Lion Country Safari. No tropical greenness here. Of course, it's been a very dry year—water rationing, reduced pressure, etc. Maybe world climate *is* changing. Just as long as hurricanes don't reach equatorial waters this year we'll weather the change.

The contrast between Radio Fiji and Radio Samoa doesn't speak well for the American educational system. Announcers on Radio Fiji are trilingual (English, Fijian, Hindustani); those on Radio Samoa can't even read English without stumbling. And they don't appear to understand what they're reading.

We've met several tourists out here—yachties and otherwise—who remind me of the flower children of the sixties, those overindulged products of the middle and upper-middle classes who played at being poor. These tourists bewail the changes in the islands—the corrugated tin roofs instead of thatch, the cement block homes, etc. They want "the culture" to remain as it was. Of course, they wouldn't want to live in it. They want warm, dry houses, electricity, piped water; but they want the "primitive" (i.e., "poor") to remain that way so they can visit for a week or so once a year. Naturally, I'd rather see a real firewalking ceremony than the show that's put on for hotels and cruise ships; but I don't fault the villagers of Rukua for capitalizing on their only marketable export. Firewalking profits are bringing a new water system and better housing to the village. In other areas cash buys electric stoves and outboard engines. I don't recognize any special virtue in doing without these things—maybe because we have to pump our water and scrub our laundry by hand. "Roughing it" is fine for a vacation, but I don't extol it as a way of life.

Modernization does pose problems. The brightest, most adventuresome, most aggressive are leaving the outer islands in all the groups and migrating to the larger population centers, overcrowding the cities and leaving only the most unskilled in the outer islands. All the young people on Pitcairn, in the Cooks, Tonga, here in Fiji, see New Zealand as their hope. But last year New Zealand had a net loss of three thousand people—mostly skilled or professional people seeking a brighter future elsewhere, primarily in the U.S. 'Tis a puzzlement and a problem, but I don't begrudge anyone the comforts of the twentieth century.

Speaking of electric or gas stoves, they do look funny here. Kitchens aren't contained in the houses but in a separate lean-to, usually unwalled or at least open on three sides. I hate to think of what those stoves will look like after three years' exposure to the weather—especially those nearest the ocean.

Especially on the outer islands, what we consider a "home" is little more than a family's sleeping quarters. The entire village complex is the home, and you don't traipse through it uninvited without getting people as upset as you might be if a stranger took a tour through your living room. It's not that the people are unfriendly, but the courtesies must be observed. If anyone is "at home" you'll be invited in; thereafter it's O.K. to walk through that village.

For you other Americans also too lazy to have learned foreign languages, these former British colonies are great places to visit—once you get used to the traffic coming at you on the "wrong" side of the road.

November 9, 1977

No quote or quip for this. Early yesterday morning in the dark of a quiet, starry but moonless night, we ran the boat aground on the reef at Wallis Island. Donald had just taken the watch and I was climbing into my bunk when there was a crunching, grating sound and the boat shuddered. I first thought that the engine, like the wonderful one-hoss shay, was going to pieces; but in the same instant I remembered that we hadn't turned on the engine all day. With a sinking feeling (sorry) we all realized simultaneously what had happened. "Oh, shit," said Donald, "we're aground." (Donald denies this comment, but Don swears to it.) What happened next and how I can't tell you exactly. Although we turned on the deck lights so that everything was brightly illuminated, the events remain dim to me.

Donald was dressed and Erik had scrambled into a pair of pants as he bolted out of the aft cabin, but Don and I hadn't even thought to get dressed. The breakers—gentle, thank God (or perhaps not; had they been bigger and louder we may have heard and seen them in time)—pounded on our port beam, only sometimes washing over the deck. We turned on the engine, pulled down sails, and made our first, probably instinctive, mistake. We tried to turn or at least back off the reef. Of course, we couldn't, but we had to get out of the surf. We raised sail and with the help of the engine, a fortunately rising tide, and Providence, we bulled our way into the lagoon, still aground, but not in the surf. Next (I think) came the setting of anchors to keep us from drifting back into the surf.

Don rowed the dinghy in search of a spot deep enough for us—preferably over sand, though at that point we weren't being fussy. But even with searchlight and flashlight he really couldn't see under water. And his soundings showed an uneven bottom—four feet, six feet, two feet. A bit of a moon rose, and we followed her beam on a rising tide until we rested—temporarily safely and quietly—in seven feet of water. How we accomplished this I can't really tell you. It involved casting off and picking up two of the anchors we had set and transferring one from stern to bow so that the boat would move bow first. It involved Erik's getting glasses and glasses of water for Don; his medication ordinarily dries his mouth, and under tension the dryness becomes suffocating. It involved bandaging a finger I mangled in the anchor chain, not daring to look at it, just stopping the blood and keeping everything together. It involved shouting and weeping, fear and calm. The process took a little more than two hours.

By 0330 we could sit a little calmly and think. If we stayed where we were we'd be aground in coral again within hours. We couldn't go back. Which direction forward? If "at night all cats are gray," so are all coral heads invisible—except the ones that threatened us on all sides. So with the light of false dawn and before the glare of the rising sun (which would have made the coral heads harder to see than the darkness did) we moved slowly east. Erik stood in the ratlines, trying to read the deeps and shallows; Don steered, needing lots of muscle to turn the wheel, for the rudder shaft had bent. By sunrise we were safely anchored in sixteen feet of water in a beautiful lagoon near what looked like a village and school or government offices. We collapsed in sleep.

Not for long. Natives came by with a stalk of bananas, a huge pineapple, and some drinking nuts. For an hour we couldn't make them understand that we'd had a problem getting to their village—until they went spearfishing and Don went underwater to assess our damage. Then we learned that someone had seen the flares we'd set off but had been scared off by the noise of the shotgun.

Don found sections of the keel missing, as expected, and the rudder shaft bent. The keel, being hollow, was filling with water, and some of it was leaking into the bilges. We repaired the leaks into the bilges and slowed the one into the engine room with underwater epoxy. We figure that we won't have to man the pumps more than twice a day on the way to Samoa—maybe not that often. Today we dropped the rudder a fraction of an inch so it will move freely. The moment of truth is at hand.

We got off cheap, considering what could have happened, although we'll have to haul out in Samoa. How did it happen? We didn't, after all, hit some uncharted obstacle; the island and surrounding reef were plainly indicated on our charts. It turned out that our dead reckoning was way off; usually it's pretty close to Don's sun sights. When it wasn't, he couldn't believe his figures; we *knew* we'd traveled farther and faster. And the sight hadn't been a very good one. Normally, Donald would have taken a sight, too, if Don's gave him problems; but Donald was having fun with the radio, so... Next time——but there won't be a next time. And should a reef get under us again we'll not try to back off. Forward, the Light Brigade.

Tellingly, I think, nothing helped us in our emergency but our own efforts. The old army flares (not surprisingly) didn't go off. The new flare pistol (surprisingly and disappointingly) wouldn't fire until it had been repaired. And who has time for repairs in an emergency? Even when repaired, the flares it sent up didn't attract help—nor did the noise of the shotgun nor the SOS Don flashed with the searchlight. (By then all we wanted was a local boat to show us the way to the channel and deeper water.) Donald got on the radio but couldn't raise anyone, anywhere (although he heard several African stations loud and clear). We'd read it everywhere; we had it confirmed. Out here you're on your own.

The experience gave us more reason to be thankful we'd chosen a multihull. If we'd been a monohull with a six- to eight-foot draft, we'd be living ashore and making long salvage trips out to the reef.

Though we've come through each situation with only minor bruises, this has not been our year. It began with the thefts and hit/run in Peru, through my dumping of the antenna and ripping the mainsail, to this. I think we should sit in a hole with blankets over our heads until the new year brings in a new cycle.

And as usual, we have no pictures of this excitement. It was too dark and we much too busy.

We'd decided not to visit this island. Now I'm glad we have, although I'd have wished a more conventional entrance. The island and the lagoon are beautiful, the water clear and warm, and the people the most attractive Polynesians we've seen. We plan to go ashore this afternoon and learn more. As to what real natives wear under their sulus, lava-lavas, whatever-they're-calleds, here on Wallis Island the answer apparently is nothing—or so Don says and so it appeared to me from the looks I was given, the very careful walking and sitting of the men who visited the boat, and the fact that they all went swimming clothed when it was obvious that they usually unwrap before diving in. Now that we're here, we intend to stay a few days and enjoy ourselves. We don't want to arrive in Samoa on a weekend, anyway; it being "U.S.," we'd probably be charged overtime.

November 11, 1977

The natives have continued friendly; they've brought us bananas (too many!), papayas, fish, coconuts, pineapples; every day it's someone with something, and most of them won't wait to receive gifts in return.

The school is the elite of the French islands in this area—three hundred of the best scholars. And if all the French were like the teachers and gendarme we've met here, I'd change my mind about the French. Yesterday Jean-Claude and Andre drove us to the main village for sightseeing and official checking-in. We saw the king's house with his pigs rooting in front and the cathedral, both looking like Norman fortresses, built of imported French limestone. When we visited the gendarme (Jean-Claude's friend, of course), he wasn't interested in doing any paperwork, just plied us with Johnny Walker Red. Then back to Jean-Claude's for more Johnny Walker, excellent French wines (red and white; I'd forgotten how good good wine is), and roast beef. And when Andre said that the islanders would be better off learning English than French in this English-speaking part of the Pacific, I knew we'd found a pearl without price. And this is a "hardship" post for the French, bringing extra pay and lots of perks.

November 16, 1977

For good reason do ships not travel in this direction. "Beating into the wind" describes the situation all too aptly. Wind and waves flog everything. Actually, we're no longer beating. The steady southeast trades have turned into an eastern gale. We're fore-reaching, no more than three miles from shore (Western Samoa); it's but sixty-five miles to our landfall (Apia), but at this rate we won't be there for two days. And I thought (hoped) we'd left this behind us in Chile!

I've been taking a lot of guff over my sun hat, but you won't catch me with sunburned lips and nose. I never found a straw hat to fit—brims were always too big and crowns too small—until Tonga. There I got a straw coolie hat decorated with two large purple raffia pompons, sewed in place with circlets of shells. Since the straw chin tie broke, I had to replace it with the ribbon I have—orange lace. It's quite fetching, actually. Don has threatened to fetch it overboard. "At least get rid of the pompons!"

November 17, 1977

"Cheer up; things could get worse. So I cheered up—and sure enough, things got worse." We've moved about thirty miles closer to our goal in the past twenty-four hours. It's hard to tell exactly because it's been too cloudy either to take a sun sight or to see the islands (two). National weather service says there are no weather warnings for this part of the world. And the local radio stations aren't mentioning anything, either. But if it gets much worse we'll have to run with it instead of trying to sit it out. Remember Eliza Doolittle's song from *My Fair Lady*—"All I want is a room somewhere..."? Ditto—and in spades.

Robert Louis Stevenson came to Samoa for his health. I'd have stayed in California. I suppose that's not fair, since I haven't even been ashore yet (haven't even *seen* the shore of the island we're looking for); but at times like this I wish we'd emulated Thoreau and "traveled much" in our backyard.

November 18, 1977

Remember the old joke "You can't get there from here"? It's no joke. We're back where we were Tuesday morning when we first sighted this island. Last night's gale blew us offshore. And this morning what's left of our mainsail ripped again. I've patched it, but we don't dare put it up until the wind abates at least a little. So we're flying our two infinitesimal storm sails, which are *not* made for beating into the wind. We've tried powering, but the workhorse Volvo is only an auxiliary after all; we're a sailboat. In these seas the engine doesn't do any better than the sails. *And* we're low on fuel—as well as on lots of different stores and propane. More of a problem, though, we're even low on water, although there's usually enough rain to count on catching some. We are, of course, giddy, cracking really stupid jokes—too little sleep, too much anxiety. We'll certainly have a lot to be thankful for come Thursday (Thanksgiving). The irony is, as we found out by talking to the airport control tower on Upalu last night, that on the smaller island they're having good weather. We just can't get to it. The control tower could "see that little storm system sitting out there. You must be in it."

All of the boats that left Fiji for New Zealand when we left to come this way have arrived. Sixteen have checked in on the radio. Of that number, one had fifteen hours of sixty knot winds, one rolled over in the same storm (but is now safely in port in NZ); near Tahiti, a boat lost its rudder and was trying to make any port; we went aground at Wallis and have now come up with this; and yesterday a boat hit the reef and burned in Apia harbor (where we're headed). Please send some statistics about freeway and airplane accidents and cheer me up.

Later (while standing night watch)

"Everything comes to him who waits." Even wind shifts? We certainly hope so—especially since our official books and charts say that the wind shouldn't blow with this force from this direction at this time of year. We could also use a sea sifter—get the lumps out of these waves.

Last night another regular on the ham net had trouble. The steering broke as they were approaching Suva. Somehow they got help (maybe "how to fix it," maybe just moral support) from stations in Australia and California. Again, everyone is O.K. Still, . . .

November 19, 1977

And worse. The wind never let up, so we couldn't raise anything more than our storm sails. Last night at dusk we were back where we had been last Tuesday. All night long we tacked, a saw-toothed, zigzag course, trying to get to the southeast, where the wind was blowing from. This morning we found out that we'd lost ground to the wind and current. We're farther west than when we started. I don't think any of us has ever been more discouraged—many silent tears (and curses) and a few visible (and audible) ones. The wind has died a little, so we've put up more sail and are trying again.

Maybe the wind won't shift until we bathe. No one could stand to be downwind of any of us. But until we *know* that we'll get to Apia, it's saltwater washing only. That's no problem; every time we go out to steer we get a shower. This is a wet, hard, bumpy ride.

Later

Twelve hours later and we've made good about sixteen miles (traveled about forty). We had to reduce sail again, but we're continuing to move. We hope to reach Apia in about twenty-four hours.

Apia, Western Samoa
November 23, 1977

The wind had died a little, we were sailing along nicely, everyone had cheered up—and sure enough, things got even worse than worse. Again at change of watch at 0100, Donald had just taken the wheel—and the steering went out. We were left drifting in the channel between the islands, the current setting us toward the reef we had just left behind. We pulled up the bed in the aft cabin to get at the steering mechanism. For two hours Don and Donald struggled with nuts and bolts and fittings. Erik struggled with sails, and I held the quartz lamp, illuminating the aft cabin. It was like an operating room scene out of *M*A*S*H*. The light got so hot that I melted one of my gloves. After repeated failures—finally success. We had again lost ground, but at least we hadn't drifted as far as the reef; and the wind and seas died, leaving us some breathing room.

By 0600 I was sure we had it made. I was on watch. The wind had finally shifted to a favorable direction. We were traveling at only two knots, but as soon as everyone was awake we'd motor the fifteen miles to Apia. I bathed and felt even better. (For those of you still faced with the water shortage, I used two quarts of water to wash my hair and bathe. A word to the wise? the prudent? the ecologically minded? And what I wouldn't have given for a tub full of about forty gallons of *hot* water!)

By 0830 the steering had loosened. By 0900 the wind had shifted again to on the nose; it had also increased and whipped up big seas. Given the almost broken steering and the wind and sea conditions, there seemed no chance of getting to Apia. Under power we couldn't make more than about a knot and a half; under sail we'd have to tack, traveling forty miles instead of fifteen. We headed toward shore for more protection; then we thought of turning downwind and sheltering at a small harbor near the airport. The barometer kept dropping and the clouds kept building, indicating a real blow. Donald stayed below, tightening bolts on the steering, while Don and I took turns at the helm and Erik fed us. (I couldn't eat. The *only* good part of the past two weeks is that I've finally lost weight.)

By noon Don decided that we could make Apia harbor. The rest of us argued, shouted, cried; but the skipper had his way. We poured our last reserves of fuel into the tank, turned on the engine, and headed east. At times the wind died and the sun came out; we traveled at four to five knots, feeling happy. Then wind and seas built again, clouds covered the sun, and depression returned. We next welcomed a heavy rain, which flattened the seas and washed us salt free. From then on it was moderate to heavy wind and seas and encroaching darkness. We entered Apia literally as the sun set behind a hill, put our anchor down in the remaining half light.

Flat and calm! We ate a quick dinner and were abed within an hour. Don and I had had about seven hours sleep in forty-eight and the boys not much more. We did, after all, have a lot to be thankful for that Sunday evening, even if Thanksgiving wasn't for another few days.

Monday we were checked in by a pair of very courteous officials. One took off his shoes when he noticed that we were barefoot. The second got rid of his cigarette.

Surprisingly, the general population hasn't been very friendly—the first time we've found officials more polite than "regular" people. Practically no one on the street smiles; and when we rowed ashore to the market to get water, we had bananas, cans, and other refuse thrown at us. It was closing time, and the debris was being dumped into the bay anyway, but much of it was thrown to splash around us, rather than just dumped. We feel distinctly unwelcome. We've completed our chores (some shopping, sail repair, steering repair, getting propane) and will leave as soon as the wind dies. It started last night, blowing a gale.

Don thinks that the problem might be a real case of "haves" and "have nots." Officials obviously "have." So do the tradespeople who've been courteous and even gone out of their way to help us—making a piece for the steering gear and fixing up a way to fill our propane tanks, whose fittings are unlike the ones here, for instance. The market people are "have nots." Many of them apparently live in the market. At least, they're sleeping there on the cement floor at night. Maybe they bring their produce, baskets, etc., from outlying village homes and just stay in town until it's sold. Whatever the reason, we won't be sorry to leave.

November 24, 1977

Happy Thanksgiving. We're ready to leave. The line on the second anchor we set out yesterday to hold us in the blow chafed through. We are now anchor hunting. I feel jinxed.

Later

Donald found the anchor on his first dive. Does that mean our luck is turning good again? At any event, we're on our way to Pago Pago—Thanksgiving dinner afloat. Erik has already made the pumpkin pie (*my* recipe requires fresh eggs and a refrigerator). We have mashed potatoes and our last canned turkey. Unfortunately, no wine, since we'll be sailing tonight.

The weather here is only a little short of oppressive—that is, if you want to do anything. I can understand why people work slowly—or not at all. Pago is supposed to be even worse—more humidity, *no* sunshine. Do not remind me of the complaints I made on the "long underwear route" from Chile to Tahiti.

Pago Pago, American Samoa
November 26, 1977

We've been in Pago twelve hours. It's been raining ten. I need windshield wipers for my glasses. But we've already had hamburgers; and tomorrow we get a ride to church, lunch, and use of washer and dryer. *Palagi* (foreigners) here are very friendly.

Your friend,
Joanne

Pago Pago
December 3, 1977

Dear Friends,

Remember "If it's Tuesday, this must be Belgium"? Well, if it's raining, this must be Samoa. Actually, that's not exactly right. If it's raining it must be a weekend in Samoa. Last Saturday and Sunday were rainy and overcast. From Monday to Friday we had bright sunshine. Today—it being Saturday and we being ready to paint—it's rainy.

At least it didn't rain on Santa. He arrived by fire engine today, blocking traffic for miles. With only the high school band as escort, the parade didn't quite match Macy's. But the children were as excited as kids anywhere at home. I just wish he'd been throwing marshmallows instead of hard candies. I was beaned by a raspberry sour.

December 6, 1977

I'm waiting for my phone call home to go through—and waiting is something I do badly, even after all the practice of the last two years. Since it's an on again, off again rainy day, we can't do much repairing or repainting, so we're off doing errands. I suspect that my whole day will involve hurrying up to wait. A deep breath and relax, right?

Boatyards are the same the world over. We're hauled out in the government yard (the government runs almost every large enterprise here), a big place that handles the Korean fishing fleet and most of the repair work in this area of the Pacific. But the same nonwork and big talk that we saw in Fountain Valley in Trimaran City occur here, and the shade under the trimaran is still the gathering place for the talkers and beer drinkers. We're often working around half a dozen inert bodies.

Our folding prop is also a big attraction, especially with the Korean fishermen. Hardly an hour goes by without at least one of them stopping to examine, fold, unfold, spin, and wonder. Through sign language and simple English (number one, number ten) Don explained to three or four of them. Since then it's been "each one teach one"—and at all hours, including after the bars and whorehouses close.

I wonder at the state of the head. Either Oriental cleanliness and fastidiousness don't extend to Korea or an American-type bathroom is too different. Its having been built with the drain in the high point certainly doesn't help. The floor is always wet. The toilet stalls are crammed with trash, most of it unflushable "toilet paper." Only the shower is clean, because no one uses it. The Koreans prefer to bathe and do their laundry at the basins. Or so say the men in the family. I go there only late at night with Don as escort and watch. During the day the women's office bathroom is available. Since the facility was built for (and maybe by) the Korean fishing fleet, no one here at the shipyard will clean it up.

December 9, 1977

Waiting again, this time at the hospital. Everything is clinic here—general check-up, eyes, teeth. Signs are plastered on all walls: "You space your coconuts; why not your children?" These Pacific islands (Samoa and Trust Territory) apparently have the fastest growing population anywhere. They don't space their coconuts, either.

Well, yes. They told me to be here at eight o'clock, but nothing opens until nine-thirty.

December 17, 1977

No grass grows under his feet—nor under my toenails. We've finished painting the bottom; and although I removed all my green freckles, I just can't get the antifouling paint out from under the nails. More and more I'm getting to resemble an islander. The feet give us away. *No* islander has clean feet—not even the most fastidious, well-groomed palagi lady. *If* shoes are worn, they are flip-flops or sandals, and always without any kind of stockings. When roads are either dust or mud, depending on the wetness of the day, you can't keep your feet clean.

"It's a small world," Samoan division: On Cocos Island we met people from Ft. Lauderdale, Florida, who knew my uncle and his whole family. On Pitcairn Tom Christian and I reminisced about Glendale. Here the local hamburger joint is owned by the Langkilde family. Joe Langkilde went to Costa Mesa High School, where he was in one of my classes. The restaurant (The Icewich) gets its plastic glasses from a company in Huntington Beach owned by the father of a friend of ours.

January 11, 1978

Flip-flops are aptly named, though backwards. As you flop along in them, they flip mud up on the back of your legs.

Getting money here can be a problem. Money cabled from a bank in the States takes a week or more. Out-of-area personal checks take three weeks to clear—and you don't get your money until they do. Out-of-area checks deposited to an account are not added in until they clear at home. Most palagis have accounts peppered with "hold" stamps. But not "reverends." No holds are placed on reverends' accounts. "We trust reverends," the bank teller told us as the Lutheran pastor and I exchanged checks and money. Should I tell them to put *Elmer Gantry* on the reading list?

Nowhere else, I think, is it more apparent that "the medium is the message." For unknown reasons, television programs do not arrive here when broadcast, via satellite—though the station can receive such transmissions—but come on tape, a week later. Now, except at holiday times the delay of "Happy Days" or "Laverne and Shirley" poses no problem; and even seeing Christmas shows a week late isn't too disorienting. But *news* programs are also telecast a week late—at the same time that the radio station is broadcasting the current day's news from UPI. And while the radio is encouraging visits to Soli's restaurant or the Rainmaker Hotel, the TV is plugging Transamerica and other San Francisco concerns. I wonder if schizophrenia has become more widespread here since TV arrived.

Apparently less widespread than before but still common in the more isolated villages is the making of homosexuals? pseudo-homosexuals? transvestites? In a society where social roles are not interchangeable, there has to be a balance of males and females. We're told that when there is a shortage of females, some males are simply raised as females; they dress as women and perform women's chores—cooking, marketing, child-caring, etc. Such men are not looked down on; they do, after all, perform a vital role. What their sexual behavior is I don't know, nor why there is apparently no need to raise girls to perform male roles. Perhaps males are not so necessary?

January 13, 1978 (Friday)

I *never* thought I'd see this day—wishing for *colder* water in the shower. But the trade winds have stopped and the weather become very hot and humid. Even the natives are sweating.

The most surprising thing about Samoa—especially after Mexico, Peru, and Tahiti—is that people drive courteously. Speed limits range from twenty to thirty-five miles per hour—and most drivers obey them. Pedestrians not only *have* the right of way, they are given it. Sometimes even a bus driver will stop to let someone turn left in front of him. It's very pleasant—but unreal.

Picking up again the theme of the sociology of buses—— Buses here are, as they've been elsewhere, brightly painted; but here that just means multicolored, not sporting scenes, slogans, etc. All are privately owned and run at whim, from wherever they come from to the market and back. Usually they operate from around seven in the morning until about four in the afternoon. *Sometimes* you can catch one outside those hours, especially if there's a bingo game in town. No regular runs are made on weekends, but you can sometimes flag down a family bus on the way to church on Sunday. There are never any standees; the buses aren't big enough. Most have been converted from old pick-up trucks. Benches the size we sat on in third grade have been installed. Imagine a two-hundred-pound Samoan mother sitting on a kindergarten chair on back-to-school night and you'll have an idea of the buses. How sad it will be to come back to sterile Greyhound buses!

en route to Ellice Islands
January 20, 1978

We're paying the price of "civilization." When we put the boat back into the water, we were able to tie up to a dock. Not for us rowing ashore, tying up the dinghy, locking up the oars. Instead, one step and we were on dry land. The insects found it convenient, too; we are infested with cockroaches that crawled over from the U.S. fisheries boat we were tied to.

Since we stayed longer than we'd planned (and what else is new?), we got to see the inauguration of the first elected governor of Amerika Samoa (A-mer-i´-ka Sa´-mo-a). Jimmy couldn't come (although he did send greetings via TV), so he sent Jeff and his wife. Unfortunately, the U.S. contingent wasn't too well briefed; they had only one Samoan name to pronounce (Tufele), and they mispronounced it. Wars have been fought over less. But apparently no one minded, and the inauguration proceeded as scheduled, complete with American and Samoan traditions—marching bands, floats, baton twirlers; kava ceremony and the presentation of fine mats and pigs. Only the Boy Scouts marched in step, and only they and the tuna cannery women all wore (matching) shoes. I found it hard to think of "Amerika Samoa" as having "spacious skies" and "amber waves of grain," but the band played in tune and in tempo.

All in all, we rather enjoyed our stay, though with all the work on the boat we didn't meet many Samoans, just palagis who loaned us tools, fed us, let us use their washers and dryers and baths, took us to church, etc. I can't understand why so many yachties bad-mouth the place. Or maybe I can. It's called "American Samoa." They arrive, expecting the stress to be on *American;* they are disconcerted to find the place *Samoan.* Customs and idiosyncrasies that they'd think "quaint" in a "foreign" country are simply annoying in a place they expected to be like home. Maybe the answer is not to have expectations?

We sailed out the day after having taken some of our new-made friends—including one who'd lived in Westminster (small world, again) and one we'd met in Mexico in 1976—sailing. To the surprise of the monohullers aboard and the delighted expectation of the captain, the boat behaved beautifully, and we all had a good time. Then, as always, came the sadness of parting from friends with the promise to "keep in touch."

We stocked up with every one of the "for trade" paperbacks at the library—a motley assortment. I started on the longest first, Taylor Caldwell's *Captains and the Kings.* This is a bestselling author? "He was inexhaustible. He never seemed to tire.... He never appeared to weary." Has the lady not heard of redundancy? Dickens had an excuse, but payment is no longer by the word. Our hero is also "suave, evasive, refined, casual, easy, intellectual." Stringing adjectives together is good writing? Then, this hero has the ability "artlessly" to relax his "lower eylids [*sic*]" (what are the "lower eylids"? where?) to appear more boyish, more charming. All this is not to mention the absolute claptrap of the novel; the distortions of philosophies and political theory; the quoting of Bible verses favoring money, the omission of those that berate it; the "Christian" excoriation of socialism and communism with no mention of "Sell all you have and give to the poor" or the first church in Jerusalem, which "had all things in common; and sold their possessions and goods, and parted them to all men, as every man had need." Oh, well, probably more people are watching "Laverne and Shirley" than are reading this book or any others. Who am I to expect them to have good taste? I have little in music and none in art, I'm told. Just the English teacher breaking through—and the student, trying to learn what is "publishable." I'm afraid I'll never make it.

Funafuti to Nukufetau, Tuvalu
January 28, 1978

We've just listened to the weather reports on WWV and found out that "there are no weather warnings for the tropical South Pacific." Would that we had two-way communication. We're sitting in some real weather here off Nukufetau (no, it's not a new ice cream flavor; neither is Funafuti), waiting for rain, wind, and seas to calm down so we can enter the lagoon, unseen, but only two miles distant.

We spent four days on Funafuti, hobnobbing with the "power elite." Just a few days before I'd complained that President Carter, on his world trip, met kings, premiers, prime ministers. On Funafuti we did, too. Don and I went ashore to see what was happening at the only bar in town, the one at the four-room hotel. We stumbled into a "governmet [*sic*] drink party" (according to the sign on the door) and were welcomed in by the island's chief minister (I don't know how that equates with prime). It was a farewell party for two commonwealth advisors working with the Tuvaluans on their independence (scheduled for October). Everyone who "was anyone" was there—except for the Queen's Commissioner, and we met him the following evening at a cocktail party at his house.

Nukufetau
January 31, 1978

(The trouble with coming from Southern California is that you're always surprised by bad weather.)

We did not totally endear ourselves to the British community. "Tom" greeted us at the door when we went to the cocktail party. Later in the evening we talked to him for some time, and Don asked what he did. He was the Queen's Commissioner. Oh, well, everyone knows that we Americans ain't got no couth. At least some of the community feel that they got their own back with that remark, no love being lost between them and the commissioner.

The next evening the assistant finance minister and his wife were to come out to see the boat before we went ashore to have dinner with a native family. We were already ashore when David and Ann arrived; but since our native host hadn't come, Don said he'd take them out to the boat. Seas were a little rough; there was no way they'd get to the boat dry, but we assured them that it was safe enough. You know what happened. The dinghy swamped, and the three palagi were left swimming above a sinking boat, much to the delight of the native children who'd been swimming off the pier. It was more entertaining than the weekly plane arrival. I asked some adult men driving by on a tractor if they could help. They drove the tractor down to the pier and joined the other spectators. By then some of the children had swum out to help; finally an old man went home to get his paddles, and he, Erik, and Donald took out one of the big canoes, the boys paddling like natives. Don, David, and Ann had managed to get themselves aboard *Anduril* (we still have no boarding ladder; we use the dinghy for a step, but they had no dinghy), so the canoe first went after our dinghy and oars, then brought the wet ones ashore. As I'd suspected from watching the fiasco, Ann couldn't swim; Don had had to float her to *Anduril*. Fortunately, she followed directions and calmed down before he or David had to knock her out. Also fortunately, she didn't lose her expensive and hard-to-replace-on-Funafuti glasses. But she was a gallant lady, very British foreign service, very stiff upper lip. We had coffee with her the next morning and she said that the adventure had decided her; she and David would get an outrigger canoe. Even if it did capsize there was nothing to worry about. But she'd wear a life jacket so that David could worry about the boat, not her.

Our dinner with Hope and Siulia was enjoyable but anticlimatic after that. We had pleasant talk and very good food, sitting on the floor like natives. The moon rose full above the palm trees, shining on the almost bare but immaculately clean room. The wind died, became a soft breeze. We were taken home one at a time on the back of the motorcycle.

Nukufetau
February 1, 1978

What a difference between the district center and here! At Funafuti only those people we invited came out to see the boat, and not all of them. Here we've had visitor after visitor after visitor—almost more than we can handle, especially since dozens of them have been children, dripping seawater and rain. School lets out at 1315, and at 1330 the invasion begins. A few of the children come in canoes; most swim or paddle out on logs or anything else that floats. Only a very few girls come; since they're always encumbered by sleeves and skirts, most girls don't swim. By 1630 the men are coming in from fishing in the lagoon, and they stop on the way. Yesterday we had nine canoes tied on aft and fifteen or twenty children down below plus a dozen topside.

We've been waiting for sunshine; but it looks as if we won't see any for a while yet, so today we braved the elements and rowed ashore. The village here looks like every idealized South Pacific village picture you've seen. Only the school, hospital, and mission house are of concrete block and wood. All the *fales* (homes) are the traditional posts and thatch. Steeply pitched pandanus leaf woven roofs shed rain water, which is collected for drinking. "Walls" of thatch or split tree branches rise about three feet above the floor. The rest is open, although woven blinds can be lowered to keep out rain or wind on any or all sides. A few of the homes have some furniture, but most of the people live on the floor—not as uncomfortably as I thought, because the layers of mats are surprisingly soft. I still can't get used to sitting cross-legged, though, just as they can't get used to sitting in chairs. Even in school the children sit on the floor, their legs crossed under short-legged desks.

We delivered a letter and a bottle of lighter fluid to last year's president of the island from his cousin (the one we had dinner with on Funafuti). The ex-president is a very big man who rolled and smoked many cigarettes as he fed us coconuts and bananas and told us his war stories. He worked with the American forces on several of the islands during the war and rescued a three-man crew that had ditched a plane and been adrift for twenty days. When we leave here we'll take a letter to his son on Tarawa.

After we left Toma's, the children picked us up again (the Pied Piper in spades), and we walked around the village. Everything is neat, tidy, swept, orderly. There are beautiful big breadfruit trees and a straighter hardwood tree, the puka, from which they fashion their canoes. We saw only a few chickens and pigs (we'd been told that most of the pigs are kept on another island in the atoll), and even they looked tidy.

The children scattered when the teacher invited us in for tea. The conversation reminded me of home—not enough paper and pencils, children have to share textbooks, the library is inadequate, etc. And of course there are too many children for too few teachers.

We left, picked up our retinue, and ended our visit at the mission house, one of two places, the hospital being the other, with indoor plumbing. Then, it being low tide, we walked a quarter mile across the sand and coral to the dinghy and rowed home. An hour later the last of our guests left, and we collapsed to dinner. Except for having hordes of children around for four hours or more every day it's an idyllic spot—friendly, English-speaking people; no resident Europeans; no hotel; no air service; no night clubs. You couldn't find a more picturesque tropical island "away from it all."

February 5, 1978

Yet I couldn't spend long there. (We left yesterday). People speak English; from second grade on schools are taught in English. Yet few people really understand it. English as we know it is a language of the modern world, and these people are not part of it. Even most of the teachers have only a hazy conception of the rest of the world. And why should they know more? Most of our "knowledge" is useless information on a small, remote atoll. With no other knowledgeable people around and precious few books, the information isn't even useful as an intellectual exercise.

I couldn't live with the lack of privacy, either. The open fales make sense in this climate, but I would find such public living difficult. And there's no concern about "private property"; there is none. We lost a bottle of deodorant and Donald's watch to some light-fingered child. It wasn't like the "theft rings" in South American countries; it's just "I like it, I'll have it." And vice versa, "you'll like this; take these coconuts, the breadfruit, this chicken." Its clucking aroused Bigfoot only momentarily. We "let" the native children who brought it out slaughter and clean it for us. They made a good, tidy job of it.

February 8, 1978

If, as we taught in semantics classes, nothing *is,* everything is changing, is it possible that the laws of physics are evolving—not that we're learning more, but that the laws themselves are changing? Such are the thoughts of silent, starry nights.

February 11, 1978

What do you do when your world crashes down around you? Why, you pick up the pieces and put them back. This morning a half-inch stainless steel bolt, five inches long, sheared off inside the mast, and the lower shrouds came crashing down. Fortunately (fortunately, there's always been a fortunately so far in our near-disaster stories), we'd reefed down in a squall, so we were in no immediate danger of losing the whole rig. But somebody had to go up and fix it. Donald tried, but the seas were so bumpy that it was all he could do to hold on. So we hoisted Don up and, swaying in what then was only a light wind and a slightly swaying mast, he managed to re-bolt the stays. He came down only slightly less green than the mast. Since then we've raised sails four times and had to take them down just as often. When we decided to motor for a while we found that our folding prop is folded shut—won't open. And we can't go down to check it out in this weather. But then, you people at home have just as much trouble with your cars, right?

As Erik says, "A squall means wind and rain and 'Take down the main!'"

February 13, 1978

There's good reason that the folding prop won't open. It's gone. Probably nothing ate it—it's just another case of a bolt giving way. And the batteries aren't charging properly and the engine is running too hot. Yes, I know all about Columbus. I'm also beginning to understand why people who retire from the sea often go to Montana or Alberta. Anyone for Omaha?

By all the standards of the Newport-Mesa Unified School District, we've fulfilled our obligation to Donald, at least. He could pass the high school equivalency test and he has a saleable (or, as he says, sailable) skill—two of them, in fact. He's a navigator and a radio operator, knows both theory and operation. So there are some things to be said in favor of the learn-by-doing school.

I forgot to mention how we found our way to Nukufetau without proper charts. We had our pilot book, but that was all. The Tuvalu government boat has charts, which we'd have been welcome to copy; but the boat wasn't in Funafuti when we were. Luckily for us, the government hopes to support itself by selling stamps to collectors. We bought several sets; one of them had excellent maps of the islands—better even than the restaurant place mats that we were told served as charts to Hawaii for at least one boat. And that's how we got to Nukufetau.

The Tuvalu government is also selling coins to collectors. The one dollar piece is nine sided (nine islands make up the country)—the first we've seen.

You may be reading about Tuvalu come October and independence. For years the U.S. has claimed the islands but hasn't pressed the claim against our allies, the British. Rumor has it that the day after independence every Tuvalu citizen will write the U.S. saying, "The British have left; we're yours. Send passports and money." Already the chief minister has been disappointed because a U.K. naval demolition team came last year and blew up the forty U.S. mines in the harbor. The minister had been hoping to get the U.S. to do something—preferably send money. Now his only claim against the U.S. is the holes the Army dug during World War II. He wants them filled in. Don suggested that the Army Corps of Engineer might do just that, taking the dirt to fill them in from the airstrip, where it went. The minister frowned.

These Polynesians, like the Peruvian Indians, can't get used to our family. Only two boys? No girls? No other children? No children "at home on your island"? They're very unhappy about it and can't understand that we're not.

If you're tracing our journey, you probably won't find Tuvalu on your maps. It's a new country, formerly called the Ellice Islands. Great Britain administered them and the Gilbert (soon to be Kiribati) Islands. Separation came in 1975; independence comes this year. Soon this group of nine atolls, population 8,000, will have its seat in the UN, too. I don't see how it can be a viable nation *if* it wants to join the twentieth century. If people there want to live a traditional life with only a minimum of twentieth-century trappings (basic medical services, transistor radios, indoor plumbing), it might work. Maybe it could even be opened up as an alternate world for those fed up with the twentieth century.

February 14, 1978

Today's lesson concerns probability theory. Donald checked into the mobile maritime ham network today to see if someone could get us information about getting another prop. A Hawaii station and a Malibu station went to check with marine stores. Then an Australian station came on. This was better yet, since the prop is Aussie-made and we could order direct. The Australian went to get his phone books and look. By the time he got back on the air, something had gone wrong with our radio. We could receive but not transmit. We heard him calling us but couldn't reply. Maddeningly frustrating. Donald disconnected the radio and began repairs. Apparently it had become too hot and just quit. When the meters started reading again he called a station coming in loud and clear on another frequency. They received us fine—in Portland, Oregon. *And* they had the message from the Australian station with the phone numbers we needed. Chances?

February 15, 1978 (0300)

The Big Dipper is visible again. It's like coming home. I never did learn the southern sky, but I know parts of this map. We're also getting Voice of America and Armed Forces Radio, as well as some stateside stations. Tonight, for the first time since Panama (September 1976), we heard the old philosopher: "faster horses, younger women, older whisky, more money." I enjoy these country and Western songs (which I never liked before) because they're so distinctly and uniquely American.

Today we labored mightily to stay in the same place. In a very light wind we were making about a knot and a half northeast (our desired course) while the current pushed us a knot west. Tonight we can see the glow of lights from Tarawa, but fifteen? thirty? miles away. Naturally, the westerly that hindered us for a week is no more—now that we could use it. Que sera, sera.

Tarawa
February 16, 1978

Now that we're in port and would like calm seas and light winds what do we have? Of course. The wind howls, and pushes the sea into lumps, whitecapping the lagoon. There's no way to get ashore dry.

Here's another famous quote: Cruising sailors are boat owners who like to do their repairs in foreign ports where the supplies they need are unavailable or excessively expensive.

Majuro, Marshall Islands
March 2, 1978

You should have seen us leaving Tarawa. Setting anchor under sail isn't too difficult; but getting it up can be, especially when it's the big storm anchor, more especially when the Gilbertese naval training ship is sitting practically atop it. Tack to port, haul in five feet of anchor line; tack to starboard, haul in another five feet. Each of those maneuvers took five minutes; we had out 125 feet of anchor line. So we decided to winch it in, alternately backing and loosing the sail, a process that took only a little less time. By then everyone aboard the training ship was lining the stern rail, watching. Finally, we broke the Danforth loose and pulled free, scarcely a boat's length from the stern of the training vessel. The sailors cheered, waved, and smiled good-bye as we quickly raised more sail to give us enough speed and power to tack away from the reef fringing the shore. None too soon for me, we had left Tarawa behind.

We made good time on the way up, covering almost four hundred miles in three days. If we'd been running instead of beating, we'd have made it even sooner. But here we are and here we'll stay until our prop arrives from Australia and until we get our alternator fixed. It's almost as windy here as at Tarawa, but the waves are small; there's not so much fetch in this lagoon.

Mail was waiting, and it was fun to read your Christmas cards and letters. Happy Easter.

Flash! another small world item: I've been sitting in the Gateway Hotel restaurant all morning, writing. A few minutes ago I asked the couple who sat down at the next table what time it was, and we began to talk. He teaches at USC and does indeed know my sister-in-law, who also teaches there.

March 4, 1978

We'd been a little disappointed in our slow time from Samoa to Tarawa—twenty-three sailing days. Then we learned that the two previous boats had taken forty-five and forty-two days. (One, it must be said, had a broken or nonexistent rudder, and the other hit two bad storms.) And we halved the unofficial record from Tuvalu—eleven days instead of twenty-two. Still, I hope the 20,000 remaining miles sail faster, or we won't have much time ashore.

This place is a slum. We haven't been yet to the "suburbs" down at the "white man's end" of the chain, but there's no other word to describe this—especially after what we've seen elsewhere. Causeways have been built, joining several of the islands (the better for jeeps to travel during a war); but no provision was made for drainage. The self-flushing lagoon is becoming a stagnant septic tank. Water is in short supply (it's turned on only four hours a day now), but many buildings don't have water catching systems from the roofs. All do in the British parts of the South Pacific. I understand that the *Time* article (December?) was quite favorable. I can't imagine why. The one redeeming feature is that the "yacht club" (actually a public bar and pool hall) serves excellent pizza. We've been disappointed in every pizza we've had since leaving home—until now. But this is a heck of a long way to come just for a good pepperoni pizza.

Rains finally came, so we've been able to launder and bathe. I just wish the heaviest rains didn't come in the middle of the night; that means getting out of bed to fill the tanks. It hasn't been enough rain, though; the water is still turned off most of the day. Think of being a hotel guest here with an inaccurate watch. You could be all soaped up in the shower and then unable to rinse off. And just when you thought you were out of range of time's tyranny.

I'm told that homes and public buildings all used to have water catchments. But when piped, central water was put in, catching water was somehow deemed unnecessary. I don't know why; no matter how it gets to the house, it still has to come from that sky faucet.

Water rationing meant no ice cubes at the hotel bar—not because there isn't water for ice cubes, but because the bar uses a new refrigerator with an ice-maker. No water flowing through, no making of ice. Seems no one's heard of an old-fashioned ice cube tray—you know, the kind you fill with water and put into the freezer for a few hours. Never mind. Drinks are only eighty cents, and the bar Scotch is Black Label.

I know I've had it before, but I think I'm having mumps again. There's no doctor on the island (and this is the administrative center of the Marshalls), so I can't get a professional opinion. But my right cheek is chipmunky and itchy. Whatever it is, penicillin seems to be curing it.

Trimarans forever—— The keel boat that left Tarawa a day after we did arrived here six days after we did. And the same weather system sat over the area the whole time.

The prop arrived yesterday. We'll beach the boat on Monday (low tide is at a reasonable hour then) and leave—if our charts, bolts, and money have arrived. If you've seen one atoll you've seen them all.

Just so you know how things are out here—Log Cabin syrup comes in bicentennial bottles and the C & H brown sugar box sports a Revere-ware offer that expired on December 31, 1975. Have you ever aged brown sugar? It's strong stuff.

The sociology of buses continued—— There are none on the island because, we're told, only "poor people" ride buses. So all but about half a dozen of the many (too many) cars are taxis. A taxi ride costs twenty cents. We've also been told that the culture interprets kindness as weakness; to get anything done, you have to "kick butts." Maybe; we haven't seen enough to say. Politics is a big concern, especially now with the stirrings for "independence"—as long as Uncle Sugar foots defense and certain other expenses.

March 11, 1978

Small world items: Last night we visited with Dave Oleson and family. He's principal of a Protestant high school (boarding) at the other end of the islands. We "met" him on the radio last November. His living room couch and chair are upholstered in the same material as our boat cushions. On our way to his house, we stopped to look at a small sailboat he wants to buy. The guy selling it used to live half a block from us in Oakland.

Dave told us incredible things about the school system. Apparently so that we can't be accused of destroying a native culture, all primary schools are taught in Marshallese. Few books, however, have been written in Marshallese; even the Bible is a poor translation; besides, the culture is oral. Practically all school work, therefore, is recitative. The children have no books—until they go to high school, where they are given books and instruction in English, because Marshallese is a useless language for anyone who wants to join the twentieth century, learn about physics, computers, genetics, etc. Wonderland looks rational.

I don't like riding in the taxis. Automobiles are an "intimate" form of transportation. It's uncomfortable being crowded into one with strangers. I think it's a combination of the low seating (compared to the high seating on a bus) and the American view of the automobile.

Housing here seem inappropriate—very different from Polynesia. Homes are closed up; they resemble (and are often made from) packing crates. There are very few doors or windows, and what windows there are are open to the ground, either because the shutter is hinged at the top or because the window is actually part of the eaves. What building materials were used before the war brought corrugated iron and packing crates I don't know. I do know that the style depresses me. It looks really slumlike from the outside; and while we've not been in a native home, I can't imagine it's anything but dark and poorly ventilated. We don't know if it's missionary or U.S. influence or just tradition, but it's certainly unattractive. We have been in a few of the restaurants, built in the same fashion. Electric lights need to be on all day, and woe if the air conditioning doesn't work. And it's not dark in the sense of a romantic, expensive restaurant. It's just depressing. Only the hotel restaurant is different; it's been built like a Samoan fale—walls two feet high and screens from there to the pitched roof, about fifteen feet above the floor. I've spent many cool, restful hours there, drinking fifteen-cent coffee or iced tea and writing.

March 14, 1978

Again and yet again we've been shown the basic (I'm convinced) goodness and kindness of people—one of them a corporation. We had sent the broken bolt from the lower shrouds to the manufacturer, Famet Marine, asking for replacement and spares and a guess about why the bolt broke. We enclosed a ten-dollar check and told them to contact mother for more money. They used the ten dollars for postage and very partial payment on a fifty-dollar order. Send no more money. Account closed.

Today we went to pick up our alternators. Buddy has had them for ten days, trying to scrounge up the necessary parts. He got one of them working. No charge. Absolutely not. If we're not going to leave right away, he'll keep working on the other. I have a hard time believing in original sin and the natural depravity of man. Also a hard time believing what I read in the newspapers. We have been treated so well everywhere that reports of bad news seem unreal. We seem to be living in a different world—or at least a different dimension.

Visiting the high school today brought me back to the previous world, only more so. This one didn't do the homework, that one didn't have a pencil, another one forgot his book. The books designed to teach English as a second language were developed for Puerto Ricans in Harlem. Some Pacific islands material has been developed, but mainly for the primary schools, where English is supposed to be taught (though instruction actually is in Marshallese, as we were told). The Catholic school gets the best students.

March 15, 1978

Don noticed an interesting trait as soon as we'd once been in town, and it was confirmed by what the teachers said yesterday. In Tahiti, Samoa, all the Polynesian islands we visited, the natives were loud and gregarious, at least among themselves. Always, the buses were full of laughter, talking, singing. People would shout out the windows at their friends on the street. Here—silence. The teachers I talked to said it's very difficult to get students to talk—even in Marshallese, even when they know the answer. The class (or perhaps a third of it) will recite in unison, as I saw yesterday; but only the Catholics can get individual students to talk. I admit, I've never seen a quieter school (not, at least, since the dark ages when I was in grammar school and the mourning Miss Wilbur ruled); even just before the dismissal bell rang students were silent. The Gilbertese teacher told us the same thing in Tarawa, and he was teaching adult merchant seamen.

I retract my Reaganistic comment about all atolls being alike.

The new Sears, Roebuck catalogs have arrived, and I've been given one. Is it just Sears, or are we into a new fashion trend? Those models are *hippy*. I mean, I could come back and do the girdle ads, at least.

This place might look like a slum, but it isn't poor. Erik's found fifty-eight cents already. He's found money on the streets everywhere except El Salvador and Tonga. I thought that perhaps now that he's taller (almost my height) and farther from the ground he'd be like the rest of us. But he's still a good treasure finder. I found a penny.

Another round of "here we go again." The fittings on our propane tanks don't fit the ones here (they haven't fit anything since Chile), so Don will spend all day running around trying to scrounge up fittings that will work. Another of the joys of cruising.

Guess what the highest paid job advertised in the Guam newspaper is? Greyhound trainer—$13.66/hr. Gambling is the big business the world over.

March 18, 1978

Today we'd planned to try spear fishing and shelling down at Laura, the village at the end of the chain. But the weather is putting a crimp in the plans. Rain, rain, and more. No one, however, is complaining. Water supply was down to one week's worth. Starting Monday, the water was to have been turned on only an hour a day instead of four. Ironically, we had filled up one set of tanks with the horrible chlorinated stuff from the pipes. Now we have all his good stuff coming down and no place to put it. This doesn't mean much to most of you, water rationing at home never having come to this point. But it should sink in like the rain, my friends, especially those of you in Southern California. You're living in a desert, stealing water from elsewhere for your overpopulated cities and towns. When Southern California breaks off and drifts away from the mainland, you'll be even worse off than Majuro—even if you drift into the rainy part of the Pacific.

Unfortunately, I'm sure the attitude here will be "saved again," and people who don't have them won't install gutters and water catchment. I'm sitting in the hotel dining room watching hundreds of gallons cascade off the tin roof—wasted, almost all of it, because once it seeps down about a foot, it mixes with sea water and becomes brackish. You can't dig a well on an atoll.

Another question came to mind last night. Why isn't the sewage pumped into the ocean instead of the lagoon? Answer: it's always been pumped into the lagoon. No matter that the situation has changed with industrialization (copra plant), tourists, increased population.

March 21, 1978

"They also serve who only stand and wait." We're not always standing, but we seem always to be waiting. Our charts still haven't arrived, and if we don't wait we'll never get them. They certainly won't catch us.

March 22, 1978

Not yet; but I just heard the plane from Honolulu. More mail will be at the post office this afternoon.

In spite of the rain, that part of the island served by the municipal water system is on one water-hour per day—1730–1830. Try running a hotel, restaurant, laundromat under those conditions. Now, if they had water catchment—— Robin, who used to live near us in Oakland, caught five hundred gallons last Saturday from her two roofs. That's nearly six months of water for us. It's all so unnecessary and irrational. No island that gets 186 inches of rain a year should have a water shortage. And no area that gets barely a foot should waste as much as you do in Southern California.

Explain/define a waffle. One of the waitresses here was reading a magazine and asked me what the word meant. I started with pancake; then the next morning we came in with our waffle iron and took over the kitchen for a while. I think they prefer breadfruit.

March 27, 1978

Happy Easter! It will *not* turn into happy April Fool's Day here.
We're leaving, charts or no. We did, after all, get to Nukufetau on a postage stamp, and we have rounded up two charts and a copy of
another—enough for safe sailing to Rabaul.

English is beginning to seem like a foreign language to me. Take an
ad I read in *Smithsonian* about wanting to be a beachcomber and live in an
island cottage. This "cottage" is "affordable" because it's "only"
$49,800. I have trouble with that definition of "affordable." It's on Fripp
Island, South Carolina, "an unspoiled place" that has excellent tennis
facilities, a championship eighteen-hole PGA golf course, a restaurant,
bar, and marina. I have trouble with that definition of "unspoiled." It
doesn't compute. Or maybe it does, and I just need a computer instead of
my abacus.

Kolonia, Ponape (Caroline Islands)
April 13, 1978

"Strangers bearing gifts"—we've had a steady procession for the
past two days. Three Japanese fishing boats put into port to get water and
fresh fruits and vegetables. Literally dozens of men came by to see our
boat. I had assumed that Don invited them aboard, but no. They just
came. One morning half a dozen arrived before we were even up, clump-
ing around, peering, smiling. At least they'd taken off their shoes.
They'd visited Jim's boat first, tracking mud and dirt aboard; he made
them wash the deck. Nothing daunted, they came aboard *Anduril,* but
shoeless. With a smattering of English ("number one engineer, number
one cook") and eloquent sign language (the finger through the circled
thumb and forefinger translates the same East as West; Kipling was
wrong) they established communication. Sometimes they just sat for an
hour, watching our lives. And every time they came they brought
something—outstanding sashimi, a dozen frozen fish, package upon package of noodles, canned tuna, canned whale (I know, I know; but the conservation argument doesn't translate well into gestures, and these men
aren't whalers), a flashlight and a dozen batteries, and two enormous jars
of instant coffee. They noticed the origami birds that our Japanese friends
had made for us in Tonga, asked for paper, and folded intricate kites. We
were overwhelmed. We were told that they really like Johnny Walker

Black Label; having none, we sent back oatmeal cookies, banana bread, and *Playboys*.

We arrived Saturday morning after a fast downwind (it's not a myth after all) sail from Kosrae (Kusaie). We were greeted by the Hagerstroms, who sailed from San Diego and are here indefinitely while Jim practices law. As it has with all the kind people we've met, that meant a car to take us shopping and, since they're house-sitting, showers. They also loaned us their extra ice chest and showed us where to get free ice. In return for our being around and thereby discouraging thieves, they leave their boat open so the kids can watch TV; Donald and Erik lock up after the late show.

Yesterday we went to open house aboard the *Micro Chief,* the newest Trust Territory boat. There was lots of Scotch and rum punch, tuna sandwiches, sashimi, potato salad—and Christmas napkins. No plates or silverware. Potato salad as finger food? You scoop it up with a cup and eat it as you would an ice cream cone.

Sunday we planned on spending the day with the Hagerstroms at The Village, Ponape's fanciest. Instead, we fixed chili aboard *Garuda* —all because of the way things are done in Micronesia. Ponape is a high island, laced with rivers—real rivers, not like the Santa Ana. The island also boasts (?) one of the world's highest annual rainfalls—four hundred inches. These two facts spell "bridges." To get to The Village, which was built in a quaint village five miles from town, you have to cross a bridge. For some reason, the road to the village (and The Village) is being rerouted and a new bridge built. The old bridge is being torn down (or repaired; it's hard to say which). One firm has the construction contract, another the demolition. The old bridge has been closed down and partially destroyed; the new bridge hasn't been begun. The road fords the river at the site of the new bridge. The river rises rapidly whenever it rains. Enough said? Through it all, The Village tries to operate a first-class hotel. When the river road is impassable, the truck lets guests off at the old bridge, which they walk across; then they are picked up on the other side by a second truck. (I assume that the hotel provides umbrellas and someone to carry luggage; Air Micronesia does at the airport.) "Ah, Wilderness is Paradise enow!"

en route to Kapingamarangi
April 23, 1978

After months in the atolls, we delighted in the high islands. We could smell them even before we could see them—the sharp tang of green, the heavy honeyed sweetness of the pikake flowers. Ashore, rivers again, and waterfalls, swimming in cool, fresh water, surrounded by trees looking for all the world like California live oaks. The price you pay is no beaches and murky water in the bay. The mangroves march to water's edge, and the rivers deposit load after load of silt. There's clear, inviting water only around the outer lagoon islands, and those are hard to get to without an outboard—awfully far for rowing and no good anchorage for a big boat. A serpent in every paradise.

Kolonia, the main town of Ponape, is squalid. Homes are more open than they were on Majuro, sort of a cross between Polynesian and Marshallese, with a little U.S. thrown in. There's no zoning, so even the nicest homes can be surrounded by pig sties. The pigs have a good thing of it; since the roads aren't paved (they were when the Japanese were here) there are plenty of wallows. Cars usually succumb to rust in salt air; but in Ponape the suspension goes long before the first rust appears.

We did, though, welcome the variety of fresh produce, unattainable on atolls—oranges, limes, tangerines, avocados, cucumbers, eggplant, cabbages—not imported, cold storage vegetables, but fresh, and reasonably priced. If you could convince the natives to like tomatoes, you'd have it all. Come the deluge, you couldn't find a much better spot.

We spent two days at a harbor on the other side of the island and were amazed. No one stopped to see us. Some waved, and joyriding teenagers in a hot motorboat sped close to see us rock in their wake—but no visitors, the first time it's happened in twenty countries. We don't expect visitors in the main ports, but when we stop where sailboats seldom go, especially in our trimaran... How different from our experiences with the Japanese fishermen!

Before Ponape we spent a few days at Kosrae, where we were entertained by the last king's grandchildren and the Baptist missionaries who were renting their house. Ted (the native) "insisted" that all yachts tie up to "his" LCM instead of anchoring out. Every day he or his wife brought us something to eat—breadfruit chips (which she cut into thin, even slices with Ted's wood plane, never mind a Cuisinart); a delicious soup made from coconut milk, breadfruit, and fish; fried bananas; and delicacy of all, mangrove crab fritters. This lady could cook! Then the Baptist missionary, who is teaching the natives how to fish, of all things, gave us part of the catch every day they went out and a chicken when they didn't. His wife kept us supplied with ice and let us use both washing machine and shower, for which we gave them a shower head we've been inexplicably carrying with us all this time. Again and again, it's not the places but the people.

Kapingamarangi
April 26, 1978

Have I mentioned clear water? balmy weather? fantastic shapes and colors of coral? of fish? Paradise? Forget it all. *This* is it. And you can't get here from there.

For all we were glad to get to the high islands, we're finding this atoll a delight—a bit of Polynesia in Micronesia. Like Nukufetau, Kapingamarangi sports thatched roofs, open air houses, swept paths. But it's even neater, less "commercial" (*not even one* motorcycle), yet strangely "cosmopolitan." Maybe "tolerant" is the word I want. We have apparently broken a few customs (I first sat on the men's side of the church, for example, and went swimming in my bathing suit instead of a dress), yet people don't seem to mind. They're very friendly, open, smiling, generous. Many of the women (most often the old) go topless, but in deference to our customs they usually cover up when we walk by. And unlike Nukufetau, the children are very disciplined. They come to visit only when adults say they can, leave when told, don't come down below. They have exuberant but not raucous fun.

Kapingamarangi, then, is every cliché about the idyllic South Pacific come true. Sea-green foam froths on the reef, but the water in the lagoon is liquid glass. It laps a golden shore. Friendly natives greet the few visitors. There is much singing and smiling.

We were warmly received, and enjoyed our first several days, welcoming visitors on the boat, visiting our new friends ashore. One old man, noticing my crudely woven Tongan hat, presented me with his own finely made one. Another brought one for Don. Then suddenly, inexplicably, relations chilled. There were few visitors and fewer smiles. We had obviously offended, but we couldn't imagine how; and our hosts were too polite to tell us—polite, but no longer friendly. Finally, one of the younger men, who had been exposed to Western "telling it like it is" while working in Ponape, explained. People didn't believe our story about building the boat and sailing from America. It wasn't the sailing they disbelieved, but the building. Anyone who claimed to have spent two and a half years building a boat by himself wasn't to be believed. And the islanders didn't want to be friends with people who didn't tell the truth.

We didn't understand, but at least we proved our truthfulness by bringing out the scrapbook. There, as the children grew taller, *Anduril* grew from one hull to three. The empty oil drums supporting the floats were recognized as "just like we have here [for the generator]." But those pictures that showed turning over the main hull, for which we borrowed a crane and enlisted the help of every available friend and acquaintance, drew the most comment. Several days later we realized why.

We had seen posts stuck in the ground on the beach and for days watched canoe loads of palm fronds dumped nearby. One morning, as Don and I set out to walk through the village, a crowd gathered on the beach. All the men on the island seemed to be there. As we watched a house being built, we realized why our story had sounded untrue. The old men sat inside the area bounded by the posts, twisting coconut fiber into rope that was used to tie the palm frond "siding" and roof into place. Middle-aged men planted themselves in the sand and threw fronds to the young men, perched on the roof beam, who placed and tied down the thatch. The building was completed in less than an hour. No wonder these people had not believed our story of nearly six thousand hours of solitary building!

May 2, 1978

Last night the lagoon was so still that we could read the constellations reflected in the water. The melodious strains of Polynesian harmony drifted across the water from the church, as they do every night. An enormous lopsided moon rose behind the lacery of palm trees, winking out the fading stars and silvering the water.

Our Kapingi friends brought us the usual—coconuts, fish, breadfruit—but their generosity extended far beyond that. Naturally, we wanted to buy some handicrafts, and we were given the Kapingi price (less than Ponape) and then a "friend's" reduction. In addition, the co-op manager gave us two of his carvings and offered a fine woven mat, which Don insisted on paying for. When people heard that Donald collected shells, they brought out half a dozen of the bull mouth helmets, their "specialty" and one we hadn't found.

On and on and on—we shall return! I'm really annoyed now that the U.S. Mail and/or Air Micronesia took *two months* to air mail our charts from L.A. to Majuro and so kept us there when we could have been enjoying Kapingamarangi.

And in addition to everything else, we had another "small world" incident. One person on the island had visited the States. He'd attended school there in 1972—at Orange Coast College.

Apropos of nothing—— Throughout Micronesia there's a new title—Distad—ranking along with the traditional ones. You see the process of language here. Everything from the States shipped to the district administrator arrived with the stencilled abbreviation DIST. AD. And a new class is born.

Your no class friend,
Joanne

Rolling On

Dear Friends,

The kids love it here at the yacht club—pinball machines and a pool table. The pinball machine goes "tilt" and gives free games easily. Pool is free, except at night. Then you have to put money in the slot to make the electric light work.

Customs clash here, as throughout the Pacific, always more noticeably in an urban area. In indigenous culture it's polite to leave your shoes outside and go barefoot indoors; in Western culture, only slobs go shoeless. Restaurants, bars, etc., adhere to Western standards, effectively keeping out many nationals. Shorts on men are O.K., but only if worn with long socks. And I've never seen so many bearded men anywhere.

National dress is the wrap-around skirt (here a *laplap*) topped by a shirt for men, a smock for women. The men carry small woven purses, usually triangular. The women carry large mesh or woven bags. These have a long strap, which hangs on the forehead; the bag rests in the small of the back. It's usually full of groceries or child—or both.

We're anchored in the crater of an old volcano. The area is still quite active. An eruption in the bay in 1937 created two islands and a tidal wave that destroyed the main part of town. There's a vulcanology lab in the hills, which we hope to visit, as well as numerous hot springs, the likes of which delighted me at Mammoth but interest me not at all here. It is HOT—and still.

May 11, 1978

It's Thursday—payday. That means no package sales of any alcoholic beverages. A place with a liquor license can be open only from noon until one and from four-thirty until six-thirty. Maybe most of the wages will get home.

Here in Rabaul there's sometimes a shortage of small change, as there was in Mexico and Central America. But here, instead of candy for change, you get a small plastic bottle of Kikkoman soy sauce.

Donald thinks we know everyone in the world. Not quite, but we've just met two women we've heard about and read of in the Seven Seas Cruising Association monthly newsletter. They've been cruising the Pacific off and on for the past seven years. One of them taught drama at Glendale College when I was there; the other teaches at Long Beach State and read my master's exam; she, too, grew up in Glendale—albeit the Hoover side of the tracks.

We leave this side of the tracks today or tomorrow.

Mt. Hagen, Papua-New Guinea
May 18, 1978

Literally fantastic: unreal; created by the imagination. I'll try to describe it; I hope to have vivid photographs to show you. But the reality is so overwhelming that neither can do it justice.

Again we're in the highlands, and as usual I find them more enjoyable and interesting than the coast. We flew from Madang to Goroka, then took an eight-hour bus ride from there to here. The ride was slow, because recent landslides have washed out long stretches of road; but it was never dull. We were eight Europeans and at different times various numbers of locals, most in native dress—or undress. Part of the way they entertained us with chants. All along the road we saw groups of people—sorting coffee beans, weaving, playing cards, just watching. They stared as hard as we did, all of us grinning widely. Whenever we saw something we wanted to photograph, the driver stopped. Whenever the driver saw something he thought we should photograph he stopped. Try that at home!

Today we visited the Saturday market—a superspectacle. People came down from the hills in hundreds, not to huckster tourists, of which there are few, but to market their produce and pigs. We saw women wearing straw belts with a length of cloth tucked fore and aft, on their heads a terry towel pad to soften the pull of the net bags hanging around their foreheads and down their backs. Men wore wide girdles (ten inches or more) made of leather, wood, or rings of bamboo. Tucked in front were lengths of netting, bright cloths, or woolen swaths. Behind—feathers or leaves (ass grass to the Aussies), making the strut like a Banty rooster's. Most of them had pierced noses, the better for wearing feathers, bones, or shells. And in one pierced ear I saw the extra cigarette. After a while you can begin to sort people into groups. The men with the wooden girdles and green leaves are ash black and almost hairless. The bamboo-girdled men are darker, and covered with curly black hair. Men wearing leather girdles are more coppery. A very few of the people are blue-black. And smiling, everyone. And gawking, just as we were. If we could have charged admission, we could have paid for the trip. We had trouble taking candid photos; everyone wanted to pose.

Walking back to the hotel, we noticed more and more people in *National Geographic* regalia—with painted faces, wearing elaborate feathered headdresses, carrying spears and axes. We followed along to the park, where they were gathered in the hundreds. Faces silver painted, eyes red masked, noses blue shadowed—the designs were too numerous, too unbelievable for me to describe. And the headdresses! Peacocks are nothing compared to birds of paradise.

One group danced, and when it broke up we followed a pole of money to another part of the park. There we sat in the circle of natives for nearly two hours, listening to spokesmen from two different villages. "Big fella killem pikinini." A child had been killed in an auto accident—only a female, worthless. No, she could have been the mother of many warriors. The money pole was compensation, presented by the tribe of the man who had been driving the truck. Bad words were said, and harsh ones. Nervous old men picked blades of grass to chew while spirited young men spoke loudly and gestured violently. Two native policemen looked on warily. But the mediators finally settled the matter. The money pole and a little more were presented to the girl's village. Hands were shaken, and arrangements made to kill several pigs for a feast the following Thursday. Then each village climbed onto its flatbed truck for the long drive home.

en route to Bali
May 31, 1978

Mountains soothe my soul—angles, planes, heights, distances, coolness. We're kin. I can't identify with the coast—hot, moist, close, curves. What are we doing here?

Papua-New Guinea is another place we want to visit again, walking. We'd have lots of company; everyone in the highlands walks. And—is this getting to be a monotonous refrain?—everyone is friendly. Our only complaint is that everything except locally grown food is expensive. Even second- and third-class transportation, accommodations, and restaurants are dear. But if you don't come prepaid through some tour group, you can get discounts. Don didn't have enough cash in his wallet to pay for the bus tickets, so he sent Erik to me to get some. Immediately, the price was halved—no charge for Erik, ten percent discount just because, and some additional fiddle-faddle. You can't do that with air fares, of course, which are regulated by the national government, or with the fancy tourist hotels. But the "two-talk" system is very real.

Book review #?? *The Deep* is not only simple-minded; it's poorly written, full of explanatory appositives that wouldn't be necessary if it were well written—not to mention "had swam." If it had been submitted under my name instead of Peter Benchley's, it would have been rejected.

June 1, 1978

About the climate here—you're always dripping, either with rain or sweat. Nor is it very healthful. Nearly half of the people who've been here a year or more have had malaria or some other mosquito-carried fever. Even the smallest cuts become infected, taking an inordinately long time to heal. More good reasons to stay in the highlands.

June 8, 1978

I detest sailing dead downwind! With one big sail billowed out on each side of the headstay, you can't see what's ahead. And around here what's ahead is usually a big log washed down from one of the rivers. We've already hit several; one dented the stem enough that we had to stop and patch it. Besides, it feels really hot sailing downwind, with no wind blowing against you. And if you turn on the engine, diesel fumes wash all over the boat.

Manokwari, Irian Jaya
June 8, 1978

You find out where it is; I'm not going to tell you.

Deliver me from the "picturesque"—tin roofs, dirt floors, outdoor privies, pigs and chickens living as intimate members of the family. And children, children everywhere. I'm more than ready for the "civilized," looking far ahead to Singapore. At this point it can't be too clean, too sterile for me.

June 10, 1978

I think I've sworn off zoos. We've spent too much time living in one for me to be comfortable on the other side. People in canoes surround us by 0600, hanging on the side of the boat, peering into ports. As soon as they see anyone awake, they clamber aboard. We practically have to throw them off bodily. A few are light-fingered. We've lost three pairs of socks and a pair of shorts that we'd left in the cockpit to be rinsed off by the rain, a short piece of line, and all the pushpins that were stuck in our cork bulletin board by the hatch. Even Don, who's much more tolerant than the rest of us, is tiring. Don't know whether it's a result of different tribal customs or the British-style training of Australian administrators, but people on the other side of the island are much "better behaved." And I mean that absolutely, not relatively. Call it provincialism, if you will; but I can't believe that this behavior is good manners anywhere. Certainly these people would be upset if we came into their homes this way and walked off with things.

We're back into a land of thick wads of bills. I shuddered to spend a hundred for a loaf of bread, then remembered that it's equivalent to a quarter. I hate having to work with thousands; makes it hard for me to keep accurate accounts. I never did learn eighth-grade math very well; we moved that year.

en route to Singapore
July 14, 1978

Ah! exotic, erotic Bali—jets whine and screech overhead; long strings of motorcycles belch down the road; *bimos* careen along city streets, deftly avoiding (usually) pedestrians, bicycles, and horse-drawn carts, trying to outmaneuver fellow drivers and be the one to pick up the next group of passengers waiting for a bus. Of course we have room for three more; our Datsun 1300 pickup is carrying only sixteen—three in the cab, six on each seat, and one hanging off the rear step. Kick the turtles forward (watch your toes!) and shove those hundred-pound sacks of rice against them. Draw up your knees; inhale; *plenty* of room! Two more stops and we reach maximum capacity—twenty-two (well, twenty-three, but you can't really count a baby, can you?). Then whooee! pull out all stops, lean on the horn, and away we go. Wedged in as you are you can't slide forward or back when the driver slams the brake pedal to avoid hitting cow or goat, but watch your tailbone; coming down on the metal brace holding the seat in place is painful, though if you've cracked your head on the way up you may not notice it at first.

But Bali is more than this. Get out of Denpasar into the countryside to see the "real" Bali—terraced hillside after terraced hillside of green, green, green rice paddies; walled compounds of thatched or tile-roofed houses, each with its corner of temples/shrines—seven for the lowest class, eleven for the Brahmins; and lining the village streets, souvenir shop after souvenir shop after souvenir shop. Never before have we seen so much huckstering and hectoring of tourists.

Not that the experience was entirely bad. Eating out was cheap, unless you wanted Western food and fancy service. A big plate of fried rice or noodles with eggs, meat, and vegetables cost less than a quarter. (Of course, the beer needed to cool down the fiery peppers cost a buck.) And we got to see a real village dance.

The traditional dances are performed at hotels and theaters for the tourists. We went to such a Ketchak (monkey) Dance. It was well done, though somewhat marred by the flash pops of camera-toting tourists (including us). Several hundred sat on tiered rows on three sides of the stage, talking about Proposition 13 (the California tax initiative to reduce property taxes), lazy teachers on sabbatical, welfare cheaters, etc., until curtain time. At precisely 6 P.M. the show began, and precisely fifty-seven minutes later it ended—just enough time to clear the auditorium and parking lot before the next show.

But the village dance! Some of the hustlers, boat boys, fishermen came by one afternoon to invite the yachties anchored in the harbor to their island village for a Barong Dance celebrating the restored health of several boys who had been sick. We were no more than a dozen outsiders among hundreds of Balinese crowding the dirt of the village square. Local boys who had hectored us with carvings all week long played their bamboo instruments and brass gongs with fierce concentration. Kerosene lanterns alternately glared and sputtered, eerily illuminating the story of the victory of white magic (the barong) over black (the witch). Children were frightened; old men were seized by fits. No spectator sport, this; except for us yachties, everyone was a participant in a genuine religious observance. The impact was incredible, and will remain my measure of Bali long after all the tawdriness has been forgotten.

Several days later we went to see a traditional cremation. An enormous temple tower and black bull (containing the corpse) were carried on bamboo platforms through the streets to the cemetery/park. There vendors hawked drinks, eats, batik, baskets, paintings, and postcards for several hours until the flames were lit. It was a mob scene such as I have never seen—tourists from everywhere, locals from almost everywhere, and a monumental traffic jam, with cars parked along both sides of a one-and-a-half-lane road while traffic tried to move in both directions and the skies poured. The fire-lighters seemed well stoked on something, and ghoulish tourists of all nationalities elbowed one another aside to get pictures of the corpse burning inside the belly of the bull. Forest Lawn now seems to me benign and reverent.

The last chapter in our Bali experiences was another "small world" chapter. We were walking down the main street of Denpasar, spending the last of our rupiah before our planned departure the next day, when I almost collided with a young man. Double-take. Kevin! Mrs. Sandstrom! And so I met another former student. He came back to the boat for dinner and spent the night. He'd been in Indonesia a year, working with Volunteers in Asia, a group with headquarters at Stanford, where he had spent a year learning that his high school experience had not prepared him for the big time. He was on his way to teach school in South Korea.

Those of you who still think of trimarans as unusual or minority boats ought to visit Bali. All the small fishing canoes are tris—more accurately, double outriggers. Most are brightly painted, and each bow extends an open dragon's mouth. The outriggers are long bamboo poles, often bright red, attached to the main hull with high, gracefully curved bars. But since the hulls are most often unseen behind the sea swells, it's the sails that leave the unforgettable impression. They're patchworks of bright nylon, some gaudy, some bold, some muted, all striking. Skittering along the crests of waves and swells, the boats move like waterbugs on a placid pond, but their bright wings call to mind exotic butterflies. There are hundreds of them, and to see "the fleet" come through the pass into the harbor is a sight never to be forgotten—especially if they're jockeying out of the way of an ill-kempt, rusty freighter (the only kind we saw in Benoa harbor during our stay).

We'd intended to stay longer in Bali and spend some time on Java, but visa problems (we have none and chose not to spend upwards of $150 to get "emergency" ones) have sent us on our way early. We'll probably spend more time than planned in Singapore and hope to take the train to Bangkok. Then it's across the Indian Ocean and on our lonely way north to the Suez. Every other boat we've met is going south around Africa. As from Panama and Fiji, we've chosen the road not taken, and that has made all the difference.

July 16, 1978

"And the dawn came up like thunder." Actually, it came up with thunder, and for the first time I could imagine giants playing at ninepins.

They were long, rolling peals. The rising sun made the western sky shine dove gray. Against it glowed a high-arching rainbow. Occasionally, a silver wire of lightning flashed, and the white underbelly and wings of a noddy gleamed. Some recompense for being up at 0500.

July 29, 1978

Singapore in the morning. Maybe we'll even find showers.

Odiferously,
Joanne

Singapore
August 6, 1978

Dear Friends,

"No admittance to males sporting long hair" at the fire station; "males with long hair will be served last" at all government offices; and we saw *Saturday Night Fever* cut to eliminate ALL vulgar language (yes, it was a short film). There you have Singapore.

Like those of us who continue our high school hairdos no matter how unfashionable or unbecoming or those of us who oppose any change in the way things were done when we went to school, Singapore is still tilting at the windmills that exercised it in 1965, when it became independent. And yet, and yet—— According to those who knew Singapore when and who know much more of the Orient than we do, great strides have been taken. As cities go, it is clean, though I certainly wouldn't call it "sterile." Even with 2.3 million people in 616 sq. km (most of them within the 97.4 sq. km city), the city has only a few shanties and no real slum areas—yet. The government has embarked on a massive housing campaign, raising high rise after high rise. These warrens are certainly preferable to shacks and shanties, but already the older ones (five to ten years old) are showing signs of deterioration, on their way to becoming vertical slums. And they're so *ugly*. Ticky-tacky Daly City rates high, compared to this. I know I made fun of that lone palm tree in every front yard, but at least it was living green. Here—nothing. The only color is provided by the ever-present laundry. Each apartment sprouts a long pole, rather like a flagpole, out a window;

threaded on the pole is the day's laundry. Were it not for this laundry, you'd see nothing but the unrelieved gray of the concrete jungle.

Generalizing from limited experience, we'd say that lower and lower-middle classes are comparatively well off and generally well satisfied. Those higher on the social or educational scale chafe at the restrictions (censored films, banned books and magazines, controlled press, one-party elections). The best housing and recreational services provided are reserved for the military and other government personnel.

Still, health care is good and health offices vigilant and well equipped. No cholera epidemics here. Stores, restaurants, bars, etc., are open at all hours, seven days a week—a pleasant change after the complicated pub hours in the other former British/Australian colonies and the blue laws of the Pacific islands. And there are supermarkets—genuine ones, worthy of the name, stocking cat food, peanut butter, and chocolate chips, all at reasonable prices.

Speaking of supermarkets, we saw *Oh, God!* the other night. What heaven—scenes of a big, Burbank supermarket! We enjoyed the film but wonder if it was roundly berated in some quarters at home. Of course, we don't know what might have been cut. It seemed a simple film with a simple message. Or was it a simple message? "Love one another" seems inordinately difficult.

Wednesday is National Day—no mere excuse for a long weekend, being celebrated on August 9, whatever day that may be, but a full-scale national celebration. As in all controlled countries, there will be much marching and many banners. We know this because we got caught in the rehearsal the first Sunday we were here. Yes, a full rehearsal—all streets blocked off, all buses and taxis stopped. And although businesses are allowed to stay open on public holidays, I suspect we won't find many open next Wednesday.

August 20, 1978

And so, to celebrate Don's birthday, we leave the sybaritic splendors of Singapore. No more daily showers (after twenty-four straight days) or cold beer—just six thousand miles of ocean with only two or three stops. Friends already out in the Indian Ocean report good sailing—lovely trade winds (late in arriving this year) and gentle seas. We're looking forward to it, hoping it holds.

We saw a government project that explained why there is no unemployment in Singapore. One man stood on the second step of a ladder, eighteen inches off the ground, using a very small brush to paint the red trim of a street sign. A second man held a small can of paint for him. Two others held the ladder.

National Day ceremonies were colorful and drumbeat stirring. Military units, of course, marched, and tanks trundled by as jets screamed overhead. Then came unit after unit of civilians—police, firemen, telephone workers, airline stewardesses, schoolchildren, fraternal groups, athletic associations. All carried scores of colorful banners. Dragons danced, lions pranced; gongs clanged and drums thumped. A stirring, colorful sight, it began precisely on time and was very orderly. Still, the procession of armaments and stirring martial music always depresses me, and the number of times our passes to the cricket club viewing stands were checked was oppressive.

After leaving the padang (central staging area) the marchers took to the streets, which were lined with hortatory banners: "Adapt, innovate, and prosper." "Bilingualism for harmony and progress." "Waste not; be thrifty." "Work better to live better." The Protestant ethic is alive and well in Singapore.

Judging from the recent courtesy campaign, I'd say that the banners will have little effect. Signs proclaiming "Courtesy is our way of life" were plastered all around the city during recent months, but we've never met such bad-mannered people. Individual Singaporeans were very nice, but in the mass they were extremely rude. We never before encountered the shoving, elbowing, and body blocking that we experienced on Singapore's buses. And the rudeness of the children in groups surpasses that of any American teenagers.

Other slogans seem to be more effective. "Girl or boy, two is enough" posters are omnipresent, and family planning seems to be making headway. Tax disincentives for having more than two children make the slogan meaningful. "No smoking" say signs in elevators, government offices, on buses—and generally there isn't. Common signs in restrooms: "Gentlemen: If you *stand closer,* you can *aim better.* Ladies: Please *remain seated* during *entire performance.*" There are also other signs about flushing after use to keep the air fresh smelling.

Such official graffiti is the only kind of writing on the wall allowed.

August 28, 1978

"Having been brainwashed as a child into believing that if you can't say something good, don't say anything at all, I have no comment about the Indian Ocean." Knowing my penchant for adverse criticism, you'll realize that the saying isn't mine. However, I subscribe to its sentiments about the Indian Ocean—and we've been at only eight hours. Bounce, bounce, crash; bounce, bounce, crash—and we have five thousand miles of it to look forward to.

August 29, 1978

Although we're traveling less than ten knots, the sensation is of great speed. The whole boat thrums against the pressure of wind and waves. Shrouds on the leeward side sag, while those on the windward side hum with tension. And everywhere, the water sound—sibilantly sliding along the hulls, often splashing on the decks, sometimes crashing at the underwings. Outside, as we slide down a wave with the wind echoing hollowly in my ears, I know we're flying. Inside, the sensation is even greater, for every sea sound is magnified by our hollow box. We made nearly two hundred miles yesterday and would have reached that long-sought (by Don and Donald) number except that I insisted on reefing the mainsail for the night. (Do you understand choosing a slow means of travel and then trying to go fast?) Maybe tomorrow.

September 9, 1978

We're making our best distances ever, averaging 170 miles a day. If we wanted to be bounced around a little more (and if I didn't get frightened), we'd leave up all sails and average better than 200.

It's a wet ride as well as a fast one. The decks glitter in the sunlight, as if, instead of sand, we'd mixed diamond dust in with the paint for nonskid. Alas, it's only salt crystals, washed away by today's rain.

And it's cold. We have to wear clothes again on night watches—not long underwear (yet), but long pants, socks and shoes, and sweaters.

We stopped at Cocos Keeling Island last week and nearly froze. The water is beautifully clear and vibrant with fish and coral formations, but it's not much warmer than the water off Laguna Beach, and that's cold to us now. Also, the trade winds, which make for good sailing, make for lousy loafing, creating a real wind chill when you get out of the water. Ashore, dense vegetation keeps the wind from ground level, so it's hot, still, and pestiferous with flies. Still, it was pleasant just to stop, and we renewed acquaintance with old friends and made some new ones. We also scraped Singapore's barnacles off the bottom, but couldn't get Indonesia's oil off the waterline.

September 11, 1978

Well, we finally did it—a 200-mile day—and carrying only a staysail and reefed main. Can't say it was *comfy*.

I'm now the smallest (well, shortest) member of the crew, Erik having passed me on his fourteenth birthday. Even his shoes are too big for me now. Looking at the passports, we learned that both boys have grown eight inches since we left.

I discovered the big disadvantage to having a multihull instead of a monohull. People on monohulls, being less comfortable, eat less. Also, in trying to stand upright while rail under, they're constantly exercising. Even staying in bed is exercise on a monohull. Consequently, they get thinner on long passages, while I just sit and spread.

September 12, 1978

The sea is jewelled today. Pearls of foam edge necklaces of transparent turquoise accented with occasional diamond sprays. This all around us. Looking ahead to the horizon you can imagine late summer in the Sierra, with only the highest peaks still snow topped. As you can see, it's not flat today. Beautiful, but not the most comfortable. Now, if I were running things (here we go again), I'd manage flatter seas with good wind—or at least a middle ear that could better handle the lumps.

Though but halfway round, we're already home, anxious to get back to living ashore—and planning the next trip. Donald is going on a boat that is built right (you can't imagine how much is wrong with this one, according to him) and by himself, so he won't have to put up with people who are afraid of going fast.

Seychelles
September 28, 1978

It must be time to come home. I'm getting tired of: people shoving and crowding at counters instead of lining up; hawkers trying to unload shoddy souvenirs; open-air markets with their unrefrigerated fish and meat—and their flies; bags of rice and beans that are full of rocks, twigs—and bugs; officials, officials, officials, and paperwork, paperwork, paperwork; chauvinism (both *pro patria* and *anti femina*). Yes, indeed.

The Seychelles are beautiful islands, but we're here too late. The airport opened in 1971, and tourists have become big business—in fact, the only business. Independence was achieved in June 1976; liberation was won on June 5, 1977. The first president (English background) was attending the Queen's Silver Jubilee festivities in London; his vice-president (French Marxist background) told him not to return. Royalty Avenue has become Revolution. Other street names have been similarly changed, although maps still bear the old designations. Boats are not allowed to travel between 1800 and 0600. (Can't you see a flotilla of yachts mounting an invasion?) Staying in the harbor costs money (no services are provided); getting permission to leave costs money. And I'm tired of tourists. What a scruffy lot! They go around town in the kind of rags we wear when changing the engine oil. At least the French navy now in port are spiffy.

Enough complaints—we did visit another delightful atoll. Unfortunately, the U.S. Navy got there first. Diego Garcia is British owned and controlled, but we lease half for Indian Ocean naval operations. Yachts are not given permission to stop, but most do and are treated hospitably by the Brits (all five of them) in charge. No fraternization with the Navy is allowed, although personnel off duty are allowed to repair electronic gear—and are delighted to have something to do. We had our speedometer fixed, another boat its autopilot, etc. As on Pitcairn, supplies are cheap, though canned goods not suitable for most yachts, being commissary-size tins. We came in shortly after a yacht that had been nothing but trouble; but instead of tarring us with the same brush, the Brits went out of their way to be hospitable. I put it in writing with the British representative—if the Navy ever leaves, I want to be on the buyers' list.

Bigfoot became a swimming cat a few nights ago. I thought I heard something go into the water; and though Don assured me I was hearing things, I got out of bed to check. There, just aft of the dinghy, was a dog-paddling cat. I don't know whether or not he'd have been able to climb into the dinghy; I pulled him dripping aboard. We don't know what happened—whether he tried for a bird and slipped, couldn't resist the land smell and decided to jump ship, thought the water was solid ground, or what. It's hard to believe it was accidental. He has a real sailor's stance and has never come near to falling off. Even on the crossing he was out on deck on his sea legs, snapping up the flying fish that landed on deck. I don't suppose we'll ever know what happened, but at least there hasn't been a repeat. We'd be sorry to lose him.

"Seychelles time" is half an hour later than zone time before lunch, half an hour earlier, after. You try figuring out when shops are open.

I haven't done justice to these islands. They're granite mountains and beautiful, surrounded by warm water and colorful reefs. We rented a car yesterday and drove the eighty miles of road (Erik shuddered every time the speedometer reached twenty; I vowed to remember the scene and remind him of it when he's sixteen), delighting in all we saw. People are friendly, for all they're after the tourist dollar, and people in even the lowest-level job are bilingual (English and French)—trilingual, when you count the native patois. It puts an American to shame. Next week we'll visit the outer islands, then head for Djibouti, Port Sudan, and the Suez, thankful for the Camp David accords. We hope to be in Jerusalem around Christmas, but the Red Sea may alter our plans. Some boats have logged as many as 4,400 miles traveling its 1,200-mile length.

Already waterlogged,
Joanne

Interlude: The Whole Truth

Most of the whole truth comes from my journal and my memories, in spite of my attempts to repress remembrances of the unpleasant realities. But I did once write of them in a letter, never mailed, to my mother:

Although Don apparently finds us enough company and really enjoys the temporary "friendships" we form in this life, both the boys and I miss the settled life of friends and family ashore. We'd be just as happy to come home now, but Don wouldn't be. There doesn't seem to be a solution that would satisfy all of us. We had such trouble with Donald a few months ago that we seriously considered a boarding school; but he decided that would be even less bearable. I think Don would call it quits if I insisted, but I can't. Completing this voyage is very important to him; and I can't tell him he has lots of time yet, because I remember dad and Nora.

Don's suggested that the boys and I fly home and he bring the boat round as fast as he can. But being the sole parent to two teenage boys—even temporarily—doesn't appeal to me; more importantly, Don isn't well enough to be a single-handed sailor—or I don't think he is, and that's what counts in making my decision. I can't tell for sure whether or not the tremor is getting worse, but I think it is; the side effects of the pills he takes—which include blurred vision and a dry mouth—are a problem; and he definitely doesn't have the strength and stamina he used to have. I won't leave him alone at sea.

And I'm afraid that finding jobs when we return will be harder than Don seems to think it will be. Resigning a secure teaching job [I'd been on unpaid leave for the first two years] wrenched my stomach. Getting another one may not be easy; teaching is no longer "something you can always fall back on." Taking into account our ages, Don's health, and my lack of preparation for anything but a profession that doesn't need me, I can't help but be apprehensive.

Intending to mail this letter, I spared even my mother the details.

Don's tremor was not only growing worse, it was beginning to affect his right side as well as his left. And the physical effects of the drugs were not my biggest concern. Don became moody, and his downs were very down. Since he'd always been the optimistic one, sure of himself and encouraging the rest of us to be self-confident, this change was unsettling. So were the explosions of temper from the man I'd known for twenty years as the most even-tempered of men.

From the little I'd read before we left, I attributed these changes to the chemical effects of the drugs he was taking. He needed to see a doctor and be reevaluated, but there was no chance of that while we were at sea. We would simply have to weather these internal storms as we did those that came on the south wind from the Antarctic. Both kinds frightened me at a deep, almost primitive level I'd never experienced and one I'd not choose to experience again.

The generational problems we were having didn't help matters. We arrived in American Samoa with a fifteen-year-old capable of handling the boat as well as the captain and first mate—and only too happy to tell them so. The shouting, silence, and tears occasioned by the telling didn't make harmony. Nor did the togetherness. The mail waiting for Donald didn't help, either. Friends from home wrote of girl friends, football, learning to drive—"normal" teenage activities engaged in by people whose parents didn't force them to do some weird thing just because the parents had always dreamed of doing it. My letters told of spending long times waiting at the phone company. They didn't explain that I was trying to unload our older son.

Donald couldn't stay with his grandmother—and not only because he wasn't old enough to live in the retirement community. If he couldn't get along with his father and me, he certainly wouldn't be able to get along with my stepfather, a generous man but a martinet where children were concerned. And to him, fifteen-year-olds were "children"—without discussion. So I called my brother, who, understandably, didn't want to take on someone else's problem teenager. He and his family had recently moved and were just settling into their new place, which didn't have a spare room. In an emergency or for a short visit he'd have made room, but this was neither. He suggested an alternative we'd already thought of—a boarding school—and promised to get information to us right away.

I next called old friends who had predicted some of the problems we were having and had said we could send the kids "home" to them when things got unbearable. But C. G. had torn up his knees and undergone surgery; he was on crutches and would be "semi-invalided" for months. The family didn't need another problem. His wife thought a boarding school would be a terrible idea; instead, she found a neighbor who was a state-licensed foster parent and who agreed to take Donald. He'd be in a house where he would have his own space, and near enough to visit our friends (daily if he wanted to), attending a good high school. But—we'd have to give up custody.

We weren't ready to—as we saw it—admit our failure that way. Donald wasn't incorrigible. He got along with everyone else we met.

Sailors and landlubbers alike remarked about how knowledgeable, well-informed, and competent both boys were, and how much fun it was to have them around!

Donald was as confused as we were. Except for "going home right away" none of the alternatives seemed better than the situation he was in. In the end, thanking friends and family for their efforts to help solve our problems, we did nothing. We left Samoa as we entered it, a family of independent, often prickly personalities, bound together by blood *and* water, with lots more water to cross.

Bumping Along

Dear Friends,

I should have known that they weren't rushing things in the Seychelles with their Christmas cards and decorations displayed before the end of September. It *is* later than we thought. The monsoon season has changed, and we're beating around the horn of Africa.

These past few weeks have conclusively proved that we're significantly faster than our friends in monohulls. We've taken only seven or eight days for every trip that took them ten or twelve. Then when we left the Seychelles, we joined the yacht club race to one of the outer islands. Next to last across the start line, we had sailed through the nine o'clock starters (our division) within twenty minutes. By the time we reached the finish line twenty-six miles away we'd passed all but one of the eight o'clock starters—and had the race been a quarter mile longer, we'd have passed her, too. Not too bad, when you consider that since we live aboard and had just provisioned for a long trip, we're much heavier than the day sailors.

Then just yesterday we met a friend out here. Unusual enough in itself, even though we are traveling the same route—but Jack left the Seychelles three and a half days before we did. Yesterday he caught up with us. (There was no wind, and when we saw a sailboat steaming up astern, we just waited.) We spent about an hour sitting and talking, then the rest of the day within a few miles of each other, drifting. Then the wind came up, and within two and a half hours Jack was so far behind we lost sight of him. Yes, isn't our boat wonderful! And if it wasn't, do you think we'd tell?!

The Seychelles, as I noted, achieved independence and liberation. Some day they may even get freedom—but don't hold your breath. The present government fears a coup (takes one to know one?)—specifically, an invasion by sea. Read *The Dogs of War;* notice that life imitated art when the Comoro Islands were recently invaded (now I understand why the CIA hired Robert Redford to read all those novels in *Three Days of the Condor*). Government restrictions become understandable, though still not laudable. Oh, well, next year there will be an (one party) election. And why should the U.S. care? Well, we have a tracking station there, and the Russians a large embassy. Beijing is going to open a cooking school. The U.S. Indian Ocean naval base was almost located nearby, on Aldabra Island; but the giant tortoises live there, so the environmentalists wouldn't let it happen. Instead, the British moved the people (they had no lobby) off Diego Garcia and leased us the atoll. I do hope you understand all this political maneuvering; I don't. But I do have a question. Of all the countries that have been "liberated" since 1960, especially in Africa, is there one in which the general population is better off—i.e., has more political freedoms or a higher material standard of living—than it was when it was "oppressed"?

en route to Sudan
November 5, 1978

Sailing in the Red Sea is like sailing in Death Valley—only more so. Death Valley is more colorful and sprouts more vegetation than the shores along the sea. Here, on both the Arabian and African sides, the color is dun, occasionally trimmed by the basic black lava of dormant volcanos. At least it's the cool season (hasn't been above ninety yet); and the nights, like desert nights in California, have been comfortably cool.

Our first African stop was Djibouti, former French colony, now independent nation. As with any place the French have been or are, it's very expensive. Food is flown in daily via Air France; a pound of beef (whether hamburger or rib roast) costs $3.90, a pound of ham, $6.00; ice cream is $5.00 a half-gallon. Those native families that have a male employed by the government (French colonial salaries set a high standard) or a female self-employed in the world's oldest profession (more than two thousand ships call here yearly) can afford to shop where the colonials do. If they live less well, one employed person can support thirty to forty people. But even local food isn't cheap. Nothing grows in Djibouti. The nearest "garden" is Ethiopia—oranges $1.50 a pound, tomatoes $1.20—and war is devastating it; only local fish is cheap. Water, from underground sources, is costly. Ask for a glass in a restaurant and you'll find a charge on your bill. (If you're not careful and explicit, you'll be brought a bottle of imported French water at $3.50!). And if you think Glendale water tastes bad, this stuff is terrible!

Still, the town has compensations. It is clean, even though scores of Ethiopian refugees filter in from the walled camp outside of town to beg in the streets and sleep on cardboard boxes outside the stores. The people are friendly, especially toward whites who don't speak French. There is no paperwork for yachts entering or leaving the country. Although many of the men have adopted Western dress, the women still wrap themselves in yards and yards of colorful and diaphanous material. Many of these women are beautiful indeed. They look like some African-Arab-Indian mixture with fine features, flawless complexions, and wonderful dark eyes.

We sailed from Djibouti to the only Arab country on the Red Sea that tolerates yachts. North Yemen, in fact, likes us nomads. Maybe we remind them of their old days. The country was first opened to outsiders in 1951, and since then has become "cosmopolitan." Foreign customs are at least tolerated in the larger cities, especially in the port of Hodaida, where camels, donkey carts, motorcycles, and Mercedes-Benz sedans share the streets, creating a deafening cacophony. Foreigners are allowed to show arms, legs, necks, and faces. Looking like Nazgul, the traditionally black-clad women stalk the streets, trudging along on their errands. Some wear see-through veils and a few even bare their faces; but most are shrouded from head to ankle, only hands and feet indicating a human presence inside the black wrappings. Unlike most other places we've been, the women here don't carry heavy loads. My backpack provided a great source of conjecture. By the time we finished with the vegetable man, we'd acquired a dozen onlookers. Then "ahh!" as we put our bargains into the pack and set off.

Unlike Djibouti, Hodaida was very dirty—the first place on our travels where we wouldn't eat food prepared by street vendors. At least the country has its own agricultural region in the mountain valley, so we could buy excellent and cheap potatoes, onions, carrots. Even imported frozen and canned foods were cheaper than in Djibouti.

After leaving Hodaida, we stopped at Jazair Az Zabayi, an island off the coast. The landscape looks lunar. Young volcanos have spewed black lava waste over almost everything, although a sand beach and some low-lying shrubs give some relief. Boobies nest all over this outcropping, and we saw the skull of one of the antelope that somehow survive here (obviously this one didn't).

In contrast to the bleakness of the land is the richness of the sea. We saw large, fantastic coral formations of all kinds—fan, brain, mushroom, etc. And fish, fish, fish, glittering like Tiffany's window in the sunlight—turquoise, emerald, ruby, ebony. Just before sunset the rays came to feed, huge mouths straining plankton out of the water. When we were sure we were seeing manta rays, not sting rays, and no sharks, we went swimming among them. Though not as playful as the dolphins, they move just as gracefully, giant wings waving slowly and smoothly. Half a dozen were feeding around the boat, the largest about twenty feet from mouth to tail tip and ten to twelve feet from wing tip to wing tip. The others were only slightly smaller. Swimming among them was an enthralling experience.

Port Sudan
November 10, 1978

How our general expectations set us up! Erik and I were in town last night, spending our money before the four-day Moslem "Christmas" shut down the town. Coming home, we walked down a poorly lighted, empty street. Midway we veered to walk around a cement mixer—only to find that the shadowy bump was not a machine but a camel! Like Yemen, Sudan is a land of contrasts—camels and donkeys jostle Jeeps and Mercedeses. Like Djibouti, it seems to have more water than the coastal Arabian peninsula. At least there are bushes and trees—cat's claw acacia, oleander, bougainvillea, date palm—to catch some of the blowing sand. And the country is definitely more African than Arabian—fewer women wearing yashmaks, more in those bright Christmas wrappings.

The streets around the harbor are almost deserted, yet three blocks inland, in the market area, you take your life in your hands crossing the streets. If the camels or donkeys don't get you, the bicycles or trucks will. I haven't yet figured out whether it's American or British traffic system. Cars come with steering wheels on either side, and everyone tries for the middle of the road.

November 21, 1978

Brr! And our hot water bottles rotted during the last two years in the tropics. We knew we'd be sailing into winter in the Med, but we didn't think we'd crash into it this far south and so soon. The air temperature isn't much below sixty-five, but the wind chill factor decreases that considerably. And it has been windy—eight days of beating into at least twenty-five knots, seas short, choppy, and confused, just as if someone had stirred them up with an egg beater. The passage is living up to its reputation as one of the most uncomfortable anywhere. If we can't get the waters parted, at least a calm would be nice.

The Sea also lives up to its reputation as one of the saltiest. Lines are so stiff with salt that we can't coil them, can hardly bend them. With salt crystals coating everything, in the sunlight we glitter like a Christmas tree. The rime of the ancient mariners—and we're aging fast, too.

The Sea is living up to its reputation as a freeway. Nearly two hundred boats transit the Suez daily, and we've seen a lot of them. A few, including a Norwegian cruise ship, have altered course to look at the crazies in the toy boat. Today an Israeli warship circumnavigated us, then went off to play games with two jet fighters.

Working on the theory that the problems that arise are not the ones you worry about, I got in a good session of worrying last night: we'd get run down by a freighter, capsize, hit a reef; the rigging would go and the mast fall, the engine would fail, the propeller fall off again; one of us would suffer a bad accident and fall overboard. I thought I'd covered all bases. This afternoon we blew out a headsail.

November 23, 1978 (Thanksgiving)

It is hard to be thankful for sailing in the Red Sea. Today we're fighting a holding action, running hard to stay in the same place. Our sails litter the deck, surrender flags shot down by the wind; we have only the two small stormsails up, beating into thirty-knot winds, ten- to twelve-foot seas. Just fifty-one weeks ago we were doing the same off Samoa, but this is worse. Seas are bigger, we've much less maneuvering room, and there's much more traffic. Wish we could hitch a ride aboard one of these freighters!

We don't know about water pollution (except foam and spray!), but there's plenty of air pollution here—clouds of sand, of course, more of gas and oil pollutants. We didn't realize how much oil drilling there is around here—rigs along both coasts and out in the channel, not prettied up like those off Long Beach, and flare after flare of wasted natural gas. At night these orange infernos are visible for dozens of miles; even when you can't see the flame you can see the pale glow; the rigs are outlined with hundreds of lights. Moon and stars are no match for this show.

November 25, 1978

We acquired some unpleasant pollution the other night—great gobs of tar. Don't know whether they were air- or water-borne, but they gummed up the deck, sheets, and sails.

To our thankful list we add having filled our second propane tank in Djibouti. Otherwise our Thanksgiving dinner (and every subsequent meal) would have been cold, out of a can. And thanks also for the extra meatballs in the can we opened for Thanksgiving dinner.

This must (I devoutly hope!) go down as our worst sailing experience. First, it feels ruddy cold. True, no one ever got frostbite in sixty-degree weather, but we haven't experienced this for several years. And for the first time since leaving home, we're sailing into winter instead of away from it. The sun shines, but such a pale, anemic light! But more discomforting than the temperature is the wind. Here in the Gulf of Suez it always blows from the north or northwest, supposedly not so strongly at this time of year, but twenty-five to thirty-five knots is strong enough when you have to beat into it. We fight for every inch. And when we have to raise the storm sails, it's a holding action. If the weather's marginal we have a Hobson's choice—leave the bigger sails up and go faster in misery or reduce sail and take longer but suffer only discomfort.

Suez Canal
December 2, 1978

Ho, ho, ho!—and you can see each "ho." For the first time since the Peruvian Andes we have visible breath. The temperature fluctuates between fourteen and eighteen (centigrade)—"balmy" we would have said when we lived in Minnesota, but it feels cold to us now.

Unfortunately, we arrived in Egypt "forewarned"—i.e., full of other peoples' prejudices. Our experiences, though, have been much happier than the ones we were told of. Yes, everyone is on the take and tries to cadge cigarettes (no one smokes more than Egyptians; it's terrible); but if you don't let that bother you, you're O.K. We did hire an agent for the first time, figuring it was easier to join than fight the system. He did in two days the Canal paperwork that would have taken us two weeks and an ulcer to do—and was entertaining in the bargain.

Everyone here likes Americans now. "Welcome, welcome," is a pleasant change from "Yankee, go home!" Sadat and Carter are the heroes of the hour.

Port Said
December 4, 1978

The two sweetest words in the English language—hot showers. And did they feel good.

We've been under "house arrest" here for the past two days. Immigration officials came on Saturday when we arrived, took our passports—and never returned with our shore passes. A Norwegian yacht traveling with us is in the same boat—on their boat. *Many* calls to immigration produced no results. Calls to our respective consulates were equally ineffective. Then the Norwegians called the Norwegian seaman's union, and tonight at five we were given our passes and allowed to disembark. It seems that regulations tightened up December 1, and Egyptian officials are checking passports closely and requiring photos for shore passes (they sent a photographer out with the passes this afternoon; if it weren't for Polaroid, we'd be waiting for developing). The Palestinians have threatened to sabotage the Canal if Sadat goes to Stockholm to accept the Nobel Peace Prize; of course, they'll come in on a small yacht.

You can tell it's cold. Bigfoot no longer stretches out full length but curls into a circle, his tail keeping his toes warm.

And guess where we've run out of sand for his litter box.

Having seen the Egyptian soldiers who are manning the Canal posts and another group marching to the train station in Ismailia, I can understand why Sadat wants peace. Or maybe they're just decoys, and a crack fighting force lies just over the ridge.

We leave for Cairo and Luxor in a day or two. The next letter should be full of "ruins." Until then,

> From this ruin,
> Joanne

> Cairo, Egypt
> December 8, 1978

Dear Friends,

If you know the sci fi story "X Marks the Pedwalk," you know all there is to know about Cairo traffic. Today we saw a taxi make a spectacular broken field run after a bicycle, and a station wagon take out after a young man carrying a tea tray from a restaurant kitchen across the street to the sidewalk cafe. There were no casualties, just near misses, but only because the unmotorized were very nimble. We have not yet figured out exactly how much faster a vehicle moves when the horn is blowing, but Egyptian drivers apparently think that it gives them extra power. After two and a half years in uncontested first place for having the most crowded buses we've seen, El Salvador has been defeated by Cairo. Not only are seats and aisles so crowded that it's literally impossible to move; not only do passengers balance on two toes on the steps; people hang out of and onto the windows, many of them missing. There is not a stretch of unbroken sidewalk anywhere in the city (not even along the Nile near the Sheraton and the Hilton); cracks, holes, pits, and mounds of dirt, sand, and trash are everywhere. You cannot walk in a straight line. They ought to send the Forty-Niners here for practice in broken field running. Visiting Cairo, you begin to appreciate the "sterility" of Singapore.

Unfortunately, the dirtiness extends into the buildings. The Egyptian Museum houses some of the most spectacular and glorious antiquities anywhere. They deserve a better home and better display, which the country can't afford. But surely they could afford to have things dusted. One of the floor mosaics is covered by a protective sheet of plastic that hasn't been swept or washed in, I'd guess, several years; you can't see anything of the mosaic. A sarcophagus lid, carved on the underside, is raised and displayed above a mirror so you can see the interior carving; but the dust and sand of weeks cloud the mirror. During our day in the museum four guards asked us for baksheesh (tip; bribe); wish I'd had mops and brooms and scrub brushes to give them!

The mosques and other monuments are in the same sad shape. I can understand not having enough money for renovation or even for repair; and I know how hard it is to keep dust out when you live in a desert; but a high pressure hose and a vacuum cleaner would do wonders, and there are plenty of people around who apparently have nothing to do. The men spend all day sitting in the coffeehouses, drinking coffee and smoking their waterpipes.

Tel Aviv, Israel
December 16, 1978

Remember the musical *Don't Bother Me—I Can't Cope*? That's me, here in the land of pizza stands on every corner (and I wanted a pastrami sandwich!), supermarkets (but no laundromats), girls in skintight pants (if that's the new style, please buy up the last of the straight leg pants for me, size 10) and high boots (think I could start a trend with my sea boots? or my hiking boots?), women in furs and flashy diamonds. Take me back to the mismatched pajamas of Egypt. I can't stand the culture shock of civilization.

If you visit Egypt, don't miss Luxor (ancient Thebes), ancient capital of "lower Egypt." Never before or since such grandiose statuary, such exquisite monuments to the life beyond death. That so much magnificence should have been dedicated to death and buried with the deceased seems a waste. Yet if it hadn't been, we would be the poorer for not having it. And at least this dedication produced works of art, while ours spends itself in bullets and explosions. Ah, but we are yet young, measuring our time in hundreds, not thousands of years. I'll try to describe it all later, when there's more time. For now, Champollion said it all—"Thebes is the greatest name in any language."

Larnaca, Cyprus
January 3, 1979

And, of course, there are cultural differences. In Tel Aviv I was hustled by a twenty-two-year-old, here in Larnaca by an eighty-two-year-old Greek Cypriot.

To back up and try to bring some coherence to this letter——

We had no sooner started into the harbor at Suez when an agent came out to guide us—the very agent we'd been warned against by half a dozen people. After two days of unsuccessfully trying to shake him (he appeared in every office where we went to do the paperwork ourselves) and find another agent (it's not *impossible* to transit the canal without engaging an agent, but it's not pleasant), we resigned ourselves to our karma and hired "The Prince of the Red Sea." He did a good job for us, charging only twice the actual fees and not hitting us up for extras. In Egypt that's unheard of. And that's why this letter began so negatively. After ten days of every hand outstretched for baksheesh, I'd had it. Then we visited Luxor, and all other impressions faded. Not that hands weren't outstretched or importunings made to take a camel ride, a donkey ride, a ride in a hansom cab—"Very cheap, very cheap!" But the glories of the ancient Egyptians overwhelmed the annoyances of their descendants.

"Egypt" means the pyramids and the great sphinx, the only remaining seven wonders of the world. But they are not particularly impressive. (More accurately, they did not much impress us.) Giza lies not far outside Cairo, in the shadow of high-rise apartments and hotels. The splendid site is an unsplendid sight, littered with trash and surrounded by the kind of tackiness that surrounds Disneyland—only dirtier. You can't take a step without being besieged by drivers and "guides." And perhaps the familiarity of schoolroom study and postcard art bred contempt. We were not impressed—except at the light show we saw one evening. Then, as the moon sailed over Cheops' pyramid and the cold desert wind whistled around its corners, modern Egypt faded, and we sat in the glory of the pharoahs.

The sites at Luxor were glorious both day and night. I can't call the statuary and temples beautiful; they're too massive for that, rather ungraceful; the columns are squat, not soaring like Greek columns; the roofs (the few remaining) are flat, not arched like those in Gothic cathedrals. "Stupendous" probably best describes the Egyptian artifacts. Practically nothing is as small as life-size.

Nobody knows how many tombs there are in the Valley of the Kings, but dozens have been excavated during the last century, and we visited about eight of the "most impressive"—the ones they let tourists into. Of these, Tut's is the least impressive—down a short flight of stairs into an outer room, a right turn into the inner chamber, and that's it. Simple, large, painted figures adorn the walls of this small room (no bigger than our main cabin). The stone sarcophagus is there, its lid removed, the masked mummy staring sightlessly into eternity. What it must have been to have found that room jumbled with gold, to have gone through four gold boxes before getting to the sarcophagus! And to think that all of that was rather hastily done for a minor king who wouldn't have made the history books if his tomb had been rifled as the rest were.

The tomb of Amenophis II (Amenhotep III) was the most impressive. It appeared to be locked (many were; even though you buy tickets of admission you have to find the caretaker and have him open things for you—baksheesh, of course), but Donald managed to open the gate. We walked down as far as the daylight from the entrance reached. I flicked all the light switches, but nothing happened. Determined to see at least some of this tomb that was high on our tourist list, I was taking the flashlight out of my purse when Donald came down.

"Why don't you turn on the lights?"

"They don't work."

"Well, first," picking up something from a shelf above the row of switches, "you have to put in the fuse."

And there was light. We walked perhaps a quarter mile, always descending. The walls on both sides were covered with the best preserved of the tomb paintings. We crossed two bridges, made several turns, and came into the burial chamber. Walls, pillars, and ceiling were covered with perfectly preserved paintings—the complete text of the Egyptian Book of the Dead. Unlike those in the other tombs, which were bright, almost gaudy, these paintings had been done with few colors and were all the more impressive. Skin and clothing were left the natural buff of the sandstone, but beards, collars, crowns, and girdles had been painted. And those eyes—hundreds of those Egyptian eyes, dark outlined, black-browed, brilliant whites.

The lights went out.

There really wasn't any problem. We had a flashlight, and you couldn't take a wrong turn because the dead (!) ends built into these places hadn't been opened. Still and all, we were in a death chamber hundreds of feet below the ground in an Arab country. By the dim beam of our Singapore flashlight with its weak batteries, we groped our way to the edge of the burial chamber. From the hallway we heard voices, and the lights came on. Donald lingered (he said later he'd rather have discovered that tomb than Tut's), but Erik would have none of it. We surfaced, meeting the caretaker who was having trouble with the lights. He knew he had to throw the switch and was surprised when doing so made the passage dark rather than light. They don't hire these guys for their brilliance.

Visiting Luxor was Donald's idea. His interest had been stirred by a report he wrote in the sixth grade; in his opinion, the only reason to go to Egypt was to visit Luxor. After looking at tour prices, we gritted our teeth (in Cairo this is a literal expression every time you open your mouth) and took public transportation with the locals—and were pleasantly surprised. The buses were very clean, the train adequately so. It was the first time any of us had traveled on a sleeper, and we all agreed that the motion of our boat is more comfortable.

As at home, train food was very expensive and looked terrible, so we had none. Instead, we bought from the street vendors. Mostly we ate "Egyptian sandwiches"—flat rounds of bread hollowed out and filled with fish cakes, eggs, cheese, lettuce, tomato, eggplant. Bought from a mobile vendor or one in the market, they usually cost from three to five cents; bought from a man who had a few chairs where you could sit, they cost seven to ten; bought in a real restaurant, fifteen cents. One was enough for me, but the boys usually ate two. Never have so many eaten so much for so little.

We even learned Arabic from "a" to "z"—*aish* (bread) to *zebda* (butter). Don was haggling with a vendor over the price of some cookies when the man asked if he knew any Arabic. Don said yes: aish, zebda—and baksheesh. That brought a loud laugh and half price on the cookies.

Your cookie,
Joanne

P.S. Regarding the way the cookie crumbles, consider our chance encounter with Nat. We were eating our cookies on the station platform in Cairo when he spotted us as probable fellow Americans and came up to chat. He was on the modern version of the nineteenth-century young English gentleman's Continental tour. Having "temporarily" dropped out of Cornell, he was backpacking "wherever I get the urge to go" on a journey of self-discovery. Nevertheless, he was enthusiastic about college and, giving us his mother's phone number and address in New Jersey, assured us that Donald could stay with her when he went for his interview at Princeton. Princeton was not on Donald's list, but Nat's enthusiasm was infectious, so it is now.

Maneuvering in the Med

Larnaca, Cyprus
January 5, 1978

Dear Friends,

"Slow as molasses in January" isn't a cliché; it's true, true, too true!
Neither the honey nor the molasses pours. It's cold—only six degrees
(centigrade) inside this morning; frost slicks the decks. It's time to head
south until the butter melts again. Instead, we're going north to Greece.
We've been trying for the past three days. For the first time since leaving
home three years ago, we've been forced back into port. Actually, we
weren't forced; we could have fought on, making twenty to thirty miles a
day. But why, when there's a nice marina here—and when the freighter
we were "following" listed when she turned the corner into the full force
of the wind, turned around, and steamed back? It took us nearly four
hours to get to that point; we dropped sails, ran back under bare poles in
just under an hour. Unless we get a gale from the east, we won't be in
Athens next week to meet Don's brother. Maybe things will improve
tomorrow, Epiphany, when the archbishop throws his cross into the sea.
    Cold as it is, I like it here.

January 9, 1978

So much that we're staying for six months. It was a quick decision,
but when the archbishop's blessing brought only more adverse winds (of
course, keeping a line attached to the cross doesn't show much faith), we
thought we'd better reconsider our plans. When Donald and Erik didn't
object to spending another ten months away or to enrolling in the
American Academy, we decided, if not to swallow the anchor, at least to
choke on it a while. So we're here until mid-June, then in the eastern

Med (Turkey and Greece) until October, thence to Gibraltar in October or November. We plan to cross the Atlantic sometime between December and March (possibly Christmas in the Canary Islands and make a few stops in the Caribbean), transit the canal (will it be Panamanian?), and beat up the coast to home. Besides not sailing during the cold in the Med, the new schedule doesn't call for flirting with an early hurricane season as the original one did. And we'll be able to see things here.

January 27, 1978

Marina life is like life in suburbia. Deliver me! We're already embroiled in a criminal case—as witnesses for our Aussie neighbor, not as defendants. The whole affair is quite ludicrous—or would be, if the officials here hadn't lifted Paul's and John's passports and charged Paul with a "crime" the penalty for which could be a year in jail and a $150 fine. We'd rather not get involved (we didn't make Nixon's enemies list; why should we get on some Cypriot's?), but he really didn't push the marina director into the water. Even more serious than this assault charge is the charge against John. He called the marina director a "silly bugger," thus affronting the director's dignity as well as using language that could provoke an assault. (No one could convince the director that the phrase was "a term of endearment.") And I thought Mexicans were touchy about "macho"! But you can't blame Glafkos too much: Paul is a royal pain (we've heard about him since Sudan); the Lebanese boats *will* cut loose any anchor that comes up with theirs when they're hurrying away on a gun/cigarette smuggling run; the ladies at the end of the dock destroy the image of a classy marina with the diapers they hang from the rigging each day; and the chicken coop on an aft deck didn't please him much, either. And I just wanted a quiet spot to hibernate!

February 5, 1978

John and Paul were talked into pleading guilty and sentenced to six months for not following the directions of a public official (marina director) and two years for assault; both sentences were suspended, contingent on the defendants leaving immediately. The accompanying fines ($75 for the first charge, $225 for the latter) and court fees ($150) were not suspended. John and Paul left for Tel Aviv that afternoon.

Tel Aviv is not on our list of places to return to. In fact, we were not impressed by much in Israel. Nothing there was as imposing as the sites of ancient Egypt, nor as old. Except for the cars and motorcycles, however, the old city of Jerusalem remains much as it was in Jesus' time—narrow, winding streets lined with shops selling wares from all over the world. We walked the stations of the cross with a Dutch Franciscan who had a heavy accent and a British sense of humor. It was very interesting and occasionally moving. You could imagine Jesus being jostled as we were by uncaring crowds, being harangued as we were by shopkeepers as he made his way to Calvary. Later, as we walked through some of the side streets we realized that the city is several levels. People are still living underground in dank places that never see sunlight.

The starkness of the Wailing Wall was quite impressive, although Donald and Erik couldn't understand "praying to a stone wall." I tried to explain that that was not what was happening, but they remain unconvinced. The most impressive of the monuments in Jerusalem, however, is the Mosque of Omar (Dome of the Rock). It is allegedly built over the rock where Abraham prepared to sacrifice Isaac, where Mohammed's horse took off with the prophet for heaven. It is a thousand times better maintained than any mosque we saw in Egypt. Thick, rich, expensive carpets cover every inch of floor; walls and pillars are of myriad kinds and colors of marble in geometric patterns—the various patterns and colors jarring to my mind and eye, but exquisitely done. The outside is covered with blue tiles, the dome leafed with gold. We saw neither Jewish nor Christian monument half so impressive.

As we were taking off our shoes preparatory to entering the mosque, we heard the guard shout, "Hey, none of that! Separate! This is a holy place!" Two teenagers walking hand-in-hand across the courtyard about a hundred yards away jumped guiltily apart. Shades of 1954 and Miss Tilly stalking the halls of Glendale High School!

Tourists visiting Jerusalem, holy city to the world's three largest monotheistic religions, have to be adaptable. Men and women both have to cover their heads when approaching the wailing wall, men to one side, women to the other. Men must remove their headcoverings when entering a Christian church, where men and women may sit together. Everyone has to remove shoes before entering a mosque. Women tourists may walk anywhere in a mosque open to tourists, but no men are allowed in the women's sections—usually the outside circle or a secluded box in the balcony.

(The shoe scam in Egypt was to provide cloth slippers to cover the tourist's shoes or a man to take them off and put them in a rack. Both services, of course, required payment. By the third mosque we had learned to enter by the side door, like the locals, leaving shoes on the doorstep or carrying them in my bag.)

Bethlehem was a bitter disappointment. We visited on the Wednesday before Christmas, knowing that if we went on Christmas we'd be crushed—literally. Everyone was busy, busy, busy getting ready to make a year's living out of the Christmas trade. Such a plethora of badly carved nativity sets made from olive wood from Bethlehem! Such a scramble in the square, setting up loudspeakers and TV screens! Such a number of children, mostly under five years old, running after tourists, asking for money! Don was afraid of being arrested for child molesting the way two little girls were patting his pockets. Big signs announced that the bank would be open until midnight on Christmas Eve. Visiting St. Catherine's, where the midnight mass is celebrated, we told the UPI reporter doing the traditional "Christmas in Bethlehem" interviews how disappointing it was. Only in the "Milk Grotto" church, where Mary is said to have suckled the Child on the flight into Egypt, did we find peace and piety. We chose not to return on Christmas Eve; and talking to friends who went and were disappointed, we were glad we hadn't gone.

It's so different here. Larnaca is a "no sweat" town—literally and figuratively. It's too cold for sweating; living is pretty easy. I can walk around the whole town and finish my shopping in an hour. The pace is unhurried and life is quiet—except on Saturday mornings. Then, what traffic jams! People come down from the mountain villages to buy and sell. Car, buses, motorcycles, horsecarts crowd the streets. Only pedestrians and (sometimes) bicyclists (of which there are hundreds) can move. Although my backpack still causes raised eyebrows and amused glances (especially when I have a leafy bunch of celery sticking out of the side pocket), I've become a part of the community. My egg and bacon lady takes the small eggs out of my carton and searches through her flats until she finds big ones; my potato man in his high black boots and black pantaloons picks up his scale, balances it at one oke (any of three units of weight varying around 2.8 pounds—and you thought metric was confusing!), then puts on one more potato; my banana, cabbage, and carrot man still apologizes because last week he was waiting on four people at once and shortchanged me three cents. A local who asked you to eat or drink with him (that's not a sexist pronoun; women hardly get out of the house, and certainly don't issue invitations to strangers) would be mortified if you tried to pay your share. I don't think there's a bicycle lock in town. The machine will stay wherever you leave it; even the groceries in the basket will be untouched. Street vendors leave their wares (luggage, shoes, etc.) on the sidewalk all night, wrapped against wind and rain but not locked against thieves. We like it here.

We had a local man for a friend when we first arrived, but Charlie (Don's brother and his wife, Wilma, came here to visit) offended him by insisting on driving home after Angelo drove off the road. It happened so: We went out with Angelo and uncle (eighty-two—yes, that one) for "an hour or two" one Sunday afternoon. First, we stopped at a friend's hilltop restaurant for a meze, a Cypriot meal rather like a smorgasbord. You get about twenty different dishes, not including the bread, yogurt, cabbage, and raw artichokes that come with everything. Copious amounts of brandy are ordered and consumed. An hour or so later you say, "Angelo, it's about time we were getting back." Everyone gets up—and goes from the patio into the restaurant. More brandy, more cabbage, bread, yogurt, artichokes, and this time, dessert—oranges and bananas. Jukebox music blares, and Angelo plays Zorba, dancing joyously. An hour later, "Angelo, it's time to go"—and we get into his car, turn away from town. "I want you to meet some of my family. No stay, no brandy." The wife's sister's husband owns a restaurant. We stroll around the grounds, inspect the pigeon coop, look at the rabbits and the three-legged fox. We walk through the restaurant on our way to the car. We must sit down, must have "a little something." We're served another complete meze, complete with more brandy. Fortunately, we're sitting outside in the lean-to—no floor, just gravel. Wilma and I pour lots of brandy on the gravel. "Cheer up," clink glasses, drink. Angelo performs something between a Greek folk dance and the limbo. Uncle maneuvers himself between Wilma and me so he can pinch us both. It's six o'clock. "Angelo, it's time to go." Out to the car and away—two miles away. We stop at George's, where Angelo produces something from the glove compartment. George is closed, but he'll let his friend and guests in. Angelo orders six plates, six forks, and a knife. He's brought a cake! More brandy—only half a bottle this time. Then George brings in another meze—and more half bottles of brandy. We are captives, unless we want to walk or try to find a taxi here (where are we?) in the hills. We finally leave George (with a full restaurant; people seeing the lights and hearing music thought he was open) at eight-thirty. Angelo runs off the road at eight thirty-seven. Charlie drives us home—and we haven't seen Angelo since. We understand that practically every yachtie gets "adopted" initially in the same way and that most such adoptions run a similar course.

We got our own wheels—a rental car—a few days later and visited some of the tourist spots. The Byzantine mosaics at Paphos were beautiful and beautifully done, but the Tombs of the Kings were a great disappointment—big holes in the ground with a few crumbling columns in the courtyards. I think I'd have been disappointed even if we hadn't seen Luxor.

Bigfoot has adapted well to the settled life. When we were here for "only a day or two" we kept him aboard—not an easy task, as he howled, yowled, and clawed at the door of his house. When we decided to stay, we knew we'd have to take our chances on letting him off the boat. He immediately took out after every cat on the dock and sprayed all over to mark his territory—making himself (and us) unpopular. He reigned for about a week. Then one morning he came home very wet and with a torn ear and scratched nose. He sneezed for a week, and even now that he's over his cold and healed, he's subdued. I think he tried to push his territory past this dock and got thrashed. Now he stays aboard all day and most of the night, doesn't go far, doesn't howl, doesn't spray—our docile ship's cat once more, interested only in his food bowl.

Apropos of nothing—— The Egyptian god of science took the form of a baboon.

March 12, 1979

Cat is uncurling. Students of signs and portents will recognize this as signaling the arrival of warmer weather. He no longer needs to curl his tail over nose and toes to keep warm. Except for that bad weather during the first half of January, it's been a mild winter—quite pleasant, except for ski enthusiasts; but unless the rainy season arrives late, it will be a long, dry, hot summer. Already we're hearing that this early good weather means an early resumption of the shooting in Beirut. Lebanese boats are beginning to arrive—the rich getting out while young Lebanese patriots? hotheads? terrorists? are paying premium prices to skippers who will take them to Lebanon—*now.* Apparently these are Christian partisans who can't fly (air fares are cheap) to Beirut because the airport is in Moslem hands. Our resident expert says that shooting is scheduled to begin on March 15. I hope he's wrong.

April 30, 1979

He was. It came later and was not so extensive—yet. This part of the world is half a dozen wars waiting to happen. In lieu of the real thing we go to see war movies. There's not much choice of pictures—one theater shows kung fu movies; the second, porn; the Attikon, "good," "recent" releases. I was talked into *The Wild Geese* by Don ("I saw the previews; it's not too gory.") and into *A Bridge Too Far* by the all-star cast. Why I do this to myself I don't know. Why people really do such things to each other I can't understand. How the depiction of such gore and violence could be judged "suitable for everyone" I can't imagine. Sick, sick, sick.

More signs—— The butter is melting and the unrefrigerated milk souring. Soon, perhaps, the water will be warm enough even for me to go swimming.

I'm writing this from work. Donald heard the ad on the radio and I applied. Lacking any other applicants (or so I suspect), they hired me. "They" is Elizabeth II. I'm teaching a crash course in English to members of the British army who are cramming for their "O" (ordinary) level English exams in June. I'm supposed to have five students; only three showed, and two of them aren't on the roster. Since I have no transport, the sergeant sent a taxi for me. The driver is supposed to show at eight-thirty tonight to take me home; but he told me that no one told him that and since he's been working since five this morning he won't be back. It's a long seven miles to the marina.

May 16, 1979

He didn't return, so I had to get my own taxi home. The major is now using a different taxi service.

Talking with people who have spent a lot of time in the Med, we've learned that "you can't do it." No matter where or when we plan to go, it's the wrong time of year. The saying here is the same as it was in Chicago: "'Don't complain about the weather; wait ten minutes and it will change."

Would you be spotted for a spy over your cornflakes? Supposedly an American was caught over his pie in World War II when, before eating it, he turned the point toward himself. Now I learn, from my German cornflakes, that I've been preparing dry cereal wrong all these years. You're supposed to pour the milk into the bowl first, then add the cereal.

June 18, 1979

The Queen's birthday. I hope no one shows up for class tonight; but I just heard a car door slam. Last week only one student showed and was glad to have some individual attention and then be sent home with the work. It's probably she. (Oh, the effects of O level cramming!)

                                                                    Later

I spent an hour with her. Now I'm drinking tea at a sidewalk cafe, waiting to go home until the dishes are (surely) done. This will be a very disjointed letter as I try to remember what I don't want to forget to say.

I remember why Washington state is green—and how much I didn't like the rain that kept it that way. But we've been six months in dry and dusty. The closest to green is gray-green, sage green. Grit blows everywhere, films everything. Yet it's humid. I'm dripping as I've done no where except Singapore.

It's time to leave. I'm tired of the smell of Larnaca. Not that it smells bad; I'm just tired of it. Last night in reverie I smelled Samoa, of all places. Wish I could be transported for a week or two (although this is the awful season there).

It's time to leave. I want English-as-a-first-language people around me. I don't want to go the aliens desk at the immigration office. Who's alien?

It's time to leave. Driving on the left-hand side of the road seems normal.

It's time to leave. The Mediterranean male mentality is driving me up the bulkhead. An unescorted woman (or two or three) can't walk after six at night without being accosted by eighty percent of the men she passes—young, old, Cypriot, UN Forces, British. It's not flattering or ego-building, just annoying and depressing. Except for some of the UN troops all the men have wives, of course. But those women aren't allowed out between six and six.

We went sailing twice last week—for the first time in five months. On Tuesday we took line honors in the First Annual Larnaca International Kataklysmos Offshore Yacht Regatta. We beat the favored boat and our arch rival on the last downwind leg, in spite of not having a spinnaker. Superior strategy (Don's) did it. We had the youngest helmsman (Erik) and the only human reaching pole (Donald and a friend, Nick, who hiked out in their safety harnesses and kept the double headsails from collapsing). Then Saturday the kids took us down to the cape for a sail, swim, and lunch—seven teenagers, two parents, and one adult friend. Forget the car. "Dad, can I borrow the boat this Saturday?" "No, you can't take the house."

Kataklysmos was horrendous—a week-long "festival" with Rose Bowl–like crowds every night. It took at least ten minutes to thread your way down one block. Cheapie carnival rides and stalls were set up on the beach. And such *junk!* And so much of it! The world could save billions of barrels of oil by not producing all the junky plastic do-dads. We saw little of it won and even less sold. Where did it come from? Where does it go from here? Why is it?

Alanya, Turkey
July 3, 1979

Reflection on "shoddy American goods": Except for three pairs of shorts that I bought in Panama, all the foreign-made clothes that we've bought have fallen apart in a short time. Sears catalog clothes more than five years old and worn over and over and over are still good. The farther we go, the more we see, the longer we're away, the more I become a nationalist, modernist, materialist. Why are hand-made goods produced by starving peasants working for a pittance "better" than machine-made goods? Why shouldn't the Indian women of the San Blas Islands use sewing machines for their molas? A computer-operated machine at Bigelow could produce a carpet every bit as good as that knotted by the small fingers of undernourished children ruining their vision in Isfahan; but nobody would pay the inflated price for it that they pay for old, "Persian" carpets. Except for a few items (notably in the Tut collection and a few Aztec and Inca pieces) the extant gold work of the renowned ancients is pretty crude. Many artists in Laguna Beach do just as well, and a few do much better. When he was beginning pottery classes, Don threw crooked pots every bit as "interesting" as those done by "primitives." I'm fed up to the eyeballs with the wonderfulness of things old, people uneducated, living conditions "natural." Really, what is wonderful about display cases full of shards of pottery and pieces of old pots? Will your "Apple Blossom" Franciscan ware and your copper-bottom Revere Ware pots grace museum shelves in the future? Will collectors vie for your Frisbees? How I long to be around in 2979 and visit a museum of twentieth-century artifacts! I suppose it's overreaction to a surfeit of "picturesque" places, museums, and ancient relics. The cure is a week in L.A.

Side, Turkey
July 4, 1979

Sky blue with bands blood red and chrome yellow, oversize wheels, deep-tread tires—it could only be a California van. No matter that the plates said "Grand Canyon State," that the jerry can of fuel locked on the rear said "Las Vegas to Istanbul," that we saw it parked outside the PTT (post office) on a dirt road in Side, Turkey. Mas was glad to meet fellow Americans, especially on our special holiday, and invited us to his hotel for coffee, tea, beer. It turned out that he meant "my hotel" literally; he's owned it for four years. A young Turk who looks like a Navajo, he is now an American citizen. He studied hotel management in Denver and now spends eight months a year working in Las Vegas, four months here. The U.S. "infected" him with ambition, and he's very intolerant of the "laziness" of his countrymen. This is a beautiful coast—sandy beaches, waterfalls, trout streams, ancient ruins—and prospects for the hotel business looked good. But the oil crisis put an end to all that, and Mas doesn't know how long he'll be able to hold on.

July 7, 1979

We held on as long as we could, then sought safety at sea, got into the worst steady wind we've encountered—fifteen hours of a steady fifty, gusting higher. Fortunately, the seas were not too steep. But we were unprepared, mentally, for the situation. We had decided not to leave Side that day. Instead we had dinner at the hotel with Mas and two Canadians he'd picked up in town. By the time we finished, the waves were so big we had to swim the dinghy through the surf. We tried to stick it out at anchor, but when waves began to break only feet behind the boat and the anchor rode to creak alarmingly with every swell, we cast off the stern anchor, struggled to get up a well-set bow anchor (Donald finally did), skirted the rocky spit, and headed out to sea. The wind built and built and built. Most of the worst of it came during daylight (0400 on). It was eerie to sit in bright, warm sunshine yet hear the wind howl in the rigging; to see the speedometer hit nine knots, then realize we were running with bare poles.

July 8, 1979

God, it's like living under siege! These Turks are worse than Israelis. Even anchored off, not tied to a dock, we have dozens of them aboard—and not just kids. They swarm, as if we were a diving platform provided by the Turkish Tourist Department. Not to be unfriendly, but it gets more than a little tiresome. Trouble is, we're too easy to board, and we have so much deck space that there's room for everyone. Wish I had the nerve to wander into one of their front yards and stare through the door. Probably I'd be invited in for tea. Well, I could handle one or two people, too, but not tens and twenties, and not all day long. We just chased off six, and three more have come! There's a lot to be said for a fenced, guarded marina.

a hillside above the anchorage
July 9, 1979

Why does the soughing of the wind through the pines sound soothing while the same wind in the rigging rubs my nerves raw?

Except that the water is salt and warm instead of fresh and cold, we're in a Sierra lake setting. A long, sandy beach (backed by truck gardens on the alluvial plain) forms the curve of the horseshoe. On either side rise steep slopes, thick with pines. Not too far behind the foothills, mountains climb three meters into the clouds. Insects throb, birds chatter. Rust-red rocks (I'd forgotten the beauty of rust *color*) glow warm in sunlight. How I'd like this for my very own! If it were at home, only the very rich could afford to live here. Here, it's the poor, scrabbling a living in a landscape to delight the eye but not the farmer. Twenty years from now, will there be a Hilton? I hope not. Not that I would doom these people to eternal poverty; but surely there's room in the world for some unspoiled places, some quiet spots.

Evidently this is already a "weekend retreat." The hordes (two dozen) of yesterday are gone, the three beach-front bars empty. A gaggle of children followed me halfway up this hill, wanted my watch, cursed me out (I'm sure that's what they were saying) when I shooed them off. But they were only little children and threw only little rocks, and those not until I was out of range. No one has been out to the boat today.

We're back among the light-fingered. Donald's mask and snorkel almost went off the boat yesterday—and with an adult. And my favorite, four-year-old Sears blouse disappeared from the washline at Mas' hotel. It's a jolt after six months in Cyprus where you could, I'm sure, leave a ten dollar bill on the sidewalk and come back a week later and pick it up—from under a rock someone had used as a paperweight. Of course, it was fair to cheat a little in business transactions—not shortchange, but give short weight, palm off shoddy goods, etc. But it's that way here, too, along with the outright theft.

I see the rock-throwing children swimming out to the boat. It's a long way, and they'll be tired when they get there. Don will let them aboard. Who has the heart to shoo them off? But it's annoying. So far they're only in the dinghy, not on the boat. It's not inhospitality (O.K., maybe it is), but I like to invite my guests. Well, I'm not there; let them handle it.

People here are hospitable—and, like the Greeks, insulted if you try to pay when they invite you for something. We ate dinner three nights at Mas' hotel. He wouldn't take any money—not for the food ("it's local, it's cheap"), the use of his washing machine, or the showers. He was even insulted when we brought out one of our remaining bottles of California wine; he had to bring out several bottles of Turkish wine. It gets downright embarrassing and uncomfortable for a Westerner. Better the yachtie style of divvying up the bill—although we got annoyed at that, too, since the custom in Larnaca was even shares, and some of those guys really boozed.

That was a culture we had trouble getting used to—the pub culture. It's typically Mediterranean, I guess, but I much preferred the Pacific style of entertainment—drinks and conversation aboard the boats. It was quieter, cheaper, less smoky, more enjoyable, more comfortable. Still, we found an inoffensive pub in Larnaca, larger and brighter than most, cheaper, run by a morose Brit who became one of the yachtie family. By the time we left, Alan had softened so much that he twice popped for drinks at his bar and gave us two bottles of good wine for a going away present—and let us buy half a dozen more, which would have impossible otherwise, the good stuff being reserved for the hotels and classy restaurants. Even Alan had trouble getting it.

Apropos of nothing: The marina manager at Larnaca was earning the equivalent of a little less per month than Don made eighteen years ago; he was paying three times as much for his apartment and twice as much for food as we paid in those days.

July 12, 1979

From "Thousand Island Lakes" Turkey. How parochial, how provincial to relate everything to home. But it is like Thousand Island Lake in the Sierra—rocky outcroppings and islets, stunted shrubbery, hot, dry, and windy in the afternoon. Only the old ruins and olive trees belie the Sierra scenery—and, of course, the water. Fresh water can be the same sapphire blue of deep saltwater, but it can't match the emerald to turquoise shades of saltwater shallows.

Impressions? Many of the small towns here on the Anatolian plain just in from the coast remind me (here we go again) of towns like Merced, say twenty years ago—fairly prosperous centers in a rich agricultural belt, dust and optimism in the air, and tractors everywhere. A car is no status symbol, but a tractor is. Mas told us that ten years ago there were no roads, only dirt tracks, and no tractors, only camels. He also said (and BBC confirms) that the country is bankrupt. No farmer owns his tractor, and few can keep up the payments. Those who can, can't afford gas. Those who can afford gas can't get it. Turkey has nothing to export, so can't afford to import oil. As all over the world, I guess, tourists have first call on available supplies. (That seems wrong to me, but I suppose tourism has to be encouraged. Tourists bring money, all of it hard currency.) We needed a permit, but we had no trouble getting ten gallons of diesel for the boat. At the same time a local truck driver was begging for five liters to get to his next stop. And in the face of all this, the customs official was agitated about our Turkish flag. I'd sewn the star and the crescent moon on one side only, so the reverse was all red, except for the outline of the stitching. Nothing would do but that we buy a Turkish flag. When the reality is in dire straits the symbol becomes all-important?

If you ever wondered what happened to those button-front, V-neck, sleeveless, floral print shifts that filled racks and racks at Penny's and Sears stores about five years ago, I can tell you. They came to Turkey. Modern Turkish women and German tourist women wear them. Far more sensible are the traditional harem pants—loose and cool like a skirt, practical like pants.

(A lizard is watching me. I can't sit as still as he.)

I hear that Iran executed its first women—prostitutes/madams, charged with selling women. If I'm right, husbands can sell wives, and fathers can sell daughters. It's only a crime when women sell women.

We're settling back into cruising with only a little difficulty. Togetherness can be trying; coupled with physical confinement, it's even more so, especially for two active teenagers who like most sports—except swimming. Don sands and paints. I read and write. Donald and Erik confess copiously to journals that I'm sure will find their way to Larnaca from each post stop. Thus we all survive. But it would be ideal to travel with one or two other boats with compatible adults and teenagers, even if we met only once or twice a week. Still, it's been a good trip. And unlike backpacking, which the boys say they never want to do again (will one of you lend me your kid?), sailing they like. They even talk about their boats, modifying this one, racing, the next trip.

July 15, 1979

It's hot, *hot,* HOT—in the nineties and windless. We know now why the great Mediterranean seafaring nations needed slaves. Someone had to row those galleys; you don't sail much in this sea.

Yesterday we visited a crumbled Crusader castle and a two-thousand-year-old necropolis. I suppose it's interesting? amazing? that the Lycians chiseled their caskets out of solid rock. But I'm less and less impressed. Will Forest Lawn be a "wonder" two thousand years from now? Will enough English have survived that the Founder's words, carved in marble, will be spoken with reverence?

It's strange to go snorkeling here and see—nothing. There're no shells, no fish, no coral. At least we get the bottom cleaned instead of being distracted by flashes of orange, gold, and electric blue.

It's strange to be in a place where it gets light so early, stays light so late—especially after a winter of late sunrises, early sunsets. We'd lived along the equator for so long we'd forgotten. The Voice of Peace (a pirate Israeli radio station) underscored it. When we began listening in December, their moment of silent prayer at sundown occurred before 1630; now it's nearly 1900.

Do you sweat when you swim? I prefer swimming to playing tennis or jogging because I don't sweat. My family insists that I do sweat but just don't notice because I'm all wet. They're probably right.

July 17, 1979

Happy fourth birthday, *Anduril.* Erik baked a cake and we opened a canned ham. I'd certainly be happy to be brought here on my birthday. It has to be one of the most beautiful spots on earth. We're stern-to to a pine tree, and the piney hillside behind us gives feathery, fragrant shade.

The water is warm—the temperature I'd have made Lake Tahoe had I been in charge of creation. High mountains almost surround us; only a 150-foot channel, fifteen feet deep, leads to the sea. The flaw in paradise? The place is no longer "completely uninhabited" as our guidebook says. Half a dozen other boats line this shore; the beach across the bay is littered with tents; and a motel is creeping up the hillside.

July 18, 1979

The fly in the ointment? Flies, followed at sundown by bees, at nightfall by mosquitos.

Cruising here is totally different from cruising in the Pacific. At least seventy percent of the boats are charter boats. They motor to an anchorage where they spend half a day, leave at three or four in the afternoon, motor to the next place, where they go out to dinner and spend the night; then they're off the next morning. Thank goodness the distances in the Pacific are too great for much of this kind of "sailing."

I was so looking forward to coming home and walking into a COLD bank, restaurant, etc. Now, I hear, under energy conservation laws they'll be seventy-eight degrees.

Later

Why must people come to a pristine place like this to listen to "The Freak" at maximum volume and dance disco? I mean, if you're going to look at flashing lights instead of stars and listen to loud throbs instead of soft wind in the pines, why bother to come here? Why not stay in Paris, Athens, Istanbul? I hope the Pacific is still pacific.

July 19, 1979

We're anchored opposite Catfish Row. Any time now I expect to hear "Summertime, and the livin' is easy." This is another "deserted" beach, full of Hellenic and medieval ruins—and summer shacks on stilts. A little apart from the others, on a rise, back from the beach, half hidden by pines is a shack of *varnished* wood, with round, glassed windows. I think a *Sunset* magazine found its way here.

Sailing the Med is like hiking up the east slope of Mt. Whitney. If you don't know better, it can turn you off sailing/backpacking for good. Or, as one of the students in the first high school English class I taught told me, like reading Henry Miller. If you didn't know better, you'd swear off sex forever.

I roller-skated around the block on my thirtieth birthday and was ridiculed. Linda Ronstadt goes roller skating and makes news. There's a message there; I'm not sure what.

Bigfoot is adapting to boat life again. After six months of being a shore cat in Larnaca, it was difficult. He enjoyed Larnaca and the ladies, but it didn't do him any good. He got flu, fleas, and worms, became just a shade of his shadowy former self. He's slowly recuperating but is still very thin and looks even thinner since he's almost hairless. As soon as the temperature rose, he shed rapidly. Since we don't want him to go ashore on our short stops, we bought him a harness. It embarrasses him to wear it. Whoever heard of a sleek gray tomcat sporting a shocking pink harness? And then being tied up so he can't go where he wants? We have to tie him short, too, or he winds up hanging over the winchbridge or down a hatch. The joys of cruising!

July 22, 1979

Separating the sheep from the goats isn't hard—tails down, sheep; tails up, goats. What's hard is preferring sheep. They're dumb, easily frightened, easily led creatures, whereas goats are intelligent, inquisitive, individualistic.

Istanbul, Turkey
August 14, 1979

For a bus terminal, it's clean. And the long-distance buses themselves are the neatest, cleanest anywhere. Two nice touches—scented water to wash your hands after each stop and bottles of ice water. I'm sure Greyhound has such amenities (handiwipes and water coolers), but we'd forgotten they existed.

Athens, Greece
August 24, 1979

I'm sitting in the *American* Cafe, waiting for a genuine BLT and a cup of "American" coffee. Greek food gets wearing after a short time; everything is drowned in olive oil, and "salad" means tomatoes, cukes, and olives. And Greek (Turkish, Egyptian) coffee—WOW, it sets my nerves to jangling, not to mention the sanding it does to my teeth when I drink too far down into the grounds. So I'm in a (large) hole on a side street instead of at a sidewalk cafe on Sintagma Square, people watching and exhaust breathing (there's more smog here than in L.A.).

Not to sound like Philistines, but we've been unimpressed with what we've seen here in the Med. Maybe, as with Egypt, it's a case of too much familiarity through history and pictures and too high expectations. Maybe we're just travel weary. Whatever the cause, it's been a real letdown.

Our biggest disappointment was St. Sophia's in Istanbul. The first things to strike your eye inside are the huge, round, wooden shields that hang around at balcony level—green backgrounds with gold leaf Arabic calligraphy. The script is beautiful, might even be termed "art," but the shape, size, and position of the shields are in complete disharmony with the rest of the building. I suppose that when the Turks "de-mosqued" the cathedral, removing the whitewash that covered frescoes and mosaics, they had to leave something of Islam. But it jars. And then, everything is so grungy, when all it would take to make it gleam is a little Brasso, some soap and water, and lots of elbow grease. All of the white marble is tattletale gray. Yes, it's an old building and needs restoration costing thousands (millions?) the country doesn't have. But a simple cleaning would at least give an idea of its former grandeur.

Crete
September 4, 1979

As for the "Golden Horn"—nothing golden remains, not even extensive commercial traffic. Istanbul is a poor city, Turkey a poor country. If you want a fifties car, visit Istanbul—especially if it's a Chevy you're after. Classics right out of our high school days—and all working, most of them as taxis, held together with spit and baling wire. I guess I just don't like cities much to begin with, and when they're poor and dirty, my dislike is compounded. The best thing about Istanbul was our hotel room—view of the Bosporus, comfortable beds, and a bathtub. If the city was dirty, at least we could get clean.

Athens, being rich (tourists) and clean (comparatively) was a little better. But the Acropolis, like the pyramids, loses much of its import (for me, anyway) being surrounded by high-rise buildings and cloaked in smog. They do not add to the beauty.

Nor do the modern Greeks. I suppose I'd be annoyed, too, if my country were overrun with foreigners dressed outlandishly and behaving atrociously, but the Greeks are downright surly about it. They're greedy for the tourist dollar, yet really don't want tourists. (We could have a wonderful school if it weren't for the students.) We were scorned in Rhodes for ordering only one large beer. (I wanted tea, but they were out of hot water, so I chose to have nothing.) I've had people (locals, not tourists) cut in front of me in lines more times than I care to count. It's very easy to prefer Turks to Greeks. Even the Egyptians were better; at least they were cordial, even friendly, when doing you in.

As for the antiquities—— Maybe contempt has been bred by familiarity, maybe we have to visit the British Museum to see the best, maybe it's just overdoses; but you can stand in wonder before just so many pottery shards and headless statues. It is a revelation, though, to learn the truth about "classical restraint." Most of those chaste white marble statues and temples were painted bright, almost garish, reds, yellows, blues. The frescoes when new must have been nearly psychedelic. What is needed to get the true feeling is re-creation, not restoration. Maybe Disney could add an ancient Athens to one of the parks. And one of the tour groups could run a simulation vacation—live a week like an ancient Athenian, citizen class costing more, of course, than slave. That's not entirely facetious; role-playing has proved its therapeutic and educational value. Trotting from ruin to ruin doesn't really give the feel of past civilizations. And it's not their architecture that's important, but their ways of living.

Not every place was disappointing. We had a delightful time in Lindos, in spite of its being a tourist town. It was our first whitewashed Mediterranean town with narrow, twisting, cobbled streets—impractical, slippery, ankle-twisting, but charming. And swimming in the bay was good, although, as everywhere in the Med, snorkeling isn't much fun—nothing to see. Not surprisingly, but unfortunately, disco has hit. You can't sit over a glass or a cup of anything and have a quiet conversation.

Delphi, too, is a tourist center, but nevertheless inspiring. It has the advantage—to me—of being in the mountains, among creeks and pines.

Even the hordes of tourists can't destroy the spectacular natural setting. And if you get up early enough (as we did) you can see most of the site before the tourist groups arrive. (Americans seem to come in the mornings, French and Germans in the afternoons.) Also, the Delphi museum houses my favorite Greek artifact—the bronze statue of the charioteer. Nothing I've seen surpasses it, and very little comes close. I'd have it. I tried to buy a reproduction, but they were so poorly done I settled for pictures and slides of the real thing.

Copies of ancient ceramics are the big things all over Greece. Never mind that when produced the originals were vividly colored; when dug up they were muted, so colors on the copies are muted. And, since many of the important pieces were found in pieces, the copies are cracked and chipped to resemble the originals—which were certainly not cracked and chipped when made. (I can't imagine the ancient Athenians admiring cracked pots. Even the charioteer was taken off display after the earthquake that destroyed his horses, chariot, and left arm. But he was given a decent burial, which preserved him for us.) I don't know how much of the stuff is bought, but tons of it are made. Can the world economy really prosper on "you buy my tourist junk here and I'll buy yours when I visit your country on the money I make off you"?

Trying to remember everything I wanted to say is making for a very jumbled letter.

If you want to go back to the adolescent custom of drag racing on city streets, visit Athens. Drivers cannot start on the green light without peeling rubber, nor can they make the simplest turn without screeching; least of all can they come to a stop gradually.

Don will disagree because he enjoyed Ephesus very much, but I think that, like Istanbul, the best thing about the place was the hotel. Not that it was anything special (well, showers are always special), but our rooms looked out on chimneys with nesting storks. Erik was disappointed because, unlike him, they do not stand on one leg. They clatter their bills, though, sounding rather like flamenco dancers rattling their castanets—not a very soothing lullaby, but an effective alarm clock.

Look at the drawings that purportedly portray ancient Ephesus and Delphi; then tell me about ostentation, status seeking, and the unplanned, ugly jumble of Harbor Boulevard.

We've fallen into what will be a bad habit when we get home—walking down the street. It's not that there isn't any traffic; but sidewalks are narrow, and filled with racks of clothing, books, shoes, etc. Every store overflows onto the sidewalk.

The longer days seem especially strange here now. We've been operating on sun time for nearly three years, and our biological clocks don't believe in daylight savings time.

September 10, 1979

Hippies live. Complete with long hair, beads, and moccasins, they throng the streets here. It's like a scene out of the sixties. Very few, though, look spaced out.

Typical Med yachting manners—— We were cheek by jowl in the marina. Then the small sailboat on our port side moved out. Soon after, a big French yacht came in, dropped anchor, and threw lines ashore. Wind made maneuvering difficult; Erik was fending them off our stern while Donald handled their shore lines. Out of nowhere came a small Belgian boat; it slipped into the spot the Frenchies were backing into. No amount of swearing would make them leave. Half an hour later, having dragged the anchors of three other boats and dumped their outboard when it got caught on the sunshade of a fishing boat, the French boat squeezed in elsewhere. Several hours later an even bigger French yacht came in. Seeing no room in the marina, they shoehorned themselves between two smaller boats anyway. Fenders squashed; boats didn't rub against one another; we were too tightly wedged for that. Guess who complained. Yep, the boorish Belgians.

Couthly,
Joanne

en route to Spain
September 21, 1979

Dear Friends,

As usual, it's been said already and better said. Listen to Jerome K. Jerome in the delightful *Three Men in a Boat:*

> Why, all our art treasures of today are only the dug-up commonplaces of three or four hundred years ago. I wonder if there is any real intrinsic beauty in the old soup-plates, beer-mugs, and candle-snuffers that we prize so now, or if it is only the halo of age glowing around them that gives them their charm in our eyes.... the pink shepherds and yellow shepherdesses that we hand round now for all our friends to gush over...were the unvalued mantel-ornaments that the mother of the eighteenth century would have given the baby to suck when he cried.

Will it be the same in the future? Will the prized treasures of today always be the cheap trifles of the day before?...

That china dog that ornaments the bedroom of my furnished lodgings. It is a white dog. Its eyes are blue. Its nose is a delicate red, with black spots. Its head is painfully erect, and its expression is amiability carried to the verge of imbecility. I do not admire it....

But in 200 years' time it is more than probable that that dog will be dug up from somewhere or other, minus its legs, and with its tail broken, and will be sold for old china, and put in a glass cabinet. And people will pass it round and admire it. They will be struck by the wonderful depth of the colour on the nose, and speculate as to how beautiful the bit of the tail that is lost no doubt was.

We, in this age, do not see the beauty of that dog. We are too familiar with it....In 2288 people will gush over it. The making of such dogs will have become a lost art. Our descendents will wonder how we did it, and say how clever we were. We shall be referred to lovingly as "those grand old artists that flourished in the nineteenth century, and produced those china dogs."

October 11, 1979

Storm at sea. The wind howls and shrieks in the rigging. The boat poises on the edge of a foamy crest, then slides down into the trough. Stays and shrouds shudder. Momentarily without wind, the stormsails shake limply; sheets snake along the deck, clattering in their blocks. Up again, and the boat is swept with foam. Then another wave, bigger than its fellows or coming from a slightly different angle, doesn't break before or astern of the boat but crashes with a dull thud into her side, hundreds of tons of water meeting three-eighths of an inch of plywood and glue. For a dozen hours the buffeting continues, wind blowing forty to forty-five knots, waves traveling fifteen to twenty, the boat, bucking both, barely making one.

October 14, 1979

And continues and continues. This afternoon we finally made the "harbor" we first spotted at dusk on the eleventh. The wind still howls, but we're protected from the waves. Tomorrow Don will go up the mast to repair the shroud that started to unravel last night. Then we'll sit here until we get a favorable change in this for once damned constant changeable Med weather. It's the longest spell of bad weather we've had—five days of force 6. At least the seas were only big, not huge.

Puerto Banus, Spain
October 26, 1979

We've been ten days now on the "Sunshine Coast" and eight of them have been rainy. We're in cheap Spain, paying higher prices for everything than we've paid anywhere else in four years. (Lobster a la carte in the restaurants is $35; kilo price in the markets is about that. We're writing $pain. Don't tell me it's as bad as U.$.)

But it's nice to be in "familiar" surroundings. After a year, we're at least back again with the Latin alphabet. Though the words aren't English, at least the letters are comprehensible. And many of the words are familiar, of course.

We settled in Puerto Banus instead of Estepona because another American boat, friends of friends in Larnaca, was here. They have a teenage boy, so we are sticking together for a while, trying to ensure sanity for all.

We had to delay our departure from Iraklion (Crete) for two days. We'd cast off the lines and were waving good-bye on Sunday night when we discovered that we couldn't back up. Because we couldn't see in the dark, we retied the lines and settled in for another night. Monday morning Donald dove into the cold murk and found—no prop. For the second time our Austral folding prop had fallen off. Donald couldn't search through the murk just free diving, so it was as lost at three fathoms as it had been at three hundred. We were preparing to be a real sailboat again (no one in the marina had scuba tanks) when I remembered having heard the announcements for the diving club on the Armed Forces radio station. So we called a friend at the air base (the commanding officer who had arranged for Donald to take his GED exam there), and within the hour we had two young airmen out. Greek harbor officials wouldn't let two men in the water at the same time (they might be stealing valuable antiquities), so the "buddy" hung over the stern, watching. After about three minutes we had our prop blades. "No charge. Happy to help, sir." ("Sir" every third word really makes you feel old.) Donald put them back on with nut and bolt instead of the "peening over" that Austral designs, and we set off.

When we arrived here there was a letter waiting for us from Austral, telling us in effect to jump. Things wear out from the very moment they're put into use, and eighteen months was a good long time. They made ten suggestions as to why it might have happened. Donald wrote back and caustically answered each one. I couldn't have done better myself.

Estepona, Spain
November 5, 1979

We came to Estepona when *Borne Free* left for Gibraltar, drying up our social calendar. In one day here we met more friendly people than in two weeks at Banus.

Donald went to Rota (the American naval base near Cadiz) last weekend to take the first of his college board achievement tests. Lacking high school records, he has to take two sets instead of one. We'll stay here until he's finished (the next one is the first weekend in December), then go on to Gib for reprovisioning with the rest of the "fleet."

November 25, 1979

We had to make do with three chickens instead of turkey, dehydrated yams instead of pumpkin for pie, and no cranberry sauce, but none of the dozen Americans, Canadians, Israelis, or Dutch at our Thanksgiving party minded. What with chocolate and apple pies in addition, stuffing, rice, sweet potatoes, homemade rolls, salad, fruit salad, wines, green beans, gingered carrots—all fixed on boat stoves and transported to a small Spanish apartment for feasting—we had plenty to be thankful for.

Gibraltar
November 9, 1979

What a glorious day it is!—sun sparkling on blue sea and absolutely clear air. "The Rock" looks just like its picture on the postcards. Two middle-aged women, obviously British, sit on the park bench facing sea and sun, skirts hiked just above their knees, blouses opened to the *second* button, faces upturned, eyes closed, fingers furiously knitting. Old Spanish couples promenade past—wizened old men, spindly as Don Quixote, their ample wives black clad. The donkey cart trails sand—a working conveyance, not a tourist attraction. Fishermen vie for the best position on the rocks, lines tangling with nets, but everyone good-natured today. Swedes and Germans spread towels on the sand and lie down to soak up the sun with as much exposed skin as the law allows. Over, around, and through, children jump, swing, roll on skateboards. No cries, no shrieks, no angry words. Everyone enjoys the feast of sun after the long fast of bad weather.

Joyfully,
Joanne

And Back Again

Los Cristianos, Tenerife, Canary Islands
December 23, 1979

Dear Friends,

It's cookie-baking time. This afternoon, if the weather stays good, will be spinnaker-flying time. Tomorrow evening, Christmas-caroling party. Christmas Day the four North American boats will have two big turkey dinners. We're getting together with *Borne Free,* the boat we met in Banus. They were just leaving Santa Cruz as we were arriving and changed their plans so we could spend the holidays together. Unfortunately, this anchorage, while a lovely spot, isn't always the best for monohulls. When the swell come in they roll a lot. We're the only ones who've been comfortable. Hooray for tris.

Later

Only Donald and Mike went spinnaker flying. It got too cold and cloudy for sensible people. Instead we took hot showers at the apartment of two vacationing Canadian girls who have "adopted" us yachties—more specifically, the young males among us.

crossing the Atlantic
January 9, 1980

Poor Bigfoot. He grew a thick coat to keep himself warm in ten degree (centigrade) weather on Spain's "Sunshine Coast." Lately it's been twenty-seven. Poor me. He's shedding it *all over.* Hair balls and fish scales are driving me crazy. Bigfoot goes fishing every night. As soon as a flying fish flaps on deck, POUNCE. Although I've convinced him that he's not to bring it downstairs, I can't convince him to eat off a bare floor. He insists on using the doormat.

The weather did clear and we did go spinnaker flying. The *idea* is to swing out over the water under the gently ballooning, brightly colored spinnaker. That's indeed what happened when I went up with Donald. It wasn't too windy, and our combined weight kept the sail from flying too high. But at different times Mike, Donald, and Erik got caught by gusts of wind, taken quite high (forty to fifty feet), and shaken off—like playing crack-the-whip with a huge troll and bellyflopping from fifty feet when you lose, according to Donald. It is not something for a mother to watch. Fortunately, no one suffered anything but bad bruises, but it could just as easily have been broken legs or cracked ribs.

Christmas caroling via dinghy is a treat not to be missed, but be sure to pick a harbor where the water is warm. It is not a dry event—not after the third wassail bowl. We ended the evening aboard *Ghida,* a British boat that we will see more of in the Caribbean. Judy and Kathy outdid themselves in baking goodies, we sang traditional carols and bawdy ballads, and toasted all friends of everyone, everywhere. We weighed anchor on Saturday, December 29, and have been enjoying a pleasant and fast sail across. If winds pick up again to what they have been, we should be in Barbados on Monday—sixteen days from the Canaries.

Barbados
January 14, 1980

We had a good trip across "the pond"—only fifteen days, nineteen hours from the Canaries to Barbados, and we would have made it hours sooner except that we reduced sail so that we wouldn't arrive in the harbor until daylight. That's fast for a cruising yacht, especially this year, when the trade winds weren't. We apparently had the last of them—at least for a while. *Ghida, Borne Free,* and *Sunbird* all waited until after New Year's to leave and have been becalmed for a week or more.

We haven't been ashore yet. Rain squalls and wind make rowing ashore a nuisance; besides, we're not checked in. Customs came out to the waiting boats at about 1100, gave us forms to fill out, and said they'd be "right back." It's 1400 and we're still under yellow flag, waiting.

It's rainy and stormy here, as it was when we arrived on Spain's "Sunshine Coast." "Very unusual weather" we're told; and where have I heard that before?

Grenada, West Indies
February 2, 1980

I can't get interested in this letter. I keep thinking that we'll be back "soon" and I'll be able to talk to all of you. Still...

As for this Caribbean—it's scenic, warm, and all that; but it's East Coast, and we're Westerners. Distances are too short, populations too large, crowds too great, manners too formal, money too old. Most of the people are chartering boats, paying thousands a week, not cruising on a scanty budget. There simply isn't the friendliness and helpfulness that we found in the Pacific. May the distances ever remain too great to turn that ocean into a resemblance of this scene!

Barbados was a welcome landfall and a welcoming country. We enjoyed ten days there, meeting old friends and making new. Our information about Grenada painted it even better. The man who is "the man" of cruising in the Caribbean lives here. Seven Seas Cruising Association members praised the place. But we forgot that The Revolution happened last February. "We welcome our Cuban comrades." "Friendship with Algeria, Libya, Syria." The best cruising grounds, on the south of the island, are out of bounds, except during daylight hours, "for security reasons." Shades of the Seychelles! Then, because charter boats work out of this bay and regularly pay customs and immigration officials twenty to thirty dollars, they tried to charge us the same. Only inadvertently did we learn that the official fee is about two dollars. Three unpleasant hours later we paid only the legitimate fee. Then we were given a receipt. The *printed* side, for which there was a carbon, said we'd paid the official fee. The other side, written and stamped but no carbon, listed the "fees" they tried to collect. Who needs this? There are too many pleasant places and friendly people in this world—maybe even a few on this side.

Praise to unisex clothing. Shirts too small for Don go to Erik, and I get Erik's castoffs. Only Donald gets new clothes. He's biggest.

Donald's SAT results were here in our mail. He did very well, outstandingly so if you consider that he's been unschooled for four years. I told you that "unschooled" is not synonymous with "uneducated."

Carriacou, Grenadines, West Indies
February 6, 1980

None of that "mi casa es su casa" hospitality around here. With so many tourists we're treated just like any other cash crop, ripe and ready to be picked. But some seed falls on stony ground and yields not, and we are soon left alone.

I must be immutably middle class. I did not enjoy Puerto Banus, Spain, one of the watering holes of the wealthy. Neither am I fond of these fishing villages populated by the poor and illiterate. Certainly we share that common humanity that bleeds when cut, knows fear, anger, etc., but we have nothing else in common. Increasingly, we leave the idyllic, isolated anchorages and seek the company of other yachts. No longer do we groan when we see another mast (unless it's a dozen other masts). It's not homesickness but people-sickness, friend-sickness, community-sickness. We most certainly don't miss smog, traffic jams, noise, the rat race, seawater too cold for comfortable swimming; but we do miss all of you. It will be good to be back—even if we don't stay long.

Cannoun, Grenadines, W.I.
February 12, 1980

Give the Caribbean its due: the water is warm. Otherwise I can't say much in its favor. We have not seen reefs anything like what we saw in the Pacific and Indian oceans, those places where it was like swimming in an aquarium. The trade winds, which keep the temperature bearable, blow incessantly, kicking up such chop in the anchorages even on the lee side of the islands that swimming is unpleasant. And the boats! I know that I said we enjoy the company, but this is ridiculous. Except for one island where we anchored in an open roadstead, we have no place had fewer than a dozen boats anchored alongside—in coves that would hold six comfortably. Most of the boats are charters—and many of the charterers don't know what they're doing; and they don't care, since the boats belong to someone else and the insurance will take care of most damage claims. Last night we were hit by one of these knuckleheads anchored *downwind* from us. Seems they turned on the engine to charge the batteries and forgot they were in gear. We were down below finishing dinner when CRUNCH—great smashing of wood at the stern. No panic, but lots of frantic behavior. Fortunately (?), they'd caught our dinghy on their bow and smashed it into our stern. No damage to their boat and little to ours, but the dinghy is pretty well stove in. The charter company doesn't care; charterers are responsible for minor damage. The charterers don't care; they split the bill six ways. So we are now in possession of a third-party check drawn on a New Jersey bank. (That will be fun to cash.) It's probably what the dinghy was worth, but we can't replace it for that—and in the meantime we're without. Yes, yes, accidents happen; but too many of these guys are accidents waiting to happen.

Mustique
February 22, 1980

I haven't stayed up all night in a long time, but tonight looks to be the night. The wind is not steady, and boats are moving every which way on their anchors. Common courtesy says that the last boat(s) anchored are the first one(s) to move if there is any danger of collision. Since we were here first there should be no problem. However, one of our neighbors is a French racing boat, another a CSY charter, and the third a gold plater with the attitude that might (i.e., bigger boat, more money) makes right. Two other boats that were anchored before he was have moved. But we have right on our side. Besides, another boat is sitting over our anchor. Don thinks we'll be O.K. So he and Donald are asleep. Erik and I, as official worriers, are keeping anchor watch. Erik is asleep on the cockpit seat. And here I sit, coffee in one hand, pen in the other. Not that I could sleep anyway. The French racing boat (0225—Might did make right; we moved.) has loose halyards that clank incessantly. We're being "rocked" to sleep out here. The disco ashore is going to "Ring My Bell" because "We Are Family." (At least there was an hour of Louis Armstrong and such songs as "Stardust.") Oops! just heard a crash inshore and the rattle of anchor chain. Can't see who it was, but not our British gold plater. (I can't believe it's a British boat; it's probably been chartered by some French.)

Bonaire, Netherlands Antilles
March 16, 1980

We spent a week living a technicolor dream—dull green of mangroves, yellow-green of ice plant, white sand spread with orange oyster shells; pale green water shading to turquoise, shading to blue-green, becoming dark blue topped with white froth outside the reefs; pale blue sky shattered by pink? flight? Yes, flamingos, sun glinting off pink feathers made more vivid by their black wingtips. No movie maker could get away with such outrageous colors, but they exist at Los Roques, a chain of islands, islets, and reefs lying off the Venezuelan coast. Conch abound, and clams and oysters and fish. There are a few fishing villages and no other yachts.

Hot, hot, hot. We're gobbling salt tablets and guzzling lemonade and tea to try to counteract the heat. And we're using our diesel breeze much more often than usual. This isn't part of the pleasure cruise but the last lap home, a hurried trip before the bad weather sets in. At least we're back in the world's best ocean again.

At the end of our journey we did find a marvelous spot in the Atlantic. It's worth transiting the Panama Canal just to visit the San Blas Islands—Pacific-like atolls and reefs like aquariums. They're visited but not overcrowded, so you can choose solitude or company. Definitely not overfished—even we caught things, whether trolling, bottom fishing, or spearing. And on our last "vacation" day Don and Erik speared lobsters and a giant crab in less than a foot of water—a delicious conclusion to a usually? often? at least sometimes? delightful voyage.

The Cuna Indians inhabit and control this part of Panama. Their villages lie at the mouths of the rivers in the foothills and deltas of the mainland and on the close offshore islands. They fish everywhere, but most of the hundreds of islands are uninhabited. They do not, however, exist on a mere subsistence level. They are famous for their molas, intricate panels of reverse applique, which in the traditional costume (still worn by the women) form the front and back of the women's blouses. These they now make for export to the likes of Nieman-Marcus and for sales to tourists the likes of us. So they are very definitely in the money economy but, most unusually, are "exploiting" themselves. Fortunately for them, Balboa was hustled off to the Pacific. Otherwise it seems improbable that they would have survived. They had and still have gold, much of it on display. Unfortunately, we spent too much time in the Caribbean and had only a week to spend in the San Blas. Next time...

We had been scheduled to transit the canal on Saturday, specifically planned so that we could attend the Lutheran church in the Zone on Easter Sunday. The port captain and other authorities assured us that the holiday made no difference to canal operations. BUT—eighteen pilots/advisors called in "sick" on Good Friday; one side of the locks was closed down for maintenance; and, naturally, the yachts were the boats bumped. So we went through on Easter Sunday, completing our circumnavigation at 1800. Nobody there was very impressed; the remark at the yacht club bar was "oh, yeah?" I guess they've seen it all too many times before.

Puntarenas, Costa Rica
April 18, 1980

Around the world for fried won ton, at our favorite Chinese restaurant. Donald and I both wanted some, but only one order remained. He deferred to age (beauty? authority?), and I shared around. It was only a little more expensive than it was four years ago and every bit(e) as good.

"Returning" has been strange. To our eyes, at least, very little has changed. Both here and in Panama all of "our" stores and markets are in their same places; the buses are the same (though fares are higher); we can get our shopping done without wasting time learning the territory. About the only noticeable change—many more bicycles here. (Later) Retraction: Even more noticeable are the ladies of the evening. There may have been as many four years ago, but they weren't so obvious. It's a sign, we're told, of a faltering economy.

en route to Acapulco
April 30, 1980

File under "Ignorance is bliss": While we were enjoying our won ton and other goodies, three fishing boats broke loose and started drifting down the channel, propelled by a five knot current. They careened off several other sailboats before barely missing *Anduril*. We didn't even hear about the episode until several days later.

Acapulco, Mexico
May 7, 1980

Ugggh. Smog, noise, dirt. I don't think we'll be able to return to civilization.

We stocked up with cheap Mexican diesel (sixteen cents a gallon) today, will leave tomorrow. So even without wind we may get home. More than likely there'll be wind—all of it from the wrong direction.

en route to San Diego
May 19, 1980

At the Acapulco Yacht Club the water in the swimming pool was too warm to be refreshing. We couldn't get the showers cool enough, either. Since then it's been iceberg city; we got out the wool hats and socks and the long undies. But everything is relative. Don's relative (brother Charlie, who lives in Anchorage) thinks that twenty degrees Fahrenheit is warm; we're freezing at twenty centigrade. In January of 1976 we thought the water at Cabo San Lucas wonderfully warm for swimming; last weekend we shiveringly withdrew our tender toes. (Not that my toes have any feeling; they're permanently frozen up to my kneecaps.) Actually, I feel better in this weather; but it's weather for walking, not for sitting and being sprayed by saltwater.

Nothing else looks like California. I know I've written about places that reminded us of home—Chile, the Galapagos, some of the Greek islands—but when we saw Cabo again it was so definitely California that I wondered how I thought that anything else resembled it. It's a certain slant of light, a particular shape of rock, a special angle of hill. It may be Baja, but it's definitely California.

Crowning indignity—too much sun in Acapulco produced a sore lower lip. I have to sip my Scotch through a straw.

May 23, 1980

Good old KFI radio. We learned that you're having a perfectly miserable beginning to the Memorial Day weekend. Well, it's even "miserabler" here. We're being battered by the same rotten weather, only we're suffering it bobbing around fifty miles or more from any decent anchorage (which would be impossible to get into anyhow). A miserable way to conclude the trip.

Working again on the old primitive magic that it's what you don't worry about that will do you in, I have a very long list of worries. Ignorance *is* bliss. When we were sailing down this coast in 1976 I didn't have any idea how many things could go wrong. Five years and fifty thousand miles later I know—and don't like the knowledge.

On the brighter side—— We've also heard ads for Safeway, Ralph's, Market Basket: prices for chickens, eggs, ground beef. We'll be able to afford eating again! Truly, we haven't seen such low prices in years.

We came close to running down a catamaran several nights ago. Don was on watch and saw her light; but since she wasn't showing running lights, he couldn't tell her direction until he was almost on top of her. We flashed our searchlight, called, whistled, etc., but couldn't raise anybody. I can't understand these people who don't stand watches, especially in crowded sea lanes like those near Cabo. But I'm sure the attitude would be "See, nothing happened; you were watching."

May 29, 1980

So I cheered up, and sure enough things got worse. If you liked the Red Sea, you'll love Acapulco to San Diego.

Another theory shot. Rigging failure was on my list of worries, yet it happened anyway. The port running backstay parted last night—fortunately, not quite all the way, and fortunately, we could repair it. Today, we developed a hole in the muffler. (Engine failure was also on my list.) Not that we can run the engine now anyway; there's too much wind and we're beating right into it. But when we do, Donald will have to vacate the aft cabin so he doesn't get asphyxiated.

We're wishing for that "cold" twenty degrees centigrade. Tonight it's thirteen down below. No telling what it is outside, especially if you include the wind chill factor. We have the oven on almost constantly, drying shoes, gloves, socks (have melted a few synthetic pairs).

Actually, the experience is salutary—reminds us of good reasons for giving up sailing, for a while, at least. Listening to the radio and reading *Time,* we sometimes wonder why we are returning.

Why, What?

Why a tri?

Jo: *Anything* to get out of Southern California!

Don: I did a lot of reading and looking at boats and was attracted to multihulls because of their speed and "daring." We bought a Sea Spray (fifteen-foot catamaran) and sailed and raced it a lot in Long Beach. By the time we were ready to build and go cruising, experience and more reading had convinced me that a tri would be a better cruising boat than a catamaran would be. We never really considered any monohull; I hadn't enjoyed sailing on them nearly as much as I had on the multihulls.

As to why a Norm Cross design, I had corresponded with virtually all the trimaran designers. The Cross design seemed best suited to our cruising needs without sacrificing too many of the features that make a good racing machine. I liked the idea of the hollow keel—it gives the boat much better windward ability, yet it doesn't have the leaks and other problems associated with centerboards and daggerboards. Norm was willing to work with us on adapting his stock design to meet our needs. His full size patterns were easy to work from. The boat did everything it was supposed to and never gave us any trouble.

Jo: Now that we've been cruising, we have even more reasons. Sailing rail under, washed with spray, may be fun for a while—but it's not my idea of a pleasant way to live. Unless you have one leg shorter than the other, I can't imagine why you'd want to live on a slant. We rarely heel enough that it's noticeable. We never have to strap ourselves into the galley or wedge ourselves into our queensize bunks. We don't get black-and-blue from being thrown around in a seaway.

Don: I'm convinced that, except maybe for a single-hander, a tri is safer. Its broad, stable platform makes sail changing both easier and safer. Being as light as it is, a tri is easier to handle; you don't have to fight so many tons of dead weight.

And because it's stable and comfortable, you can sleep, cook, and eat even in bad weather. A well-fed, well-rested crew is less likely to make the kind of error in judgment that's responsible for most accidents.

What kind of self-steering did you have?

Jo: I myself, Don himself, the boys themselves.

Don: I have a "thing" about someone being up and on watch at all times. Too many people are seduced by the ease with which a mechanical or electronic device will steer the boat. They forget that these devices have no senses and no sense; they cannot anticipate a change in the situation, only react once the change has occurred. That's usually too late. When we were in Tahiti we heard that five of six boats sailing through the Tuamotus ran up on reefs. Three of those groundings happened at night, with no one on deck. It's bad enough to run yourself on a reef, as we did at Wallis Island, but pretty stupid to let some machine do it for you— and in an area notorious for treacherous reefs and shifty currents.

Jo: We did plan to build a wind vane along the way, but we never got past an unsuccessful prototype. With four of us standing watches, self-steering didn't have priority. With fewer, I think self-steering would be necessary. Still, being relieved of *steering* doesn't mean being relieved of *watching*.

What about theft?

Don: We didn't tempt fate by leaving valuables lying around. Other than that, we took no special precautions. We generally locked the boat when we left, but figured we didn't have enough to lure a professional thief and that any professional could get through any security we devised anyway, if (s)he really wanted to.

Jo: The dinghy oars were stolen in San Francisco's Aquatic Park at the beginning of our trip. Donald's new Timex watch was taken from his cabin by one of a crowd of kids we were entertaining in Nukufetau in 1978. Later that year two pairs of Don's shorts that had been lying on deck for three days disappeared. That's all we lost from the boat.

What electronic gear did you have?

Don: Minimal, but we found it adequate. We had a radio direction finder, which was occasionally useful; a depth sounder, which was very useful; a ham radio, which proved entertaining as well as useful. We also had a knotmeter that sometimes worked and wind speed and wind direction indicators that never did. For navigation we had compass, chronometer, and sextant. Next time I think we'll get a digital readout chronometer. We found that the most common mistake in navigation was misreading the standard clockface by a minute (perhaps even the hour once or twice). Getting the exact time is critical, and a digital readout would eliminate the kinds of errors we sometimes made. Then, as prices come down, the sat nav becomes tempting. I understand, though, that the current (1983) system is due to change soon, so we'll wait.

Jo: Next time we'll also have a good cassette player—and some good cassettes.

How much water did you carry?

Don: Eighty gallons—it was a month's supply for the four of us.

Jo: While we were at sea, of course, we used seawater for doing dishes and for some laundry and bathing. We always used seawater in the head. When were in port we just filled the tanks when we needed to and never counted gallons—except where water was scarce and/or we had to pay for it. So there's no way to measure what we used—but we carried eighty gallons. I couldn't believe that people were "suffering" during the drought in the Bay Area on 280 gallons a day.

Did you carry guns?

Jo: Yes, but not by my choice. We never needed them, and they were more trouble than they were worth.

Don: We took a rifle, shotgun, and pistol that we had at home. We never volunteered the information that we had them, but when asked about "guns" we always declared the rifle and shotgun. Then we had them sealed in a locker aboard the boat or took them to the police station—whatever was required. If you're carrying guns, you should have a storage locker where they can be sealed—and you should be able to get into that locker without breaking the seal or be prepared to break the seal and suffer the consequences if you have to use the weapons. We were never threatened, so we never used the guns for anything but target practice when we were far at sea and once for hunting when we were invited along by the sole inhabitant on a remote Pacific island. But we were prepared to use them—and not to "warn off" intruders. If you shoot, you shoot to kill. If you're not prepared to do that, don't take guns. Either you'll "warn" somebody to kill you, or your own weapons will be used against you. You can only use them in a life-threatening situation aboard your own boat. If well-armed pirates are after you (and there usually aren't any other kind), a rifle and a shotgun won't deter them.

What about pirates?

Jo: We never saw any. We heard stories, but, considering the sources, we discounted most of them. One true story ended in the death of the skipper's wife.

Don: "Pirate" zones are almost as well defined as hurricane zones. You can avoid them. If you meet an "out of season" pirate, you probably can't outrun or outshoot him —unless you're carrying illegal artillery. I've thought that the best idea would be to fix up a Molotov cocktail and heave it at him when he was close enough. You could also fire your biggest flares—not to attract help, but straight at him. Fire and burns might cause him to alter course.

What anchoring techniques did you use?

Jo: Just the usual—screaming and swearing.

Don: Most Southern California sailors never anchor; we sail from marina to marina, or perhaps to a mooring. While working our way down the Mexican coast, all of us cruising boats had a lot to learn. We tried all the permutations we had read or heard of—anchoring fore and aft, anchoring with a bridle (a trimaran specialty), using two hooks in heavy weather, Med-mooring (aft end tied ashore), two anchors on one rode (either in tandem or split with a swivel shackle). The old standby of one anchor on one rode worked best for us, except in special conditions. In a reversing current we used a tandem on a swivel shackle, and in heavy weather we used two (or more) anchors, each on its own rode or in tandem. Generally, the more lines in the water the more likely you will foul one on your prop, rudder, or even your keel, especially if you're using floating line.

Setting the anchor firmly and eliminating chafe are critical. We found that once the anchor was set it did not drag. Setting involved selecting a clear patch of ocean floor, lowering the anchor, and letting out line slowly and smoothly to prevent slack and piling chain and line on the anchor. In poor holding ground it's sometimes necessary to let out as much as 10:1 scope to help the anchor dig in. We usually backed down with the engine in full reverse for two minutes. If we didn't drag, we were set; if the anchor moved we tried again. To prevent chafe we used thick-wall vinyl tubing over the first ten feet of our half-inch nylon braid, wrapping it also around the shackle (which was wired shut). We used the same tubing on deck lines to prevent chafe at the sheer and cleats. It really works!

What did you do in bad weather?

Jo: Pray and have a drink—not necessarily in that order.

Don: We finally adopted the high speed theory of storm management if we had sea room. We found that with 50–60 knots of wind we would run under bare poles at about the same speed as the wave trains (7–10 knots). This meant we had responsive steering and could pick the low places to let the wave drive by. As the wave rose steeply, we surfed away from the breaking crest, slowing down as that particular wave front passed. We never found it necessary to drag warps for control. If we chose not to run, but to fight, we found that we could fore-reach, making up to 3 knots of windward distance. With the trysail up instead of the main and the storm jib, backed slightly, on the inner stay, we locked the wheel and balanced the boat about 60° off the wind and wave direction. This provided a reasonably smooth ride and allowed us to attack the waves at a favorable angle yet eliminated any tendency to broach or pound.

What kind of construction is *Anduril*?

Don: She's cold-molded, W.E.S.T.® system. The hulls are laid up of three layers of 3mm mahogany plywood; total thickness is 9mm. We followed the system as developed by the Gougeon Brothers and used fibreglass only to tape the joints at the sheer and keel. We have only positive things to say about the W.E.S.T. system. We did have minor checking of the doug fir plywood decks, but that's the fault of the wood, not the epoxy. If I were to do it over, I'd use mahogany on the decks, too. It finishes better and seems to have a longer life. *Anduril* is a dry boat, and every indication points toward continued low maintenance (except for the paint). In addition, I think that cold-molded W.E.S.T. is both the easiest and surest way for an amateur to achieve a sound and fair hull.

Did you have much trouble with gear failure?

    Jo: Very little. Most of the things that "failed" simply wore out from use.

    Don: As Jo mentioned, we somehow sheared off a bolt inside the mast; although it was not their fault, Famet Marine sent us replacements for less than the shipping cost. On the way to Tahiti, Erik broke a Barient winch handle. It looked liked a crystallization fracture to me. We sent a snapshot of the broken handle to Barient. Within four days a new handle arrived, air freight, postage paid. Two days later we got an invoice stating "no charge." Two days after that came a letter of apology. It's never a pleasant surprise when gear fails, but it's always pleasant to deal with companies that stand behind their products.

How much money did you save by building the boat yourselves?

    Jo: "Save money" is not in the vocabulary of boat-building and cruising.

    Don: We didn't, and I don't think you usually do; at least, you don't if you're using top quality materials—and I wouldn't want to go to sea with less. You "save" only if you don't count your time in the cost. Most people would be ahead financially if they got a second job and turned that money over to a professional to build the boat for them. *Anduril* was "homemade" because I wanted the self-satisfaction of doing the job—and the assurance that it would be done right or done over.

What kind of refrigeration did you have?

    Jo: None. We soon got used to bilge-temperature beer. And much of the food that Americans refrigerate doesn't need to be. Eggs, if they haven't been refrigerated, will keep a month or more; and we never greased them or parboiled them or dipped them in wax. Cabbage, carrots, potatoes, citrus fruits, apples—all will keep at least a month if stored in a cool, well-ventilated locker. We kept margarine and even butter for up to two weeks in the tropics, much longer in cooler areas. Hard cheeses keep almost indefinitely; just cut the mold away or wipe it off with vinegar. Nuts and grains keep forever if kept dry. But you have to drink your fresh milk and eat (or can or salt) your fresh meat and fish right away.

Don: As with electronic gear, don't take refrigeration if you can't
fix it yourself or can't do without it.

What did you eat?

Don: Anything and everything that came our way. For fresh
foods, we bought what was available in the local markets.
Of course, we ate out of cans more than we had ashore; and
we ate a lot more rice and beans.

Jo: We started out with a lot of dehydrated foods. We bought
#10 tins from distributors. Some of the stuff was very
good—sausage TVP, potato dices, yams, carrots, corn; some
was edible—spinach flakes, stew blend; and some we still
have—TVP in chunk form, sour cream. We used powdered
milk a lot—the rest of the world has *good* powdered milk,
mainly from New Zealand—and powdered eggs for baking
when our supply of fresh ran low.

How did you handle your money?

Don: Briefly, as it passed by.

Jo: We seemed always to be one method behind what was best.
When we were traveling, the dollar wasn't as strong as it is
now, but American currency was acceptable anywhere. In
some countries you did better with dollars than with local
currency; in those countries such trading was frequently
illegal, however. Traveler's checks are always safe, but
they're not always convenient. In some places there's a
service charge for cashing them. And you can't haggle in
the local markets with traveler's checks. Getting the most
local currency for your dollar was the trick. On the islands
(Tahiti, Fiji, etc.) it was best to have a bank transfer and
take the full amount in local currency. You got the best rate
because there was no physical, negotiable cash that had to be
guarded on its way to wherever banks send their money.
This was one place where traveler's checks, cashed at the
bank, worked well, too, since they're nonnegotiable once
signed. In places where we could trust the mail service we
had international money orders in amounts under $500 sent
to us. We cashed them as we needed them; that way we
didn't need to turn local currency back into dollars, a
conversion that is often costly. Twice we got cash on our
Visa card—but that's costly, too. You have to play it by
ear—and always keep a stash of "Yankee dollahs."

How much did the trip cost?

Don: We spent an average of $5,500 a year over the five years.
The average was lower in 1975–1978, higher in 1979–1980,

partly because of inflation, partly because we were in more expensive areas of the world (Med and Caribbean), partly because we had to replace things like sails, line, etc. A good third of our money was eaten up by inland travel—buses, trains, planes, hotels. We own the boat, so except while on our inland travels, our housing was free. Whether too much, not enough, or just right, the wind is free. We met cruisers who spent a lot more and others who spent substantially less.

What happened to Bigfoot?

Jo: Bigfoot jumped ship when we got back to Newport Beach. He was an Orange County cat and, I guess, didn't want to be taken away again. And he was probably irresistible to the ladies—all those tales of adventures and far away places.

Desdemona, after all, was bewitched by Othello's tales, and Othello was from Cyprus, where Bigfoot had spent six months as king of the marina.

What did you do about the boys' schooling?

Jo: As I've mentioned earlier, we had an excellent study plan and schedule—only it didn't work. Essentially, we left it up to them. I told them that if they wanted to be seventeen years old and in the fourth grade when we got back it was their problem. We had all their school books aboard—and lots of other books. With no other distractions—no TV, no telephones, no football, no cars, no girls—they studied out of sheer boredom. Some subjects—especially math and science—had direct practical application in learning navigation and radio operation. We experienced different cultures instead of reading about them in social studies texts. Donald took a high school graduation exam in Crete, had no trouble with it, and received his Graduate Equivalency Degree. He took SAT's in Cyprus and Spain, scored so well that he was accepted by Cal, Princeton, and San Diego State. Erik did well in high school and is now attending Cal State Long Beach, studying marine biology. Lack of schooling never interfered with their education.

Would you do it again?

Jo & Don: How soon can you cast us off?

"I shall never regret," said Mr. Pickwick in a low voice, "I shall never regret having devoted the greater part of two years to mixing with different varieties and shades of human character: frivolous as my pursuit of novelty may have appeared to many. Nearly the whole of my previous life having been devoted to business and the pursuit of wealth, numerous scenes of which I had no previous conception have dawned upon me—I hope to the enlargement of my mind, and the improvement of my understanding. If I have done but little good, I trust I have done less harm, and that none of my adventures will be other than a source of amusing and pleasant recollections to me in the decline of life."

DICKENS, *The Pickwick Papers*